Praise for Dorotheos of Gaza and the
Discourse of Healing in Gazan Monasticism

"In this fresh, contextualized examination of Dorotheos of Gaza's collected works, Kyle A. Schenkewitz explores how Dorotheos created a new understanding of healing in monastic communities. Parting ways from much of Christian monastic thought, and certainly from his Gazan setting, Dorotheos views the monk's body as the positive locus of health because of its position as the soul's home. Schenkewitz analyzes Dorotheos's corpus in its Gazan monastic context by comparing it to the letters of Barsanuphius and John, the Asceticon of Isaiah of Scetis, and the Apophthegmata Patrum. Through his comparative literary analysis, Schenkewitz lucidly reveals Dorotheos's unique contributions to Gazan monastic thought. In reading Dorotheos's works through the lens of his position as the consummate physician, Schenkewitz widens our understanding of how Christianity appropriated Greco-Roman medicine to understand the ascetic body. This volume will stand alongside recent literature on monastic medicine and Gazan asceticism as a key analysis of Dorotheos and his novel medical theology of the ascetic body."

Zachary B. Smith, Resident Assistant Professor of Theology,
Creighton University, Omaha, Nebraska

Dorotheos of Gaza and the Discourse of Healing in Gazan Monasticism

AMERICAN UNIVERSITY STUDIES

SERIES VII
THEOLOGY AND RELIGION

VOL. 357

This book is a volume in a Peter Lang monograph series.
Every volume is peer reviewed and meets
the highest quality standards for content and production.

PETER LANG
New York • Bern • Frankfurt • Berlin
Brussels • Vienna • Oxford • Warsaw

KYLE A. SCHENKEWITZ

Dorotheos of Gaza and the Discourse of Healing in Gazan Monasticism

PETER LANG

New York • Bern • Frankfurt • Berlin
Brussels • Vienna • Oxford • Warsaw

Library of Congress Cataloging-in-Publication Data
Names: Schenkewitz, Kyle A.
Title: Dorotheos of Gaza and the Discourse of healing
in Gazan monasticism / Kyle A. Schenkewitz.
Description: New York: Peter Lang Publishing, 2016. | Series: American
University studies VII. Theology and religion, ISSN 0740-0446;
Vol. 357 | Includes bibliographical references.
Identifiers: LCCN 2015033944 | ISBN 9781433132216 (hardcover: alk. paper)
| ISBN 9781453917091 (e-book)
Subjects: LCSH: Dorotheus, of Gaza, Saint, active 6th century. Discourses
and sayings. | Monasticism and religious orders. | Healing—
Religious aspects—Christianity.
Classification: LCC BR65.D757 S24 2016 | DDC 271.00953/1—dc23
LC record available at http://lccn.loc.gov/2015033944

Bibliographic information published by **Die Deutsche Nationalbibliothek**.
Die Deutsche Nationalbibliothek lists this publication in the "Deutsche
Nationalbibliografie"; detailed bibliographic data are available
on the Internet at http://dnb.d-nb.de/.

Cover image: St. Dorotheus of Gaza. Mount Saint Dionysius, Mount Athos, 1547

The paper in this book meets the guidelines for permanence and durability
of the Committee on Production Guidelines for Book Longevity
of the Council of Library Resources.

© 2016 Peter Lang Publishing, Inc., New York
29 Broadway, 18th floor, New York, NY 10006
www.peterlang.com

Printed in Germany

Contents

Acknowlegments

This book is the culmination of a long road of persistence, encouragement, and trust from family and friends along life's way. The work has not been easy, but it has been enjoyable. I am very thankful to the support of my wife and daughter who send me off each morning with a squeeze-hug and kiss. This work would not be possible without the resources and support of Saint Louis University, its Library, and its Department of Theological Studies, especially Fr. Kenneth Steinhauser. The Church of St. Michael and St. George has been a constant source of prayer and assistance as my spiritual home and employer. I would also like to thank Timothy Chapman for his editorial skills in transforming my rough ideas into clear prose.

CHAPTER ONE

Introduction

Four great monastic teachers emerged from the fifth to mid-sixth centuries in Gaza: Isaiah, Barsanuphius, John, and Dorotheos. Contemporary scholarship has not clarified Dorotheos's distinctive place among these teachers nor fully examined his contribution to his monastic tradition. This book proposes an innovative approach to understanding Dorotheos's monastic teaching by analyzing the shared discourse of healing in the monastic school of Gaza. Dorotheos diverged from his tradition's understanding of humanity's salvation and the monastic life by emphasizing virtue as integral to a healthy life and the positive role of the body in asceticism. The comparison of Dorotheos with his contemporaries distinguishes him as a dynamic figure intent upon retaining inherited approaches to monastic living, but offering his own interpretation of the spiritual and physical healing inherent to the monastic life.

Dorotheos carefully indicated the need for health of soul and body. His conception of asceticism did not denigrate the body for the sake of the soul's health but sought to provide therapy and training for the body so that it could gain and retain its own health and be conducive to the healing of the soul. The monastic life, for Dorotheos, was not conceived as patient suffering until the release of death but the rehabilitation and restoration of human life. Dorotheos envisioned humanity as depicted in Eden: flourishing, contemplating God, and full of virtue. The monastic life was a reconstitution of humanity's health through asceticism and cultivation of virtue. The body was an important aspect in each respect. The positive role of the body in the monastic life distinguished Dorotheos from his contemporaries and established his teaching as a decisive development in the monastic school of Gaza. The discourse of healing was essential to Dorotheos's monastic vision. Christian monastics inherited an approach to health and medicine that reached back to Hippocrates and Galen. At times tenuous, health of body and soul were complementary for most early Christians. Dorotheos was able to draw upon a long custom of Christian monastic health care, for which Basil the Great stood as an important figure. The provision of bodily health care was not at odds with the monastic life but was integral to the stability and function of monastic communities themselves and the laypersons of surrounding areas. By using the metaphor of healing as an interpretive lens through which to re-consider Dorotheos's works, I illuminate new facets of his teachings that corroborate Peter Brown's observation of the importance of the body for Dorotheos and open up new avenues of research that consider how the discourse of healing, both physical and spiritual, was used in monastic teaching.[1]

Much of Dorotheos's epistolary exchange with his spiritual mentors, Barsanuphius and John, revolved around his role as monastic infirmarian. Dorotheos was concerned with the daily routine of actively enjoying and providing spiritual and physical health in the infirmary. He attended to patients, directed his own disciples, and interacted with laypersons and visitors. This duty was as troublesome for Dorotheos as it was formative. Dorotheos's monastic maturation in the infirmary reverberated throughout his leaving Seridos's coenobium and settling with his own monks nearby. Dorotheos incorporated the importance of daily living to his vision of monasticism's goal of slowly and steadily returning to a state of health. Dorotheos translated his tradition into a discourse that was familiar to him. The healing he provided in the infirmary was analogous to the spiritual healing he would provide as a spiritual teacher. Dorotheos first offered spiritual direction while working in the infirmary. His first disciple, Dositheos, accompanied him in the infirmary, providing care to monks and laypersons. In his own monastery, Dorotheos's task was to guide and direct his monastics to a life of health. Dorotheos viewed the Christian life, generally, and the monastic life, more intensely, as a daily enterprise of cultivating and habituating health within the body and soul such that the individual could prosper within the monastic community.

Dorotheos employed numerous metaphors of physical healing to illustrate the spiritual healing that takes place in the individual who sought Christ as a physician. These metaphors demonstrated his familiarity with medical healing and served as means to illustrate the similarities of healing in body and soul. For

Dorotheos, healing was more than a metaphor; it constituted a reality in which a monk's soul and body were united in the harmonious excellence of the healthy life.

This study will reassess Dorotheos's significance within the monastic school of Gaza and demonstrate that his distinctive vision complicates portrayals of the Gazan monastic tradition. More specifically, Dorotheos introduced a conception of healing in the monastic life as acquisition of virtue in conjunction with a positive view of the body's role in the Christian life. This investigation will proceed from the observations of Lucien Regnault, that "Plutôt que de nous attarder aux points de détail où Dorotheé n'est que l'écho de la tradition, nous avons préféré insister sur ce qui nous paraît les plus essentiel et le plus caractéristique."[2] Regnault recongnized Dorotheos's participation in a living tradition. He further described Dorotheos as being faithful "à *toute* la tradition, et n'en laisse rien perdre."[3] This study will locate Dorotheos within his monastic tradition and will also explore his contribution to that tradition, interpreting and contributing his own perspective.[4]

Dorotheos founded his monastic teachings upon the interrelatedness of health for body and soul, providing a distinct vision of the monastic life that emphasized a positive role of the body as he employed the discourse of healing. While Isaiah, Barsanuphius, and John emphasized a monk's endurance of illness and suffering as preparation for future union with God, Dorotheos encouraged the transformation of humanity from a state of sickness to a state of health. He asserted that Christ restored health to humanity from the sickness incurred through sin and he claimed that Christ's teachings provided the way of life free from passion and rich in virtue. The distinctive character of his monastic teaching balances his care for the spiritual and physical health of his monastics.

Dorotheos continually cast his spiritual guidance in the mold of diagnosis and treatment of a spiritual disorder. His teaching can be noted for at least three distinctive marks. First, Dorotheos held that the natural state of humanity at creation was a state of health and did not include passion ($\pi\acute{\alpha}\theta o\varsigma$).[5] The passions were a sickness incurred as a result of the fall. Dorotheos argued that the salvation of humanity was a return to the natural state at creation, rather than a completely new state. Second, Dorotheos discussed Christ's role as the physician who heals humanity's sickness but also as the teacher who provides the prescription for maintaining a life of health. In his spiritual teaching, Dorotheos emphasized that attaining virtue ($\dot{\alpha}\rho\epsilon\tau\acute{\eta}$) constituted the healthy life. Third, Dorotheos emphasized the interrelatedness of body and soul in the health of the human person rather than the denigration of the body for the sake of the soul.

Dorotheos utilized the metaphor of healing through his discourses. Averil Cameron claimed, "Metaphor is at the heart of Christian language."[6] In her study of Christian use of rhetoric within the Greco-Roman world, she observed how "increasing recourse was also made even in learned writings to such figurative tropes as metaphor and simile, and with them, to paradox, those features so deep seated in all the less formal types of religious discourse and inherent in Christian language."[7] In his 2003 study, *Krankheit und Heilung in der Theologie der frühen Kirchenväter,* Michael Dörnemann stated that metaphor is "nicht nur eine sprachliche Ausdrucksform, sondern bereits eine Form des Denkens."[8] Dörnemann explored the notion of illness and healing in early Christian writers[9] by utilizing George Lakoff and Mark Johnson's theory of conceptual metaphors in *Metaphors We Live By* combined with insights from Christa Baldauf on metaphor theory.[10] Lakoff and Johnson explained, "The essence of metaphor is understanding and experiencing one kind of thing in terms of another."[11] Metaphors characterize one's conceptual system and enable a person to understand experiences and concepts in a consistent manner. They assert that metaphors are inherent in one's conceptual system and that "human *thought processes* are largely metaphorical."[12] For Lakoff and Johnson, metaphors are more than mere linguistic expressions, but operate at the cognitive level. Additionally, metaphors are based upon the experiences of everyday life. Lakoff and Johnson hold that conceptual metaphors are inseparable from their experiential basis.[13] For example, a culture where argument is understood as war would not be able to comprehend an argument in a culture where argument is understood as dance. In the former case, the metaphor "ARGUMENT is partially structured, understood, performed, and talked about in terms of WAR."[14] Lived experience of, say, a culture where ARGUMENT IS WAR affects the way one comprehends and expresses the idea of ARGUMENT through conceptual metaphors. Likewise, Dorotheos utilized the metaphor of healing to convey his conception of the narrative of salvation and the monastic life. Baldauf described the use of metaphor as "das Verständnis kognitiver Routinen."[15] Through metaphor, one can conceptualize difficult and even non-tangible ideas through easily comprehended concepts.

Healing was used as just such a metaphor for the salvific activity of Christ. In her study, Amanda Porterfield held that "Recent historians also pointed to the interest in medicine shown by early Christian writers and to the frequent use of medical metaphors in Christian discourse."[16] Porterfield showed that though analogies between Christ and physicians were plentiful, they were "always accompanied by an insistence on Christ's superiority to any human physician or material form of medicine."[17] In another recent study, Anne Elizabeth Meredith anticipated the emphasis here given to Dorotheos by articulating how for Christians "medical metaphors used by the Greek and Roman philosophers proved to be very useful indeed. The use of medical metaphors, however, was not simply absorption of a stock metaphor. For many Christians, the analogy between philosophy

(Christianity) and medicine became a primary way in which they conceptualized salvation."[18] Dorotheos employed the metaphor of healing in his method of addressing spiritual ailments, the work of Christ, the healthy life, and the interconnectedness of body and soul. Healing became a metaphor for Christ's work in and through the individual.

Dorotheos's continual use of anecdotes and explanations of physical healing in his spiritual instructions indicated how he incorporated the metaphor of healing into his spiritual teaching. When he explained the importance of forgiveness without resentment to his monks, Dorotheos utilized the metaphor of a wound to explain the process of spiritual healing that takes place when one truly forgives. Dorotheos stated that one who forgives another "is like a person with a wound (τραῦμα). He puts a plaster (ἔμπλαστρον) on it and temporarily heals it through that and it forms a scar."[19] A monk who retained resentment toward his brother, however, was not perfectly healed. "He still retained the problem of resentment that is like the scar from which the wound is easily reopened if it receives a small blow."[20] The wound of the injured monk was not perfectly healed and left him vulnerable to animosity toward the one who injured him. Only through complete spiritual healing would one become impervious to re-injury, much like the healing of a scar where "no disfigurement remains and you cannot discern where the wound was."[21] Dorotheos's understanding of physical healing was a vital resource for his understanding of spiritual healing, but, more broadly, it influenced how he conceived the salvific healing of Christ's example and teaching.

Recent scholarship has not adequately established the distinctive character of Dorotheos's teaching in comparison to the monastic tradition of his region, nor has it given due attention to the positive role for the body in his monastic instructions. The most recent works on Dorotheos's monastic instructions suggest how scholarly inquiry has shifted away from highlighting Dorotheos as an important contributor in his monastic context by subsuming him within his tradition.

Peter Brown and Pierre Hadot noted Dorotheos's distinctive understanding of the body in early Christian monasticism and Christian appropriation of ancient *philosophia* and spiritual exercises. Brown, a social historian, and Hadot, a philosopher, have both recognized Dorotheos's marked contribution to early Christianity because of his insistence on the body's importance in the monastic life.

Brown remarked that "Dorotheos of Gaza (who died around 560) is the most attractive figure among these" figures in Gaza in the fifth and sixth centuries.[22] Interested in the impact of sexuality on monasticism, Brown expressed his view that with "the delicate and marvelously vulnerable young man (Dorotheos) we possess evidence unique in late antiquity: the inner portrait of his life over two decades."[23] He further examined how Dorotheos's early influences informed his later spiritual guidance. He noted that whereas Barsanuphius once called upon Dorotheos to "Torture your senses, for without torture there is no martyrdom,"[24] Dorotheos instead emphasized an intimate connection between body and soul in which the body could bring humility to the soul.[25] For Brown, Dorotheos's notion of the "inextricable interdependence of body and soul"[26] signaled a new emphasis on the importance of the body in the Christian monastic tradition: it is to be loved and saved.[27] Brown rightly observed that Dorotheos's focus on the value of the body was one feature of his distinct monastic vision. This study will move beyond Brown's observation and demonstrate that the interdependence of body and soul was an extension of how Dorotheos understood the connection between the body and soul from creation to redemption. Brown's analysis, though helpful, did not offer an explanation of Dorotheos's deviation from the negative teaching on the body of Barsanuphius and John. Furthermore, Brown did not explore how Dorotheos's understanding of the union between body and soul was illustrative of a larger concern for cultivating health among his monastics.

According to Pierre Hadot, Dorotheos exemplified the ancient spiritual exercises of meditation, self-mastery, and attention to oneself.[28] For Hadot, Dorotheos took up the Stoic notion of spiritual perfection as the transformation of the will that led to peace of mind. Hadot described Dorotheos's emphasis on "*apatheia* [as] the end-result of the annihilation of one's own will."[29] According to Hadot, one attained *apatheia* and peace of mind through spiritual exercises. Hadot utilized Dorotheos as an important figure in his argument for Christian adaptation of ancient spiritual exercises. He explained, "the means Dorotheos recommends for cutting off self-will are wholly identical to the exercises of self-mastery of the philosophical tradition."[30] For Dorotheos, many spiritual exercises were distinctly bodily activities. Hadot noted the "therapeutic value of writing" that appeared in Dorotheos's works.[31] Hadot also addressed the inextricable connection between the body and the cultivation of humility, which, for Dorotheos, "leads us to maintain the greatest reserve in both conduct and speech, and to adopt certain significant bodily positions, for instance prostrations before other monks."[32] Further, in *What is Ancient Philosophy?*, Hadot cited Dorotheos among Clement of Alexandria, Origen, the Cappadocians, and Evagrius as practicing Christian monasticism as a form of philosophy, a way of life.[33] Spiritual exercises were an important aspect of Dorotheos's monastic teaching as a means to combat the frustration of the passions and return a person to a state of health. Despite Hadot's helpful comparison of Dorotheos's monastic approach with that of ancient philosophy, he did not take into account how Dorotheos's understanding of creation and salvation illumined his monastic teaching.

More directly focused on Dorotheos, Judith Pauli's *Menschsein und Menschwerden* examined Dorotheos's teachings with regard to contemporary approaches to ethics. Her monograph explored Dorotheos as a singular author with little focus on the differences between Dorotheos and his contemporaries.[34] Pauli quickly surveyed the monastic setting of Gaza in which Dorotheos lived and delved into a thematic portrayal of Dorotheos's teaching. Her later study and German translation of Dorotheos's works remain important investigations into Dorotheos's work, but do not sufficiently attend to the broader monastic context in which he lived.[35] Further investigation into this context will account for the way Dorotheos's experience in the monastery shaped his later teachings in contrast to his contemporaries.

In 2005, Jennifer Hevelone-Harper's *Disciples of the Desert: Monks, Laity and Spiritual Authority in Sixth-Century Gaza* explored the monastic environment of Seridos's monastery. She acknowledged that, "Among the monks at Tawatha under the spiritual direction of Barsanuphius and John, one figure stands apart as an ascetic father in his own right–Abba Dorotheos."[36] Unfortunately, her examination of his contribution was limited to the portrayal of Dorotheos in the *Letters* of Barsanuphius and John and the *Life of Dositheos*. While these texts offer a vivid picture of Dorotheos's monastic life within the coenobium of Seridos, they do not include Dorotheos's own teaching in his *Discourses*. Her work thus provides a strong foundation to the practical elements of Dorotheos's monastic life, but did not consider his actual monastic teachings.

Recently, Brouria Bitton-Ashkelony and Aryeh Kofsky assembled a collection of their articles on monasticism in Gaza in *The Monastic School of Gaza*. In so doing, they attempted "to frame the historical development of this community and to depict and analyze the spiritual and intellectual context represented in the sources of what may be termed the monastic school of Gaza."[37] The goal of their project was to examine the monastic tradition in Gaza and construct a discernible continuity of thought that would constitute a monastic school. They studied the history of monasticism in the Gaza region and argued that between the fourth and seventh centuries "a monastic school emerged that, while amalgamating these ascetic teachings, simultaneously deviated from them in certain respects, forging its own intellectual profile."[38] Because of this broad approach, Bitton-Ashkelony and Kofsky overshadowed Dorotheos's distinctiveness.

When they did discuss Dorotheos, their appraisal of his position in the Gazan monastic tradition did not account for his development and distinction within this tradition. Bitton-Ashkelony and Kofsky were willing to note that, "Dorotheos presents ideas and concepts from Greek philosophy and theological concepts of Greek ecclesiastical writers alongside anecdotes from his personal experience. It is his adaptation of this amalgam to the coenobitic reality of his monastery that gives Dorotheos's spiritual direction its distinct character."[39] Yet, they expressed limited enthusiasm for Dorotheos's works as distinctive, disregarding his experience in the infirmary and the value of the body in his teachings. Their contradictory assessment of Dorotheos can be seen in their claim that his works "are characterized by their lack of originality and their eclectic nature, and express a predilection for preserving and systematizing monastic tradition."[40] Later they conclude, "His lectures are vivid and attractive, his topic interwoven with anecdotes and personal experience; but there is hardly anything in them that is not traditional."[41] Bitton-Ashkelony and Kofsky overemphasized the continuity of the monastic school of Gaza and failed to perceive the distinctive features of Dorotheos teaching.

Additionally, Rosa Marie Parrinello has published *Comunità monastiche a Gaza: Da Isaia a Doroteo (secoli IV–VI)*. Parrinello argued that these Gazan monastics held to "un evidente polimorfismo" in which the community was held together by the spiritual authority of charismatic leaders rather than a rule.[42] Her examination revealed the impact of Basil of Caesarea on these Gazan monastic communities through the emphasis on fraternity and salvation of the community as a whole.[43] Her chapter on Dorotheos's community elucidated the importance of concieving each monastic as an individual in relation to a community and the outside world. The influence of Basil and Abba Zosimas on Dorotheos were important in this regard. [44] This publication is important in its approach to monastic community in Gaza and reinforces the connection between Dorotheos and his monastic predecessors. Parrinello's argument might anticipate the investigation into Dorotheos's contribution to this ancient community of monastics, but not the contripution itself.

This study will examine Dorotheos's *Spiritual Discourses* within the monastic literature from the late fifth-century to the early sixth-century Gazan monastic context. Dorotheos and his contemporaries offer historians the very last glimpse of Gazan monasticism before the Arab invasion of Palestine in 634, as well as the growth and variation of a monastic tradition.[45] Lorenzo Perrone declared that, in the Palestinian monastic setting, one can observe "the process through which a growing corpus of ascetical writings contributed to preserve and transmit previous monastic experiences and teachings, conferring them 'normative' value within a very short span of time."[46] Isaiah, Barsanuphius, John, and Dorotheos contributed to the vibrant monastic heritage of this locale. Comparison with his Gazan contemporaries will demonstrate how Dorotheos developed his monastic instruction amid comparable literature from his monastic tradition.

Dorotheos's own monastic works remain at the center of this study, though several ancillary texts will also be consulted. The surviving works of Dorotheos consist of seventeen spiritual discourses, sixteen letters to his own monks, and eighteen brief sayings (*CPG* 7352–7360).[47] Lucien Regnault and Jean de Préville published the critical edition of Dorotheos's corpus in 1963 as Œuvres Spirituelles.[48] Judith Pauli published a reprinted edition in 2000 with accompanying German translation as *Doctrinae Diversae: Die geistliche Lehre*.[49] The critical edition by Regnault and Préville supplanted the previously standard Migne edition through comparison with other surviving manuscripts of Dorotheos's works.[50] This collection of texts represents only a portion of Dorotheos's discourses; the remainder has not survived. Although the date of the composition and compilation of Dorotheos's works cannot be precisely determined, Siméon Vailhe posited that his discourses were written between 540 and 560.[51]

Appended to most manuscripts of Dorotheos's *Spiritual Discourses* are four additional texts that will also be considered in this study: *Prologue*, *Introductory Letter*, *Life of Dositheos*, and *Introduction*. All of these texts are included in the critical edition published by Regnault and Préville. The translation of Constantine Scouteris is the only English translation based upon the critical edition of Regnault and de Préville and is used as the basis for this study.[52] Notably, Dorotheos was prominently featured in the *Life of Dositheos*, a young man over whom Dorotheos was given charge in the coenobium.[53] This account verified Dorotheos's role and authority as infirmarian. Dorotheos himself offered few indications of his life prior to entering the monastic life at the coenobium of Seridos.[54] The information gleaned from these resources situates Dorotheos within the monastic context of Seridos's coenobium in Gaza and elucidates the environment in which Dorotheos would flourish as a teacher of the monastic life.

The comparative literature from the Gazan monastic context is primarily comprised of the *Ascetic Discourses* of Isaiah (of Scetis) and the *Letters* of Barsanuphius and John. While other writers influenced Dorotheos, these central figures from the monastic school of Gaza comprise his monastic tradition and provide the theoretical lens through which he was trained and from which he offered his own distinct spiritual guidance.[55] The selection of these works is based upon the proximity of their authors to Dorotheos himself and will highlight his distinctive position from within his tradition.

Isaiah of Scetis lived and taught in the region of Gaza near the end of the fifth century and his *Ascetic Discourses* were available to Seridos's community.[56] Dorotheos and other monks question the Barsanuphius and John about these discourses.[57] This study will utilize the Greek edition of Isaiah's corpus, *TOY ΟΣΙΟΥ ΠΑΤΡΟΣ ΗΜΩΝ ΑΒΒΑ ΗΣΑΙΟΥ ΛΟΓΟΙ ΚΘ* that Augoustinos Hilarion published in 1911, as well as John Chryssavgis and Pachomios Penkett's 2002 translation of Isaiah's Greek corpus entitled *Abba Isaiah of Scetis: Ascetic Discourses*.[58]

There can be little doubt of Dorotheos's relation to Barsanuphius and John in whose letters he appears as correspondent on eighty-six occasions.[59] In these letters Dorotheos described his life and struggles as a young monk as well as asking for spiritual guidance from Barsanuphius and John. Their replies demonstrated the spiritual guidance he received and the sanction for his work as an infirmarian in the coenobium. Derwas Chitty claimed, "Abba Dorotheos has himself left us a body of ascetical works in the tradition of his masters, Varsanuphius and John, but in fact far better known in the West, appearing in Migne's Patrology (P.G. LXXXVIII, 1611–1844)."[60] This assessment by Chitty now requires more nuance. In light of the completed critical editions of Barsanuphius and John's letters, scholars can ascertain how directly Dorotheos adopted the monastic outlook of his spiritual guides. The collection of letters between the Old Men, Barsanuphius and John, and their correspondents has only recently been fully edited.[61] The fifth and final volume in the critical edition of Barsanuphius and John's *Correspondence* was published in 2002 and an English translation offered by John Chrysavvgis in 2006.[62] Dorotheos's interaction with Barsanuphius and John in the monastery and through written correspondence is a vital aspect of understanding Dorotheos's place in his tradition.

The two final literary collections important for this study are the Christian Scriptures of the Gazan theologians and the *Apophthegmata Patrum*.[63] Lorenzo Perrone depicted biblical learning as "a necessary prerequisite, especially for the monks who were expected to become members of cenobitic monasteries and as such to participate regularly in the life of prayer."[64] Christian scriptures served as a resource for moral teachings and practical examples from which the monks could "extract … lessons for a life of perfection."[65] If scripture was the primary written, spiritual resource, the Sayings of the Desert Fathers was not far behind.

Perrone also described the *Apophthegmata Patrum* as "a second type of authority next to the Scriptures, in order to provide a guide and orientation for the ascetics' behavior."[66] Chryssavgis cautioned readers concerning these "spiritual journeys," for they "constitute a kind of map requiring unfolding and careful reading."[67] As a resource for spiritual direction, the *Apophthegmata Patrum* displayed the "tensions and problems inherent in spiritual direction."[68] Chryssavgis expressed disappointment that the *Apophthegmata Patrum* only transmitted small portions of the lived monastic life. Regretting the loss of "the rich texture of the monastic life," Chryssavgis recognized that the *Apophthegmata Patrum* was "the distillation of wise words, without the description of the process of wise living."[69] Jean-Claude Guy asserted that the literary form and style of the *Apophthegmata Patrum* indicated "the educational method already in use. There is no legislation in it attempting to give institutional structure to a particular 'spirituality'… . Nor does the work contain any methodical teaching on the spiritual life such as, shortly afterwards, Dorotheos gave to his monks at Gaza."[70] In the Gazan monastic context, sayings culled from the monastic fathers were the spiritual foundation from which later monks could find solid guidance. Spiritual fathers employed these sayings as spiritual guideposts and authoritative dictates. In Dorotheos's works, the sayings provided substance and support for his own teaching.

The use of scripture and monastic recollections constituted the foundation for the continuing tradition of the monastic life. This life, Perrone argued, was a continual embodiment of the salvation displayed in scripture: "The new 'Fathers' of monasticism were not meant as substitutes for the old ones. They only reflected, in the eyes of the monks, a further development of the history of salvation to be conceived as a *continuum*, a unique sequence from biblical to present times."[71] In the Gazan context, the monastic life was the life prescribed by scripture. The collections of monastic sayings and stories were a further resource for achieving the monastic ideal. Each generation of monks continued to carry this way of life forth into its own day.

This literature will serve as a basis upon which to evaluate Dorotheos's assumption of the monastic tradition in Gaza and to establish the distinctive quality of his own monastic teaching. This study does not presume to incorporate every work known to have been influential on Dorotheos's thought but attempts to situate his work within the lineage of the monastic school in Gaza and contemporary to Dorotheos.

CHAPTER TWO

Monasticism in Gaza

Gaza was an important crossroad for travel and trade in the Byzantine world. François Neyt posited that Gaza was especially important for Christian pilgrims because "la region de Gaza, de Tavatha à Maiouma, le long de la mer, devint un carrefour culturel et spirituel où se retrouvèrent des chercheurs de Dieu venus du Nord et du Sud, souvent attires par la visite des lieux saints à Jérusalem."[1] The Judean countryside and Gazan coast were the main monastic centers in Byzantine Palestine.[2] The Judean desert boasted of the famed Saint Sabas monastery and association with Jerusalem.[3] Gazan monasticism was most notable because of its famed inhabitants Peter the Iberian, Barsanuphius, and John.[4] Perrone indicated that Gazan monasticism thrived for at least three centuries, "from Hilarion, the alleged initiator of monasticism in Palestine, to the great masters of monastic spirituality in the sixth century culminating in the ascetic teachings of Dorotheos of Gaza."[5] This monastic center drew upon a variety of monastic precedents and incorporated them into a distinctive monastic way of life. Chitty described the Palestinian monastic heritage as an institution "with a vast tradition and literature of its own, integrated into the organization, ecclesiastical and civil, of the Christian Οἰκουμένη–Christendom."[6] This chapter will explore the roots and lasting legacy of Gazan monasticism. The background of Egyptian monasticism lay at the foundation of the Gazan monastics, but the ascetical works of Basil of Caesarea also permeated the work of Barsanuphius, John, and Dorotheos. The life, work, and influence of the Gazan monastic leaders provides the necessary historical context for situating Dorotheos within his monastic lineage.

Palestinian monasticism, especially Gazan monasticism, was intimately connected to the great monastic centers of Nitria, Scetis, and Kellia in Egypt.[7] According to Samuel Rubenson, "The flowering of the relations between Egypt and Palestine came in the last decade of the 4th century and in the early 5th century."[8] He posited that after the 390s many visitors journeyed through Gaza on their way to the Egyptian desert. The constant travel between Egypt and Palestine through Gaza provided the literary and spiritual resources for Gaza to become a vibrant monastic center combining its own monastic ideals with those adopted and adapted from travelling monks. Rubenson contended that Gazan monasticism was intimately connected to the Egyptian monastic tradition. He reported that the continual movement of monastics between Palestine and Egypt "almost made the monasteries around Gaza and Bet-Guvrin part of the Egyptian desert tradition. But the Egyptian influence did not only come with wandering monks, a literature on the Desert Fathers was already on its way around 400 AD."[9] Similarly, Chryssavgis traced a spiritual pedigree from the Egyptian desert to Gaza through Isaiah and Barsanuphius to Dorotheos. In his estimation, if the relationships between Isaiah and Barsanuphius withstand historical inquiry, "then we have four generations of an ascetic 'pedigree,' a monastic 'succession' or evolution that beings in the Egyptian desert."[10] The spiritual links between our authors constitute a tradition of monasticism, a "school" as Bitton-Ashkelony and Kofsky have argued.[11]

Much of the monastic travel was due to escalating hostilities with indigenous tribal attacks. A major motivation for movement of monastics from Egypt to Gaza in the late fourth to the early fifth centuries was the threat of invasion. The exile of Egyptian monastics resulted in a transfer of the collections of monastic sayings from the desert of Egypt to Gaza. Rubenson recounted:

> To the monks in exile it became essential to collect the sayings that went back to the early teachers, and the first large collections were made. All evidence points to Gaza as the region where this work was done and written down into the famous Apophthegmata Patrum, a collection dominated by Scetis, but with numerous sayings derived from the Palestinian scene. Gaza was the gate to Egypt and in addition to Scetis which is the dominant scene in the saying, there is a great number of sayings connected with people who for some time lived in the monastic surroundings of Gaza and nearby Eleuthropolis. It is actually quite probable that the collections of sayings of the Egyptian fathers were first done in or around Gaza.[12]

The importance of the Apophthegmata Patrum in later Gazan monasticism will be explored below, but its significance cannot be understated. Rubenson appraised the impact of this monastic shift from Egypt to Palestine: "The silence of the desert was gone and the old disciples of the first generation looked back upon the time when they were young followers of the founding fathers. For many of them the fact that the world had moved in meant that they had to move out. Some settled in Sinai, but others moved into the deserts of Negev and Judea."[13]

The Gazan monastic communities stood in a line of tradition with earlier monastic communities. Chief among these influences was the Egyptian monastic legacy. Perrone reminded scholars that "the mainstream of Gaza asceticism derives from the 'classic' traditions of the Egyptian desert, frequently recalled by our authors thanks to the quotations of the Apophthegmata and the recurrent invitation to read the Lives and Sayings of the Fathers."[14] Perrone described Isaiah's *Asceticon* as receiving "a strong imprint from the spirit of the monastic origins" in Egypt as well as the monastic developments of Basil of Caesarea.[15] This influence was also perceptible in Barsanuphius, John, and Dorotheos.

The Gazan monastics relied upon the recollections and writings of earlier traditions. Concerning monastic pedagogy, Columba Stewart observed that

> monasticism is *lived*, and is learned primarily from living it under the guidance of those who have grown wise in the life. Traditions, whether literary or customary, may support this living guidance but they can never substitute for it.... Mediating between asceticism and knowledge stands the teacher. Aiding discernment and interpreting the Bible, the monastic teacher points toward Christ and the fullness of life found ultimately in the Holy Trinity, source and goal of all Christian aspiration.[16]

In Gazan monasticism, Barsanuphius and John based their monastic vision upon the earlier examples in Egypt. Barsanuphius and John saw themselves as successors to these monastic societies.[17] Chryssavgis described an intimate spiritual continuity between the monks of Egypt and the Palestinian tradition precisely because they prized obedience. He claimed that "Authority and obedience are perceived by the Desert Fathers and Mothers in the light of *continuity* in the tradition of spiritual direction, and in the context of *communion* between director and directee."[18] Chryssavgis asserted that the Palestinian tradition neither innovated upon nor deviated from its received monastic tradition. He fostered the view that "the sixth century teaching on this matter is very much a continuation of the fourth and fifth century desert practices."[19]

Concerning the influential Sayings of the Desert Fathers, Douglas Burton-Christie recognized the veiled spirituality of the Egyptian monks: "While the monks we meet in the *Sayings* are generally reticent to speak of their spiritual experience, we can nevertheless glimpse substantial traces of their spirituality through their interpretation of Scripture."[20] Moreover, Chryssavgis cautioned, "The revision and rearrangement of the 'sayings' over generations inevitably reduced the focus, even distorted the original, oral tradition that would have conveyed a more comprehensive vision of the ascetic mindset and desert lifestyle."[21] However, the faint traces of personal anecdote and spiritual maturation were openly displayed in the Letters of Barsanuphius and John, Dorotheos's eighty letters among them. As Brown has noted from Regnault, "What the Sayings of the Desert Fathers let us glimpse only in the form of transitory flashes, is here played out before our eyes like a film."[22] Barsanuphius and John's correspondence provided a rare window into the daily life and struggles of their monks. Barsanuphius's and John's correspondence and Dorotheos's instructions employed and displayed the monastic tradition of Egypt that the Sayings preserved. Archaeological remains and literary works from the monks of Gaza testify to their activity and way of life in the region.

The Madaba Map remains one of the most important ancient sources of the Gazan monastic landscape in the sixth century.[23] This mosaic map inlaid in the floor of the Church of St. George in Madaba, Jordan, is dated to the reign of emperor Justinian. Depicting Palestine, the area of Gaza is clearly visible as well as the accompanying villages of Θαυαθα (Tawatha) and Μαϊῦμας (Maiumas).[24]

In his archaeological review based upon the Madaba Map, Yizhar Hirschfeld reported,

> The section of the map between Gaza and Elusa shows seven large villages and provincial towns. Two important roads crossed the region in the Byzantine period, one running southeast from Gaza to Beersheba and the other leading in a more southerly direction from Gaza to Elusa. In Elusa the road forked: one branch ran southeast along Nahal Besor to 'Avdat, on the route of the 'Spice Road' along which the Nabateans transported precious cargoes from the East, while the other branch ran southwest via Rehovot-in-the-Negev and Nessana to Sinai. In the Byzantine period this road served Christian pilgrims bound for the monastery of St. Catherine in Sinai; it was, for example, the route from Jerusalem to Sinai taken by the pilgrim known as Antoninus of Placentia and his companions in 560.[25]

Of the ten monasteries in the area known from literary sources, Hirschfeld identified two archaeological sites as monasteries. These sites are the monastery of Seridos near Deir e-Nuseirat and the monastery near Khirbet Jemameh east of Gaza. These sites featured "isolated building complexes" and a church.[26] Hirschfeld reported that the continuous density of settlements in the area of Gaza and the use of ancient building sites and building stones make identification of these monastic sites difficult. His conclusion was that "poor preservation of the remains poses a considerable challenge to the archaeologist attempting to identify, as far as possible, the location of the monasteries of Gaza."[27] The five monastic settlements most closely related to the urban area of Gaza were "concentrated to the southwest of Gaza on both banks of Nahal Besor, and another three are northwest of Gaza, between the city and Maiumas on the coast."[28] Based upon the names of several villages in the literary sources, Hirschfeld noted, "The propinquity of the monasteries to the villages expresses the involvement of the monks in the lives of the rural population, as well as in the religious and intellectual life of the nearby city of Gaza."[29] The correspondence of Barsanuphius illustrated his communication with lay persons and civic and ecclesiastical leaders, indicating regular interaction with the surrounding towns and villages.

The monastic communities were also close enough for regular communication between one another. Hirschfeld asserted, "The average distance between monasteries is about 3 km, a distance that could be walked in a few hours. This physical proximity undoubtedly contributed to the social cohesion of the monks and personal acquaintances between them."[30] The archaeological evidence that survives and the material witness of the Madaba Map indicate a lively and interconnected collection of monastic communities that existed among urban and rural residents. Hevelone-Harper described Gaza as a spiritual community in which "Spiritual directors belonged to a network of Christian authority" who, rather than live in isolation, "chose to work in concert with their leaders.... In more functional networks, spiritual fathers with different gifts could both complement and reinforce each other's teaching."[31] Chryssavgis and Penkett's observation that in the late-fifth century "Gaza suddenly flourished as a center for literary studies and spiritual pilgrimage, attracting numerous students and pilgrims alike, and becoming renowned for its teachers of rhetoric" recognized the growing influence of Gaza in the sixth century illustrated by the Madaba Map.[32] The monastic communities of Isaiah, Seridos, and Dorotheos stood amid the intellectual flowering here described.

In exploring the "ascetic ideals and experiences of the monks of Gaza," Perrone points to three major sources: the *Asceticon* of Isaiah of Gaza, the *Erotapokriseis* of Barsanuphius and John of Gaza, and the Instructions of Dorotheos of Gaza. Concerning Dorotheos's works, Perrone noted that they are the last representatives of monasticism in Gaza.[33] These sources represent the most exigent background of Gazan monasticism and comprise the literature from which to discern Dorotheos's contribution to his tradition.

Isaiah's Community at Beth Dallatha

The monastic communities of Gaza with which we are concerned are those of Isaiah, Seridos, and Dorotheos. First, Isaiah collected followers into a coenobium

near Beth Dallatha southwest of Gaza.[34] Chryssavgis dated Isaiah's move to Palestine between 431 and 451. "He lived in the semi-eremitic Scetiote ascetic life until
his death."[35] Isaiah died on August 11, 491.[36]

Zachariah the Rhetor recorded biographical data concerning Isaiah in his
Syriac *Life of Abba Isaiah*, composed in the early sixth century.[37] John Rufus also
mentioned Isaiah in his *Life* (of Peter the Iberian).[38] Additionally, Chryssavgis
notes that eleven of Isaiah's sayings were included in the *Apophthegmata Patrum*,
which points to Isaiah's reputation as a spiritual guide.[39] In her study of Peter
the Iberian, Cornelia Horn claimed that Isaiah lived about forty years in Gaza
"providing spiritual direction for the monks of the *coenobium* in which he lived
and of which Abba Peter the priest [not Peter the Iberian], Isaiah's disciple and
cell-mate,... was superior."[40] Abba Peter was head of the coenobium and liaison
between Isaiah and the other monks. Written correspondence became the regular
means of communication between Isaiah and the monks. Abba Peter collected this
correspondence and "these words of wisdom form the body of what came to be
known as the *Asceticon*, a work widely read in monastic circles. It established Abba
Isaiah's fame as an author of spiritual writings and as one endowed with a charism
easily recognized by many."[41]

In their introduction to the English translation of Isaiah's *Ascetical Discourses*,
Chryssavgis and Penkett characterized the work as "a practical guide for the monk
on the life of *ascesis*, the way of prayer, the discipline of work, the fulfillment of
the commandments, and the attainment of accordance with the nature of Jesus."[42]
Isaiah provided for his monks the spiritual direction he received as a monk in the
Egyptian desert. Elsewhere Chryssavgis described Isaiah as a "bridge to an earlier generation of elders, about the teaching and conduct of monks from former
times."[43] Chryssavgis asserted that "Isaiah was remembering conversations held
between his own elders, or simply informants, and leading personalities from the
Egyptian generation of monastics in the 430s: Arsenius, Agathon, and Sisoes, all
of whom did not die before 434."[44] Rubenson similarly pointed out that Isaiah's
"teaching is the first literary product of Palestinian monasticism, and of primary
importance as a link between the Egyptian tradition as represented by Evagrius
and later Palestinian and Syrian monastic literature."[45] For Rubenson, Isaiah's
teaching displayed similarities to the letters of Antony and Evagrius, but also initiated "certain characteristics which we will find in subsequent literature from the
region, primarily the writings of Dorotheos of Gaza and the correspondence of
Barsanuphius and John."[46] Isaiah stood between two monastic locales, Egypt and
Palestine, and conveyed the monastic teaching of one generation to the next.

Chryssavgis and Penkett also claimed that the *Asceticon* "does not contain
any explicit philosophical speculation or exclusively doctrinal elaboration."[47] In

their assessment, Isaiah was intent on emphasizing the practical life rather than speculative theology.[48] Isaiah's monastic writings remained focused on the monastic life and eschewed delving into theological conjecture.

One of Isaiah's most enduring particularities was his style of living. Isaiah remained sealed off from his monastic community as a hermit and was only accessible through his cell-mate Peter. As Chryssavgis made clear, Barsanuphius and John adopted this mode of living and directing other monks in the "next generation" of Gazan monastics.[49] In their own writings, Barsanuphius and John cite Isaiah on at least four occasions. While Dorotheos does not cite Isaiah, Eric Wheeler described Isaiah as Dorotheos's "spiritual ancestor."[50]

Seridos's Community at Tawatha

The community of Seridos was near Thawatha south of Wadi Ghazzeh, founded ca. 520. From the *Correspondence* of Barsanuphius (the Great Old Man) and John (the Other Old Man), it is clear that this community was established in the reign of the Byzantine emperor Justin I (518–527).[51] This community "was located south of Nahal Besor, as we learn from the writings of Dorotheos, who lived in the monastery of Seridus. Dorotheos relates that the watercourse to the north of the monastery burst its banks and prevented one of the monks from reaching his destination in Ascalon."[52] According to Hirschfeld's description, Barsanuphius maintained spiritual authority in the community while Seridos was in charge of the coenobium. He explained that the monastery was organized "according to a formula that was typical of Gazan monasticism—a coenobium surrounded by hermits' cells. Acting with Barsanuphius and parallel to him was another monk, John, who lived in an isolated cell near the monastery."[53] The archaeological evidence yielded evidence of a central coenobium surrounded by scattered cells.[54]

In her study of the Old Men's (Barsanuphius's and John's) letters, Hevelone-Harper found literary agreement with the numerous cells indicated in Hirschfeld's archaeological survey. She showed that under the authority of Barsanuphius, John, and Seridos, there "were other fathers, experienced monks living as hermits in cells scattered through the area. These monastic fathers were associated with the cenobium, and some had their own disciples."[55] This system of spiritual authority allowed the monastery to accommodate growth.

The expansion of the monastic community witnessed to its growth and influence. Under the leadership of Seridos, the community built "a guest house to accommodate visitors, who were fed from the monastery's resources. Stables housed the horses, camels, or other beasts of visitors, along with the monastery's donkeys, which were used to transport grain and other supplies. An infirmary provided medical care to sick monks and lay people."[56] Dorotheos of Gaza joined this monastery for nine years and served as gatekeeper, administrator of the infirmary, and attendant to Abba John. His donation of books to the monastic library added to an already important collection of written documents.[57]

Barsanuphius and John led a monastic settlement near Tawatha, Gaza.[58] They lived as hermits, taking no visitors after their retirement. Abba Seridos, who functioned as head of the coenobium, conveyed their spiritual direction.[59] Seridos received written correspondence intended for the two Old Men and penned Barsanuphius's responses. Initially, Seridos was secretary to Barsanuphius.[60] John joined the community at a later date and would have his own secretary, but Seridos remained the intermediary between the two hermits. Neyt explained, Seridos's role in the monastery as "the abbot of the cenobium, in that he is the one individual who has the task of running the community and organizing its life as a whole."[61]

The lifestyle of the two Old Men reflected that of Isaiah depicted above. Numerous smaller communities composed their larger monastic community in which a father directed disciples. As Hevelone-Harper made clear, "Many letters mention the 'fathers' of the monastery, monks advanced in the spiritual life, who lived in cells outside the coenobium yet remained integrated into the community.... These other anchorites associated with the monastery were under the authority of Abbot Seridos."[62] The archaeological remains of Tawatha concur with the literary evidence.[63]

Hevelone-Harper's study of spiritual authority in the *Correspondence* of Barsanuphius and John described the Old Men's perceived relation to Egyptian monasticism. She reported, "Barsanuphius did not boast of his own spiritual pedigree."[64] Barsanuphius came from Egypt, but never mentioned "the name of his own spiritual father. Instead, Barsanuphius appropriated a wider source of spiritual authority, that of scripture and that of the *Apophthegmata Patrum*."[65] Barsanuphius was well versed in the monastic tradition represented by the *Apophthegmata Patrum* and considered himself within that lineage. Hevelone-Harper portrayed Barsanuphius as seeing "himself as part of a chain of spiritual authority, originating in Christ and passing from the apostles to the desert fathers to the fathers at Tawatha."[66] Neyt also recognized that the two Old Men of Gaza's correspondence "reflète admirablement la maturité religieuse qui régnait dans ca monastère; elle assume aussi le meilleur des traditions monastique égyptiennes, sans oublier les écrits des grand Cappadociens et la literature monastique de l'époque."[67] In a recent study, Rosa Marie Parrinello claimed that che vi sia una serie notevole di punti di contatto tra Basilio e l'*Epistolario* di Barsanufio e Giovanni, mentre molto più ridotte sono le convergenze con la normativa pacomiana: le direttive basiliane, del resto, sembrano adattarsi molto di più alla tipologia di monachesimo incarnata da Barsanufio e Giovanni, che difficilmente avrebbe potuto esprimersi nella ben più rigida comunità pacomiana.[68]

The monastic influences from which Barsanuphius and John drew were widespread. The community was centered upon the guidance of the two Old Men in a chain of spiritual authority rather than upon a rule.

In their monastic environment, Barsanuphius and John corresponded with monastics, lay persons, bishops, and government officials.[69] According to Hevelone-Harper, "The surrounding lay communities… looked to the monks to provide societal order and spiritual guidance. The monastic community was not seen as a retreat from the world but as a spiritual resource for the wider community."[70] In contrast to Brown's assertion that the holy man exercised patronage over villages and provided a link to urban society, Leah Di Segni claimed that "this pattern does not apply to the thousands of simple monks, the bricks of the lighthouse on which the holy man stood like a dazzling beacon; but in fact it is obvious that the light of the ascetic could burn only if plugged into the power system of monasteries which sustained his legend as well as his physical existence."[71] Di Segni recognized the social importance of the Old Men's written correspondence. In her estimation, most of the correspondents must have been "educated, well-off middle- and upper-class people, which is not surprising, since the two holy men could be approached only by writing, and no illiterate and inarticulate beggar or peasant could do that—or, if any such messages go through, they were not deemed worthy of preservation."[72] The compilation and preservation of their letters witnessed to the importance of Barsanuphius and John as spiritual and ecclesial figures in their Gazan society.

As leaders of Seridos's coenobium, Barsanuphius and John admitted a spiritual unity between themselves. To a monk who asked both men the same question, Barsanuphius indicated that "the God of Barsanuphius and John is but one."[73] These two Old Men supported one another's ministry by confirming each other's spiritual guidance.[74] Their unity also incorporated the authority of Seridos. As Barsanuphius's secretary, Seridos wrote to a certain monk in Barsanuphius's own words. Barsanuphius dictated, "Tell brother John, who is of one mind with us, that I have written many things to you [the certain monk] through the hand of our genuine and beloved child [Seridos], who loves all three of us equally [Barsanuphius, John, and the certain monk] and with all his soul in perfect love."[75] The unity of purpose and authority between the two Old Men and their support for Seridos was an important facet of the spiritual and practical authority in the coenobium.

The *Correspondence* of Barsanuphius and John was a peculiar collection because a monk of the monastery compiled it while the Old Men were offering spiritual direction. Historians benefit from this preservationist's work because "the compiler not only copied the letters of Barsanuphius and John, but he also commented upon each letter, occasionally naming the recipient, describing the situation that prompted the correspondence, and usually summarizing or quoting the original question addressed to the Old Men."[76] Hevelone-Harper discussed the importance of these letters by stating,

> The letters of Barsanuphius and John provide a unique view of early Byzantine asceticism. Each letter captures both a specific moment in time and the response to the query of an individual petitioner. Although the compiler's summaries of the petitions often leave the historian hungry for more information, they constitute, nevertheless, an unusual window into the lives of the sixth-century Christians.[77]

Perrone also remarked that the letters of Barsanuphius and John were "a very special vantage point from which to observe not only the practices concerning introspection and examination of the conscience, commonly recommended by both ancient philosophers and monastic teachers, but also the religious and ethical issues raised in the daily life of Christians."[78] Hevelone-Harper suggested that the letters may have been preserved to provide practical and spiritual guidance in the monastery, but the compiler also included a prologue in which he warned "that the letters were written to a wide assortment of people—anchorites, cenobites, clerics, laymen, and novices—and, therefore, a response to one individual might not be applicable to another."[79] The spiritual counsel divulged in the letters was provided for a particular individual and should not be the basis of broader regulation. They were a testimony to the spiritual dynamic that characterized Gazan monasticism.

Barsanuphius's and John's letters of spiritual guidance are a remarkable testament to their understanding of the monastic life. Perrone has provided some important insight into this monastic vision. He explained the importance of relationship to others in the monastic vision of the two Old Men. The love for God entailed a love of others. In the monastery, "when spiritual progress is assured, the questioning partner will transform himself into an answering one, thus assuming in his turn the role of 'spiritual father'."[80] The monastic life illuminated in the *Correspondence* was a spiritual journey that resulted in the transfer of spiritual authority from teacher to pupil.

The emphasis on continuity within a monastic tradition was characteristic of Gazan monasticism. Chryssavgis declared, "The context of obedience to a spiritual elder is always one of spiritual continuity, which protects the community from the inherent dangers of self-designated directors.... Outside of this line of spiritual succession, the advice is to avoid teaching and counseling."[81] The transformation from pupil to teacher was only accessible through the cultivation of obedience. Chryssavgis eloquently explained, "Obedience is neither submissiveness nor ser-vility. For, obedience is *also due from the elder*, not simply to abstract rules but to another person... Both elder and disciple are subject to the same conditions and commandments, both accountable before the living God. The two are traveling together, though they may not be on equal footing."[82] Within this understand-ing of spiritual pedagogy, the instructor and the student are interdependent. The spiritual authority passed from master to disciple such that "if the disciple is even-tually called upon to become a master, he will in his turn recreate the relation he experienced, by himself practicing spiritual direction."[83] Perrone did not hesitate to describe the letters of the two Old Men of Gaza as essentially "a 'school of Chris-tianity' and a remarkable embodiment of its religious values and ideals, as well as its possible limitations."[84] This reciprocal relationship ensures the continuity of a way of life as envisioned by the two Old Men. This relationship could mature into "the passage from disciple to master."[85]

Dorotheos's Community at Maiumas

In the late sixth-century, John Moschus referred to "the ceonobium of Abba Dor-otheos, near to Gaza and to Maïouma" in his collection of monastic anecdotes.[86] The prologue to Dorotheos's *Discourses* revealed that the teachings presented were given to Dorotheos's disciples after "having left the monastery of Abba Seridos and, by the grace of God, [Dorotheos] established his own monastery (μοναστήριον) following the death of Abba John the Prophet and the complete silence of Abba Barsanuphius."[87] However, Hirschfeld declared that the archaeological remains of the monastery have not been located.[88]

The *Life of Dositheos* related that Dorotheos joined the coenobium of Seridos at Tawatha near Gaza.[89] Here he spent many years under the spiritual direction of Abba Seridos and the Great Old Men, Barsanuphius and John. Dorotheos was from a wealthy Christian family in Antioch and received a classical education in rhetoric.[90] His education may have included the study of medicine, since Heve-lone-Harper affirmed that Dorotheos's donation of his personal books included Basil's *Ascetica* (Letters 318–319) and works on medicine (Letter 327).[91] The anonymous *Life of Dositheos*, which accompanies Dorotheos's work in most manuscripts, verified that Dorotheos was a monastic in the coenobium of Abba Seridos and lived under the spiritual guidance of Barsanuphius and John.[92] After about fifteen years, Dorotheos moved with his disciples to Maiumas.[93] His spiritual struggles and maturation in the monastery can be observed in his correspondence with Barsanuphius and John.[94] Dorotheos was also the builder and administrator of the monastery's infirmary (τὸ νοσοκομεῖον).[95] Hevelone-Harper described how Seridos utilized Dorotheos's education and experiences to aid the construction of the infirmary.[96] This duty made prayer and meditation difficult due to the constant disruption of patients.

His responsibilities expanded when he began to offer spiritual counsel to his fellow monks with the approval of the abbot and the elders.[97] Dorotheos reacted to this situation with some trepidation, but the abbot and the elders assured him that he was able to offer sound counsel. His ascension to the level of spiritual director indicated the trust that Seridos and the Old Men placed in his guidance. Within the Gazan context, spiritual direction required authority from one's own spiritual father.[98]

From Dorotheos's correspondence with Barsanuphius and John and his *Discourses* to his own monks, the particular character of Dorotheos's teachings is evident. He continually cast his spiritual guidance in the mold of a diagnosis and treatment of a spiritual disorder. He portrayed humanity as under the influence of a profound ailment for which Christ alone could provide treatment. The commandments of Christ were prescriptions that purified the lingering effects of the passions and eventually eradicated them completely.

Dorotheos's spiritual teaching, letters, and sayings conveyed his monastic guidance to later generations. These writings revealed the impact of the monastic school of Gaza on his embodiment of the tradition as well as his marked development on his tradition. Hevelone-Harper noted that within the correspondence between Dorotheos and the Old Men and Dorotheos's own spiritual discourses, "various stages of Dorotheos' life are well documented, allowing us to trace his development as a spiritual director. His training in the monastery reveals the manner in which spiritual authority was transferred to a new generation of spiritual leaders."[99] Perrone was unabashed in his praise for Dorotheos, calling him "the most cultivated of the great masters of Gaza spirituality, since he had been educated in secular studies and more specifically in medicine when still in Antioch, his birthplace."[100]

Dorotheos had other monastic contacts during his time in Gaza. In his discourses, he mentioned associating with Abba Zosimas. Parrinello affirmed that Dorotheos probably collected and edited the sayings of Zosimas. She noted that

Zosimas "potrebbe dunque essere il tramite attraverso il quale Doroteo entra in contatto con Basilio, uno degli autori più presenti nell' opera zosimiana proprio con le Regole."[101] In addition to Dorotheos's dependence upon the *Apophthegmata*, Isaiah, and Zosimas, Pauli saw a heavy influence of Cappodocian spirituality in Dorotheos's works "stärker theologisch reflektierten asketischen Konzeption der Kappadokier."[102]

Pauli also directed her readers to the way Dorotheos utilized "die Analogie zwischen Medizin und Seelenheilung, d.h. zwischen körperlicher Krankheit dem Verständnis der Leidenschaften als seelische Krankheit, findet sich sowohl in der Stoa und hellenistischen Moralphilosophie und ebenfalls bei Basilius."[103] This connection is viable precisely because, as Pauli explained,

> Dorotheos greift häufig auf die Kenntnisse antiker Medizin zurück, um geistliche Zusammenhänge zu veranschaulichen. Er folgt dabei dem Medizinkonzept des Hippokrates (Humoralpathologie), wonach Gesundheit und Krankheit als Harmonie bzw. Störung des Gleichgewichtszustands der vier Körpersäfte verstanden werden. Die Vorstellung von den Leidenschaften als Krankheit der Seele legt dieses Vorgehen zwar ohnehin nahe, doch zeigen die von Dorotheos angeführten Vergleiche, daß es sich nicht um ein wirkungsvoll eingesetztes Stilmittel handelt: Aus ihnen spricht die eigene Kenntnis und praktische Erfahrung des Autors.[104]

Pauli did not investigate further how Dorotheos's medical practice influenced his spiritual guidance, but indicated that Dorotheos moved beyond his knowledge of medicine in his spiritual teaching.

Adapting the discourse of healing to highlight his own concerns was an important aspect of Dorotheos's monastic tradition. Bitton-Ashkelony and Kofsky aptly described the monastic school of Gaza as "firmly rooted in earlier ascetic traditions, reshaping them through its interpretation and selective adoption, demonstrating that we are dealing here with a dynamic monastic culture in an ongoing process of shaping and reevaluating its own tradition."[105] However, their account of the monastic school of Gaza failed to adequately incorporate the distinctive teachings of Dorotheos. The dynamism of his tradition allowed Dorotheos to express his spiritual teaching in a form that was traditional but with particularities that were distinct. Dorotheos made use of the established discourse of healing to articulate the monastic life, while adding his own emphasis on the type of healing one should pursue. Bitton-Ashkelony and Kofsky's demonstration of the coherence of the Gazan monastics as a school overshadowed the features of Dorotheos's contribution. The comparison of the discourse of healing illumines new facets of Dorotheos's thought and confirms his account of the body's positive role in the monastic life. Dorotheos was truly a monastic teacher who promoted the health of body and soul in his spiritual guidance. Dorotheos's service in the monastery's infirmary may have, perhaps, contributed to his divergent views.

Much of Dorotheos's epistolary exchange with his spiritual mentors, Barsanuphius and John, revolved around his role as monastic infirmarian.[106] He attended to patients, directed his own disciples, and interacted with laypersons and visitors. Dorotheos first offered spiritual direction while working in the infirmary. His first disciple, Dositheos, accompanied him in providing infirmarian care. In his own monastery, his task was to guide and direct his monastics to a life of health. Dorotheos viewed the monastic life as a daily enterprise of cultivating and habituating health within the body and soul such that the individual could prosper within the monastic community.

Dorotheos entered the monastic life during Seridos's tenure as abbot of the monastery at Tawatha. At that time, he had already enjoyed a rigorous education. Hevelone-Harper indicated that his education included the study of medicine. She also suggested that Dorotheos might have practiced medicine before entering the monastic life.[107] Dorotheos also donated his personal books to the monastery's library. Hevelone-Harper asserted that these included Basil's *Asceticon* and works on medicine.[108] The introductory letter to Dorotheos's compiled works characterized Dorotheos as a bee, gathering up teachings from even pagan philosophers and applying those teachings "just at the right moment."[109] Dorotheos's education and study was so beneficial to his work in the infirmary that the author of the introduction to his discourses claimed,

> He is sweet in speech and even sweeter in conversation; he is a knowledgeable healer of every illness and cure (ὁ ἐπιστήμων ἰατρὸς ἦν βούλει νόσον καὶ ἰατρείαν). He has adapted the manifold economy of God to the rich, the poor, the wise, the unlearned, women, men, the aged, the young, those who sorrow and those of good cheer, strangers, close friends, those living in the world and those following the monastic life, governors and those under them, slaves and free. 'He has become all things to all men' and thus gained the majority (1 Cor. 9:22).[110]

In the transmission his works, Dorotheos was portrayed as a physical healer and teacher of God's salvific economy. This attribute affirmed the use of medicine as part of God's provision for humanity and pointed to the various individuals who may have sought health care from Dorotheos.

Pauli assigned Dorotheos's stay in Seridos's coenobium to fifteen years. In his earliest years Dorotheos was responsible for the guesthouse of the monastery.[111] As Dorotheos gained the trust of Seridos and the Old Men, they encouraged him to report the actions of the brothers to the abbot. This duty resulted in some strife between Dorotheos and the brothers. John advised Dorotheos that correcting the brothers was for their good and that "the sick who are being healed will even speak against their doctors; yet the latter do not care, knowing that these will thank them afterward."[112] According to the *Life of Dositheos*, Dorotheos was instructed to build the monastery's infirmary (τὸ νοσοκομεῖον) with the financial help of his "brother in the flesh" and family resources and was appointed the infirmary's administrator.[113] Regardless of his family's financial status, Dorotheos was also well poised to operate the infirmary because of his extensive education and possession of medical books. When the young nobleman Dositheos, a refined and handsome soldier, entered the monastic life, he was immediately placed under the spiritual guidance of Dorotheos who was then working in the infirmary.[114] Thus, the minimum length of Dorotheos's administration of the infirmary would correspond to the five years Dositheos lived and died in the coenobium.[115] Dorotheos spent the remainder of his time in Seridos's coenobium as the mediator of Abba John, some nine years of service.[116]

Dorotheos's administration of the infirmary was not without struggle. Through his correspondence with Barsanuphius and John, Dorotheos expressed various difficulties in balancing his monastic pursuit and providing health care in the infirmary. François Neyt asserted that "the organization of the infirmary and the care of the sick are such a burden for Dorotheos that he longs to lead a hesychastic life in which, he says, he will be able to pray without ceasing and live 'in the remembrance of God.'"[117] These struggles were often practical issues that corresponded to a disruption of his monastic life. For instance, Dorotheos was attached to certain choice vessels that were used in the infirmary. John advised Dorotheos to take and use those vessels if they were necessary but to blame himself saying, "Had it not been for my need, I would not have to accept this; instead, however, I was conquered by attachment (ἡττήθην τῇ ἐπιθυμίᾳ)."[118] Dorotheos's duties in the infirmary should not be compromised because of his personal struggles. He was commended to provide the best care he could while acknowledging his struggles. Dorotheos also admitted entertaining frequent visits from both monks and laypersons in the hospital. In Letter 313, Dorotheos asked Abba John about certain people who come to the monastic community seeking something from them and John instructed him to give them what they need. John cautioned him, though, not to engage in idle conversation outside of financial or medical needs nor did he authorized him to offer treatment.[119]

Dorotheos also worried about the quality of health care he could offer. In a letter to Barsanuphius, Dorotheos asked about applying a cure that accidentally caused a person harm. Barsanuphius emboldened Dorotheos by explaining that God will pay attention to his intention even if the cure causes greater harm, "for he knows that it was in your desire to bring benefit (ὠφελῆσαι) that you caused harm (ἔβλαψας)."[120] Barsanuphius cautioned Dorotheos, however, not to allow pride to interfere with his treatment. If an experienced person offered advice for treatment, Dorotheos should heed that advice. This particular question correlated to an anecdote in the *Life of Dositheos*. While in the coenobium of Seridos, Dositheos became deathly ill. As Dositheos's health care provider and spiritual father, Dorotheos was all the more responsible for the young man. Dositheos had heard that soft-boiled eggs are good for his particular illness but remained silent out of obedience to Dorotheos. The *Life* stated that Dorotheos was too distracted to remember this cure. Dositheos's admission of the benefit eggs could provide indicated his conflict between physical health and spiritual constancy. Dositheos admitted, "Father, I would like to tell you about something that would be good for me. However, I do not want you to give it to me, since my thoughts trouble me."[121] Dorotheos complied with Dositheos's wishes, but, instead of eggs, Dorotheos tried to give him other good food "since he had said that the idea of the eggs troubled him."[122] Dositheos soon perished, but, for the author of the *Life of Dositheos*, this episode was an indication of Dositheos's struggle against his own will.

The height of Dorotheos's anxiety in the infirmary lay in the potential vainglory and distraction of medical books. Dorotheos conveyed his uncertainty about whether to consult medical texts even though he was administrator of the hospital. He was afraid that his intellect would be distracted and give rise to vainglory. He admitted having certain medical knowledge pertaining to the use of "oil, fire, ointments, and other such simple things (ἐλαίου καὶ πυρίων καὶ ἐπιχρισμάτων καὶ τῶν τοιούτων ἁπλῶς)" to aid in healing.[123] Yet, the consultation of medical books was, for Dorotheos, a challenge to his humility. Barsanuphius urged Dorotheos not only to commit himself to study medical texts but also to consult lay doctors. According to Timothy Miller, Dorotheos's study and administration of the hospital was "essential to his Christian life."[124] Barsanuphius replied, "When you read these books and ask others about these matters, do not forget that without God there can be no healing…. The art of medicine (ἡ ἰατρικὴ τέχνη) does not prevent one from practicing piety; you should regard the practice of medicine in the same manner as the brothers' manual labor."[125] Barsanuphius's response revealed the real cause of Dorotheos's apprehension toward medical texts: a fear of misplacing divine agency in the healing of the human person. The Great Old Man stated, "We should not, however, place all our hope in these [medical texts], but only in the God who grants death and life, who says 'I shall wound, and I shall heal (πατάσσω, κἀγὼ ἰάσομαι). (Deut. 32:39)' When you read these books and ask others about these matters, do not forget that without God there can be no healing (ἴασις)."[126] Dorotheos offered no indication of which medical texts he accessed or the local physicians with whom he spoke. From the letters cited, he was certainly engaged in study and consultation on medical matters.[127]

The Old Men supported Dorotheos's work in the infirmary offering encouragement amid these distractions. On one occasion, Dorotheos inquired about attending liturgical services amid his duties in the infirmary. Dorotheos oversaw a group of attendees in the infirmary and John allowed Dorotheos to attend liturgical services "If the brothers know what to do."[128] In another letter, Dorotheos asked about the pursuit of stillness amid his bothersome duties in the infirmary. John responded that through attention to the sick and contributing to their healing, Dorotheos could cultivate stillness.[129] John affirmed that serving the sick helped to generate compassion: "It is a good thing to suffer with those who are ill and to contribute to their healing. For if a doctor receives a reward in caring for the sick, how much more so will someone who suffers as much as possible with one's neighbor in all things?"[130] Barsanuphius also communicated his trust in Dorotheos's work in the infirmary. In Letter 330, Dorotheos complained that his duties contributed to vainglory and boldness. Additionally, continually handing out food made Dorotheos gluttonous. Barsanuphius communicated his confidence in Dorotheos, saying,

> Brother, listen and be assured in the Lord that, since the time that we permitted you to assume this charge, our hand and our heart are with you.... When you fall, arise; when you err, blame yourself until the Lord shows you the mercy you desire.... The one who assigned you to this charge is the very same one who said to his disciples: 'Behold, I am sending you out'; (Matt. 10:16) and again: Behold, I am with you' (Matt. 28:20).[131]

The correspondence of Dorotheos with Barsanuphius and John, corroborated by the account given in the *Life of Dositheos*, clearly attested to the Old Men's encouragement and leadership in the building of an infirmary for the monastery. The impact of Dorotheos's infirmary experiences is difficult to ascertain but remains a possible influence on his monastic teaching.

For Perrone, Dorotheos stood as an important figure amid his predecessors precisely because he drew upon a wide range of resources in his monastic instruction. Perrone mentioned Dorotheos's secular education and "systematic treatment of ascetic doctrines."[132] He noted that Dorotheos proposed a "synthesis among differing monastic traditions: besides the authors of Gaza we find the Fathers of the Desert, including Evagrius' gnostic writings, together with the coenobitism of Pachomius and Basilius. At the same time Dorotheos manifests himself to be sensitive to philosophical inspiration. For this last aspect he represents indeed one of the most interesting test-cases for a comparison between early monasticism and the philosophical practice of 'spiritual exercises'."[133]

Whereas the *Correspondence* of Barsanuphius and John was directed at the specific concerns of their respondents, Dorotheos discussed general avenues of monastic thought. Regnault reminded readers that Dorotheos was "tout en restant toujours très proche du réel, concret et pratique comme Barsanuphe, Dorothée semble avoir eu quelque préoccupation de dégager des données de la tradition et de l'expérience, les éléments essentiels, d'esquisser les lignes maîtresses de la spiritualité chrétienne et monastique."[134] While Dorotheos's primary audience was his monastic disciples, he also anticipated a broader audience. Bitton-Ashkelony and Kofsky ascertained Dorotheos's attention to the Christian life in general, stating, "Anyone perusing the teachings of Dorotheos has no difficulty in discerning that the ideal way of life that he preached in the framework of coenobitic life was suited to all who wished to abide by the Christian faith and not solely the minority who chose a life of retreat and monasticism."[135] Dorotheos's prescriptions for Christian living were amenable to those outside the monastic enclosure, modeling an approach similar to Basil the Great, "whose ascetic writings sketch the image of the ideal Christian."[136] Dorotheos was attentive to practical monastic instruction, he also intended to provide his disciples a larger vision of the monastic life and Christian spiritual doctrine.

The emphasis Dorotheos gave in his *Discourses* echoes a shift in current methods of reading ascetic texts that Samuel Rubenson indicated. Rubenson observed that studies of Christian asceticism have undergone a shift in interpretation: "Earlier emphasis on ascetic practice as a sign of disdain for the body, related to a strongly dualistic anthropology, have given way to a reading of Christian ascetic texts as expressions for a strong belief in the possibility and even necessity of transforming the body."[137] No longer are ascetics presumed to despise their bodies, but rather the body was an important partner in the monastic pursuit of God. As Rubenson noted, research into the writings of Evagrius of Pontus and Stoic anthropology and psychology does not emphasize "any separation of soul, or mind, from body, of immaterial from material, but rather on making the body and soul to conform to the logos, the rational capacity, and thus create harmony and stability in the entire person."[138] In this same vein, Dorotheos combined his concern for spiritual health among his monastic disciples with his emphasis on providing health for the body as well as the soul.

CHAPTER THREE

The Discourse of Healing and Gazan Monasticism

In Gazan monasticism illness and healing were common themes. The Gazan monastics were aware that health care was important to the strength of their communities, and they often described the monastic life as a search for healing according to early Christian discourse on healing. This chapter evaluates how Isaiah, Barsanuphius, John, and Dorotheos discussed Christ's activity as physician, approached health and illness in their communities, and used the metaphor of healing in the monastic school of Gaza. Reactions to bodily illness were intertwined with spiritual concerns for these monastics. The portrayal of Christ as physician and conceptions of illness and healing will accentuate the unity of thought among these monastic figures. That is, Dorotheos was part of a monastic tradition steeped in the metaphor of healing to describe the monastic life. His own employment of the metaphor points to a link with his tradition. However, the meaning with which he imbued the metaphor of healing positioned Dorotheos as distinctive.

Gary Ferngren and Darrel Amundsen proposed that "the desire to remove disease and preserve health" motivated the ancient medical tradition[1] Ancient health care necessarily included concern for the body. Galen taught that "A body is healthy in the general sense when it has from birth a good mixture of the simple, primary parts, and good proportion in the organs which are composed of these.... Such a body will also be of good mixture and proportion; but it will not be possessed of the best type of mixture and proportion, rather of that suitable to itself."[2]

Disease was an imbalance of the body or a "malfunction." Again, for Galen

> What proceeds from the very nature of the best-constituted bodies is the balance of the homogeneous parts in respect of heat, cold, dryness, and moisture; and the balance of the organic parts in respect of quantity and magnitude of their component elements, and also in construction and position of each of its parts and of the organ as a whole. What proceeds from the attributes which are necessary consequences of these homogenous parts is as follows: with respect to the sense of touch, a balance between hardness and softness; with respect to the sense of sight, a good colour and balance between smoothness and roughness; in the context of activities, the perfect performance of them, which is also called 'excellence' [ἀρετή].[3]

The healthy state of the body involved proper function. The combination of internal operations and external influences must be held in a delicate balance. The role of the physician was to prescribe a way of life to restore the body to its proper balance.

The disruption of the body caused humoral imbalance and the physician's goal was to restore that balance. Risse drew a distinction between an "*iatros* (physician)" and a lay healer due to the physician's "learning and practical skills—his *techne iatrike*—including employ [*sic*] the employment of *pharmaka* and surgical instruments."[4] Ferngren offered a brief survey of healing techniques available to ancient physicians.[5] The physician's knowledge of the patient was very important because "the proper balance differed from individual to individual. Hence ancient physicians were illness-oriented, and they viewed and treated the patient as a whole person rather than the disease itself."[6] Physicians relied upon their knowledge of the individual and their experience of the effects of various treatments on bodies.

Treating diseases with ancient medicine often included religious expression. The Hippocratic text *On the Sacred Disease* showed how ancient physicians tried to move from divine origin to a rational explanation of the disease. The author explained, "I am about to discuss the disease called sacred. It is not in my opinion, any more divine or more sacred than other disease, but has a natural cause and its supposed divine origin is due to men's inexperience and to their wonder at its peculiar character."[7] He then offered a contrasting opinion,

> My own view is that those who first attributed a sacred character to this malady were like the magicians, purifiers, charlatans, and quacks of our own day, people who claim great piety and superior knowledge. Being at a loss and having no treatment that would help, they concealed and sheltered themselves behind superstition and called this illness sacred, in order that their utter ignorance might not be manifest.[8]

This classic example illustrated the move from religious explanation to medical healing as a skill to be acquired through experience and education.

Galen, too, emphasized the importance of study and rational discernment when treating diseases. He claimed, "The true doctor will be found to be a friend of temperance and a companion of truth. Furthermore, he must study logical method to know how many diseases there are, by species and by genus, and how, in each case, one is to find out what kind of treatment is indicated."[9] Diseases were understood through both their causes and their effects. The human body, too, would undergo much examination to determine how and why certain diseases affected the body in various ways.

Mere bodily study of human beings was too simplistic an approach. The skilled physician must also tend to the whole person. For Galen, the best doctor

> must be practiced in logical theory in order to discover the nature of the body, the dif-
> ference between diseases, and the indications as to treatment; he must despise money
> and cultivate temperance in order to stay the course. He must, therefore, know all the
> parts of philosophy: the logical, the physical, and the ethical…And so he is bound
> to be in possession of the other virtues too, for they all go together. It is impossible
> to gain one without acquiring all the others as an immediate consequence; they are
> connected as if by one string.[10]

Treatment was not, for Galen, the prescription of elixirs, but a recommendation of a whole way of life that would restore and retain health to a person. The best physician must attend to the body and the soul. Galen made this point very clear by stating,

> The causes of change in the body are divided into the 'necessary' and the 'not neces-
> sary'.… The art concerned with the body is thus performed by means of the former,
> not the latter. And if we make a classification of all the necessary factors which alter
> the body, to each of these will correspond a specific type of healthy cause. One cate-
> gory is contact with the ambient air; another is motion and rest of the body as a whole
> or of its individual parts. The third is sleep and waking; the fourth, substances taken;
> the fifth, substances voided or retained; the sixth, what happens to the soul."[11]

His conclusion was that "philosophy is necessary for doctors with regard to both preliminary learning and subsequent training, [and] clearly all true doctors must also be philosophers."[12] The medical tradition in which Galen stood and for which Galen would remain a touchstone followed Hippocrates, but Galen would also advocate that one "must, then, practice philosophy, if we are true followers of Hippocrates."[13]

Ferngren argued that Greek view of "health (*hugieia*) as a state of the body in which all humors operate in harmony provided an analogy for the soul in which moral virtue (*arete*) was defined as a balance of the elements of the soul (e.g., by Plato)."[14] Health was a holistic endeavor of which freedom from physical disease was merely a part. In Ludwig Edelstein's oft-quoted estimation, "medicine did serve philosophy as a means of explaining and of making acceptable to men that conclusion which philosophy itself had reached, that man can live without philosophy as little as he can live without medicine."[15] Medicine and philosophy worked together to provide the physical and intellectual remedy for human ailment. Health of body and health of soul were interrelated, such that "medicine and philosophy complimented each other by together enabling one to lead a harmonious life whose end result was happiness. The body-soul analogy was used by writers of nearly all philosophical schools."[16] Dorotheos renewed the dual emphasis on health of the body and health of the soul in his monastic teaching. He revived an emphasis on healing the whole person, body and soul.

Ferngren and Amundsen compared the Greek concept of virtue to its use by Christian authors. They noted that the Greek term ἀρετή was broadly used for excellence and proficiency of humanity, gods, animals, and things: "Insofar as they fulfill their function weapons and horses possess *arete*."[17] In reference to human ἀρετή, "health [was] to be both essential to *arete* and an aspect of *arete*. It was thus a virtue and an indicator of virtue and the *sine qua non* of the good life."[18] Plato described the four cardinal virtues as wisdom, temperance, courage, and justice in *Republic*.[19] The human person functioning or operating correctly was said to be healthy.[20] Galen stated, "I see all men using the terms 'health' and 'disease' thus.... For they also consider that person to be healthy in whom no function of any part [of the body] is damaged, and someone to be diseased in whom there is damage."[21] In his *Method of Medicine*, Galen proposed that health is the restoration of function to the parts of the body that have been damaged.[22] The function of the body as a unity of elements working together harmoniously was analogous to the soul. Ferngren and Amundsen assert, "Moral virtue, after the model of human pathology, was regarded not as adherence to an external code or standard, but as a balance of the elements of the soul."[23] Likewise, wherein health represents a balance or harmony, disease is the disruption of that balance because of "bodily fluids or material taken into the body."[24] Health of the body and health of the soul were analogous concepts; both were conceived through the lens of proper function and harmonious balance.

Virtue became the key concept to describe those who enjoyed this balance of health. Because health of body and health of soul were so intimately related, the person who was bodily healthy was believed to be morally superior to those lacking bodily health. Hence, there was a correlation between medicine and ethics: "The care of the body was regarded as a spiritual duty... Since the virtue of the soul and the virtue of the body were so intimately related, the health of the body mirrored the health of the soul."[25] Through self-control and moderation, treating the body through diet and care, one could maintain a state of health. Alternatively, the presence of disease and sickness was "an indication of the lack of proper regulation of one's life... Overeating or overindulgence of the passions not only leads to bad health, but creates an unhealthy disposition of the soul."[26] The virtuous life was a combination of care for the body and the soul. Health was the condition in which each was properly balanced and operated correctly. Health care was the response to disharmony and an attempt to return the body to its regulated state.

The rise of Stoicism, Epicureanism, and Cynicism in the fourth century B.C.E. complicated the interconnectedness of virtue and bodily health. These schools, while not denying the virtue of health, claimed "that other virtues are superior to health and that happiness may be achieved at the expense of the body."[27] Ferngren and Amundsen characterized this shift as concern for "the practice of askesis ('training'), to make his soul independent of his body."[28] These philosophical schools initiated "an ascetic tradition that eventually led to the belief that the proper attitude to disease and suffering was one of indifference, while the real concern of an individual should be the care of the soul."[29] This position turned the individual's attention inward and privileged health of the soul above bodily health to the point of disparaging bodily well-being.[30]

Amundsen and Ferngren pointed to a new emphasis in medical care in the Roman Empire toward kindness, helpfulness, and charity. This new emphasis imbued medicine with a sense of compassion or *philanthropia* (love of humanity).[31] Accordingly, for Galen medicine also embodied the ideals of a philosopher in terms of living a moral life. Stephen D'Irsay also indicated the importance of comforting the sick as "one of the cardinal Christian virtues and complete altruism became so fundamental an ethical standard that it was part of faith."[32] Ferngren and Amundsen asserted that virtue was the attribute of bodily harmony and lack of harmony signaled lack of health.[33] Emphasizing philanthropy and compassion in medical practice represented, for Ferngren and Amundsen, "a transformation of the classical concept of virtue and anticipates the new definition of virtue introduced by Christianity."[34] In their estimation, "Virtue and the virtues were seen as an integral part of the Christian life in spiritual growth, moral attainment, sanctification, perfection and eternal reward."[35] This shift and the Christian response was by no means monolithic, but it would have lasting effects on Christian approaches to health and virtue.[36]

Adolf Harnack signaled the importance of healing in early Christianity when he described it as "the religion of 'healing.'"[37] In another context, Harnack characterized the gospel as that which offers health to the world and the individual. He wrote, "Das Evangelium selbst ist als die Botschaft vom Heiland und von der Heilung in die Welt gekommen. Es wendet sich an die kranke Menschheit und verspricht ihr Gesundheit."[38]

While Christians did have recourse to the religious significance of illness and disease, Meredith also cautioned the impulse of assuming that all cases of illness were infused with such religious meaning.[39] Meredith discerned two discourses of disease. The first discourse utilized metaphor and analogy to cast Christianity as metaphorically providing medicine to religious and social disruption.[40] The second discourse considered disease as beneficial to Christians because through suffering of the body one is cured of the afflictions of the soul.[41] The redemptive and transformative properties of suffering through lack of health would have been unknown to the classical world.[42] In Porterfield's opinion,

> Part of Christianity's appeal as a means of coping with suffering is the idea that suffering is not meaningless but part of a cosmic vision of redemption.... The real genius of Christianity has been to embrace pain and disability and death and not to limit the meaning of health and healing to their expulsion. Thus, many Christians have accepted the onset or persistence of suffering as part of religious life, while also celebrating relief from suffering as a sign of the power and meaning of their faith.[43]

Indeed, Christians could continually refer back to Christ himself as the Good Physician in their discourse of healing.[44]

The Christian discourse of healing often involved a consideration of the relationship between sin and illness. For Meredith, this illustrated "the perception on the part of Christians that humans are profoundly psychosomatic beings."[45] The health of the soul and the health of the body were intimately connected. The two discourses of disease may have interpreted the relationship differently, but the intimacy was retained. Meredith signaled the importance of not only examining the cures Christians offered but also the mode of discourse they used to describe "disease, suffering, healing, and transformation to shape a new understanding of bodily ills and physical affliction."[46] Amid the Christian use of healing as a religious discourse, Ferngren pronounced that "the first five centuries held views regarding the use of medicine and the healing of disease that did not differ appreciably from those that were widely taken for granted in the Graeco-Roman world.... They employed natural means of healing, whether these means involved physicians or home or traditional remedies."[47] Timothy Miller declared that Byzantine society "drew on its own rich traditions of classical Greek medicine. Although Christian bishops surely organized the first hospitals, they readily turned to the students of Galen and Hippocrates for the expertise to make their nosokomeia effective centers of medical care."[48] Early Christians studied and used ancient medical techniques of healing. Medicine provided an avenue to physical healing, as well as an established mode for religious discourse.

Early Christians utilized ancient medicine for healing, but also adopted healing discourse to describe the Christian way of life. Teresa Shaw contended, "Many of the concepts and assumptions ... in Christian ascetic discourse and theory are grounded in the wider context of Greco-Roman medical theory, moral philosophy, and contemporary understandings of the relationship between body and soul in the human being."[49] Amundsen asserted that early Christians "inherited and exploited to the fullest the positive metaphorical value of the idea of the physician."[50] Origen and Eusebius, for example, applied to Christ an ancient formula contained in the Hippocratic corpus describing a physician: the physician "sees terrible sights, touches unpleasant things, and the misfortunes of others bring a harvest of sorrows that are particularly his."[51] Origen and Eusebius characterized the work of Christ as that of a Physician.[52]

Christian reactions to the actual use of medicine were more ambivalent. In *Contra Celsum*, Origen acknowledged that the normal recourse to medicine was less preferable for Christians. He argued that a Christian, "in seeking recovery from disease ... must either follow the more ordinary and simple method, and have recourse to medical art; or if he would go beyond the common methods adopted by men, he must rise to the higher and better way of seeking the blessing of Him who is God over all, through piety and prayers."[53] Origen's assertion did not interrupt Christian use of medicine.

Medical practice had an esteemed place for early Christians. Gregory of Nyssa claimed that medicine was honored because it combated death.[54] In *Life of Macrina*, Gregory's mother contributed medicine as a gift from God to save people.[55] Gregory of Nazianzus, too, praised Basil of Caesarea's knowledge and understanding of medicine. Through study and practice, Basil mastered the art in both its empirical and practical aspects.[56]

Basil is particularly important for this study because his medical knowledge was a central feature of his monastic institutions in Caesarea, and he was highly influential in the Gazan monastic communities.[57] Andrew Crislip affirmed that Basil "comes down firmly in support of medical healing, that is, the use of Hippocratic/Galenic medicine in monasteries."[58] Risse summarized Basil's nuanced response to medical practice as "in perfect accord with Christian virtue so long as both the sick and their healers never lost sight of the need to please God and place spiritual health on the highest plane."[59] Similarly, Nutton supposed that

Basil taught that the "careful Christian, when he or she falls ill, must carefully investigate the cause of the disease. A Christian's knowledge of his own moral failings enables him to evaluate the cause of his suffering."[60] For Basil, the Christian response to illness included medical attention as well as spiritual introspection.

The true physician, echoing Galen's emphasis above, was able to discern both the physical and spiritual ailments of the individual. The physician was skilled in healing body and soul. In a letter to Eustathius the physician, Basil commended:

> Humanity is the concern of all of you who follow the profession of medicine. And it seems to me that he who would prefer your profession to all other life pursuits would make a proper choice, not straying from the right, if really the most precious of all things, life, is painful and undesirable unless it can be possessed with health. And your profession is the supply of health... [Y]ou set for yourself higher standards of humanity, not limiting the benefit of your profession to bodily, but also contriving the correction of spiritual ills.[61]

For Basil, medical practice was an important part of the healing God provided for humanity. The physical and spiritual dimensions of humanity are interrelated, thus the attention of the physician must also be directed to the whole person.

Treating the sickness of humanity, however, required inquiry into the causes of illness and its relation to sin. Basil faced the question of why humanity was subject to illness. He pointed to the fallen state of humanity as the ultimate cause for disease.[62] In a homily arguing that God is not the cause of evil, Basil asked, "From what source are the maimings of the body?"[63] Basil explained that God created living things suited to their nature and that illness was a disruption of that state due to bad lifestyle or another cause. The diseased state of humanity was a perversion of the natural state. Basil transitioned from illness of the body to illness of the soul. These two concepts were analogues for one another, but their root is the same: perversion of nature. Basil explained, "God created the body, but not illness; and likewise God created the soul, but not sin. Rather, the soul is made evil through a perversion of what is according to nature."[64] Disease, both of the body and the soul, was produced by humanity. The physician's task was to understand and prescribe a way of life that would bring a person back to a state of health. Basil argued that God often allowed evil to persist among human beings as bodily illness so that through the curing of the bodily illness, the soul, too, might be cured; bodily illness "is brought to us by the wise and good Master for our advantage."[65] Just as the physician produced good and health in the body through painful or distressful remedies, God allowed punishments to encourage human salvation. The source of the illness remained in humanity, but the healing remedy came from the Physician.[66]

The teachings of God created peace in the soul by reconciling the mind to the passions that wage war against the soul. God also "creates" evil in that God transformed the evil that arose within humanity to become an avenue for healing.[67] For Basil, understanding and treating human illness was an opportunity to learn the source of disease in the body and the soul. Evil, as a sickness, is opposed to the healthy state of the soul, virtue. Thus, Basil contended, "the soul, without being taught, strives for what is proper to it and conformable to its nature. For this reason self-control is praised by all, justice is approved, courage is admired, and prudence is greatly desired. These virtues are more proper to the soul than health is to the body."[68] Virtue, as seen above in ancient Greek medicine, was an essential aspect of the healthy soul. From Basil's Christian perspective, the created state of humanity did not distinguish between sin and virtue, "for the age was unsusceptible of either condition."[69] After the fall of humanity, virtue characterized a life of return to the created state. This life of virtue was a life of gradual progress, from one step to the next, ascending "to the height attainable by human nature."[70] This way of life, though natural to humanity, was difficult and beset by human inclination to pleasure. Basil contemplated the goodness of God who, understanding human desire for pleasure, provided the Psalms as a cure. In the Psalms, the Holy Spirit mingled melody "with the doctrines so that by the pleasantness and softness of the sound heard we might receive without perceiving the benefit of the words, just as wise physicians who, when giving the fastidious rather bitter drugs to drink, frequently smear the cup with honey."[71]

Basil also prescribed an ascetic program in his monastic establishment. Many of Basil's ascetic works dealt with sickness and disease in the monastic communities. Longer Response 55 addressed the use of medical remedy for those whose goal was piety.[72] Basil began this response by asserting that the arts of agriculture, weaving, and medicine were "bestowed on us by God to supply for the infirmity of nature."[73] In contrast to conditions, harm, food, and distress, the medical art ordered the body by removing what is in excess or making up what is lacking in the body. In like manner, the medical art was "a pattern for the healing of the soul."[74] Meredith acknowledged Basil's use of bodily cures as an analogy for transforming the soul.[75] These cures, according to Basil, were not needed in paradise, because humanity had immunity from disease "before the Fall."[76] After the Fall, humanity was subject to illness and disease, though God also supplied the herbs, roots, flowers, leaves, fruits, metals, and the sea that have "properties beneficial to the body."[77] Use of the medical art should not entail turning one's "whole life into one long *provision for the flesh* (Rom. 13:14)," but should be used "to the glory of God and as a pattern for the care of souls."[78] Basil encouraged his monastic community to endure their afflictions because God often used trials to prove humanity.[79] When medical aid was unavailable, Basil advised: do not worry, but trust that God can heal secretly or can use substances to heal after a long period of time according to whatever was most beneficial to the soul. The cuttings, cauterizations, and bitter drugs that cure the body were analogies for the cutting of the word and the bitter drugs of penalties that cure the soul.[80]

Basil warned that physicians might be seen as saviors and their art praised as a means of pleasure. This view disregarded the spiritual function of medicine, teaching the soul to care for itself. Medicine acted as an analogue to spiritual healing and made explicit the ultimate source of healing. For Basil, Christians should always praise God as the source of healing and the bestower of healing grace.[81] Yet God also allowed illnesses to work for a person's conversion. For such situations, medical aid could offer no relief. Basil advised his reader to acknowledge his transgression, endure the illness quietly, and do without medical attention.[82] Illness could also come as the work of the evil one, as in Job's case. Additionally, Basil claimed that, in the case of Paul, illness could remind others that even the saints were within the bounds of human nature and subject to suffering.[83] In the end, the "transformation of the flesh from illness to health" should encourage Basil's readers and provide an example of how the soul can return "to its proper integrity."[84]

Basil's responses to his monastic audience reflected his approved use of medicine as a healing measure for bodily sickness and a concern for the proper spiritual comportment in seeking physical health. Temkin correctly understood Basil's position: that "Christians who love God should accept from medicine its guidance toward a saintly life."[85] The monastic audience also engaged in certain ascetical practices that championed the health of the soul. Gillian Clark noted, "Basil himself did permanent damage to his digestive system by extreme fasting in his youth."[86] In Clark's description, Christian ascetics would pursue spiritual health through training the soul and the body such that "the Christian spiritual athlete worked on the body as well as the soul, and spiritual health, for the committed Christian, came at a higher physical cost."[87] In her study of John of Ephesus, Susan Ashbrook Harvey declared, "The ascetic's care for the illnesses of others was precisely that; rarely would holy men or women, however sick, allow themselves medical treatment."[88] Dorotheos provides an example of Christian asceticism that was not opposed to medical care for healing the body. Meredith explained that though ascetics led a life that could treat the body harshly, nevertheless "ascetics were not supposed to make themselves sick.... Ascetic discipline was intended to turn one towards God but illness invariably forces one to focus on oneself."[89] Ferngren articulated the tension between physical healing and asceticism, noting monasticism's potential for curtailing the use of medicine. He stressed, "Far from denigrating secular medicine, however, monastics incorporated it into their religious vocation, a fact that is due in large part to the church's acceptance of the role of physicians as early as the second century."[90] In Ferngren's estimation, ascetic Christians' relationship to medicine was far from antagonistic. In fact, in the fourth century, medicine would play an important role in the monastic life for leaders like Basil.

Christian embrace of medicine was especially profound in Basil precisely because medicine provided an arena to practice philanthropy. Miller showed how Basil was struck by some monastic leaders who had neglected the practical works of charity (*praxis*) and devoted themselves solely to contemplation and prayer. According to Miller, "Basil understood that Christ expected his followers to clothe the naked, to feed the hungry, to visit the sick—in short, to carry out Christian philanthropia."[91] Early Christian monastic literature displayed a great concern for health care within the community. Judith Perkins noted, "With the exception of specifically medical writings, hagiographic texts focused as did no others on the particulars of disease and suffering."[92] Crislip postulated, "monastic leaders focused on problems of the establishment of a health care system and the creation of a positive social role for the sick within monastic life."[93] In his exploration of the rise of the hospital from within monastic communities, Crislip argued that monasteries offered some of the best healthcare available in ancient Mediterranean societies:

> The sick had access to a range of medical treatment corresponding to the best types available outside the monastery: dietary treatment, pharmaceuticals, surgery, rest, and comfort care; they also had access to health care institutions that were new to the monastic health care system: a corps of professional nurses and an infirmary, a proto-hospital.[94]

The health care that would spread throughout the Byzantine empire followed the pattern of care given in monastic society in the late fourth century.[95] In fact, he claimed that monastic care, in its "breadth of treatment, its organizational scope, and its guarantee of compassionate care throughout the life cycle," transformed ancient health care.[96]

Many of the fourth-century monastic communities attracted doctors who possessed the full set of medical skills. Crislip mentioned that these ranged from "dietary therapy and hygiene, to the application of pharmaceuticals, to complicated surgery."[97] Physicians lived in and among the monastic communities and were allowed to utilize their expertise within their monastic vocation. Other monks would be called upon to serve the sick in a nursing capacity.[98] Within the monastic communal structures, health care would be provided in the monastery's infirmary or in a monk's individual cell.[99]

Health care in the ancient monasteries included a combination of physical and spiritual diagnosis. Crislip explained that, in ancient Greek medicine, physicians did not offer a diagnosis of disease by giving a taxonomical description but offered a prognosis, "a future course of the disease."[100] In monastic literature, diseases are discerned. Through discernment (*diakrisis*), a health care provider was distinguishing "between various demonic afflictions or distinguishing between angels and demons" as well as distinguish between "illness caused by demonic affliction and illness from natural causes, and indeed between the truly ill."[101] Monastic elders would play in important role in the discernment process and could recommend a course of action for the sick and reprimand for those feigning illness. Every treatment, however, was tailored to the individual.[102] The types of healing offered in the monastery ranged from nonmedical healing[103] to dietary therapy[104] to pharmaceuticals.[105] Crislip surmised that "the monasteries of late fourth-century Cappadocia largely conformed to mainstream Greek medicine in the Galenic tradition."[106]

The impact of health care in monastic communities was important for social reasons as well. According to Crislip, "Monastic leaders [in coenobitic communities] thus had an obligation to keep monastics as healthy as possible, perhaps on a faster timetable than would be possible by relying on God alone."[107] Ensuring the community had access to adequate health care provided stability and constancy for the monks and also established monasteries as providers of health care as they interacted with society. Basil and other monastic innovators embraced and transformed health care in their milieu. The Palestinian monastic communities were shaped by this new development. Peregrine Horden signaled a favorable attitude toward medicine in the Palestinian context, writing, "Their resort to secular as distinct from spiritual medicine, whether their monastery's own infirmary or privately with healers roundabout, was not thought incompatible with the minimal asceticism that monastic seclusion implies."[108] Dorotheos represented the integration of Christian and monastic developments in physical and spiritual healing through his approach to the discourse of healing.

Christian adoption and adaptation of ancient medicine illustrated the importance of health care in early monastic communities. Particularly for Basil of Caesarea, medical practice and the monastic life were interconnected. In the context of Gazan monasticism, illness and healing were common themes. Dorotheos's experience in the infirmary, as evinced by his correspondence with Barsanuphius and John, was evidence that later Gazan monastics were aware of how important health care was to their monastic communities. This chapter evaluates how Isaiah, Barsanuphius, John, and Dorotheos discussed Christ's activity as physician, approached health and illness in their communities, and used the metaphor of healing in the monastic school of Gaza. Reactions to bodily illness were intertwined with spiritual concerns for these monastics. The portrayal of Christ as physician and conceptions of illness and healing accentuated the unity of thought among these monastic figures. Dorotheos was part of a monastic tradition steeped in the metaphor of healing to describe the monastic life. His own employment of the metaphor points to a link with his tradition. However, the meaning with which he imbued the metaphor of healing positioned Dorotheos as distinctive.

Gazan monastic discourse about healing was more ambiguous. Each monastic writer emphasized the role of Christ in healing, but each operated under different notions of health for their monks. Dorotheos incorporated the Gazan monastic discourse of healing into his own vision of health and the monastic life. He took certain elements from Isaiah, Barsanuphius, and John and appropriated them into his distinct perspective.

Isaiah

Isaiah's influence on later Gazan monastics was manifest in his discourse on the work of Christ to heal the illness of humanity. His monastic guidance emphasized the endurance of bodily illness for spiritual benefit, rather than seeking the health of the body alongside the health of the soul.

Christ in Isaiah

Isaiah spoke of Christ as healing "all the passions of humanity" through his ascending the cross.[109] This healing countered humanity's illnesses, because humanity was "blind, dumb, paralyzed, deaf, leprous, lame, and dead on account of everything that was contrary to nature (τυφλός, καὶ ἄλαλος, καὶ παραλυτικός, καὶ κωφός, λεπρὸς καὶ χωλός, καὶ θανατωθεὶς ἐν πάσαις ταῖς παραφύσεσιν)."[110] Isaiah pointed to the various healing stories contained in the gospels. The healing Christ provided was the resurrection of "a new person, free from all illness (τὸν ἄνθρωπον καινόν, πάσης ἀσθενείας ἐλεύθερον)."[111] Only after the healing miracles, did Christ ascend the cross. The healing offered by Christ was not the salvific healing of the cross but the restoration to individuals those particular functions they lacked. Christ offered completion of the human being, like restoration of sight and hearing, so that his followers could understand and then imitate him by ascending the cross. Chryssavgis and Penkett claimed that "ascending the cross (ἐπιβῆναι τῷ σταυρῷ)" was a favorite phrase of Isaiah and will be discussed below.[112]

In Isaiah, Christ was portrayed as the exemplar, fulfilling the commandments of God.[113] He claimed that Jesus became human to set an example for human behavior, though this example would seem both bitter and sweet.[114] The manner of life exemplified in Christ was a life of purity. Isaiah commended his audience to "put on Christ (ἐνεδυσάμεθα τὸν Χριστὸν)," turn away from sin, and, thereby, prepare for the robe of purity and adoption. The life Christ portrayed was the life of a child of God.[115] Like Christ, Isaiah recommended that each person should lead a practical life, controlling the body's members and establishing a state "according to nature (κατὰ φύσιν)."[116] Christ modeled a way of life "in his holy body (ἐν τῷ ἁγίῳ αὐτοῦ σώματι)."[117] By imitating Christ, a person could withstand temptation.

Isaiah indicated that Christ was both a model for a life pleasing to God and a healer of humanity. His practical admonitions were accompanied by more profound images. In one discourse, he depicted Christ as the bronze serpent raised on a staff to heal the Hebrew people in the wilderness.[118] Isaiah explained that Christ, as the healing serpent, came to remedy the work of Eden's serpent. Adam listened to the serpent in the garden and became an enemy of God. Christ

> resembled the one who became an enemy of God except that he did not have a single evil thought, nor the venom of malice…Our Lord Jesus took this figure in order that, extinguishing the venom (τὸν ἰόν) that Adam had eaten from the serpent's mouth, He brought back nature (ἐπιστραφῇ ἡ φύσις), which had become contrary to nature, to conform to nature (ἡ γενομένη παράφυσις εἰς τὴν κατὰ φύσιν).[119]

Through Christ, humanity could enjoy healing from Adam's sin. This healing was a return to one's created nature.

As a healer, Christ restored human nature to its created state so that one could follow Christ. As an exemplar, Christ provided a pattern of living. Consequently, the imitation of Christ involved suffering. In ascending the cross, an individual took up something of Christ's suffering. Consequently, one should not be surprised by Isaiah's meditation, "I deserve to suffer and endure for the Savior. By tribulations and insults I imitate the passion of my God."[120] One could conceive of illness as suffering in imitation of Christ. Isaiah's approach to illness and health was an extrapolation of his conception of Christ's healing work.

In a poignant passage describing his own need for bodily healing, Isaiah compared his need for spiritual healing to arrows stuck in his body. He was wounded and scarred but not yet stinking with decay. He hid his inner wounds because he could not endure the removal of the arrows. He avoided the good doctor's prescribed ointments because he was "not sufficiently strong-hearted to endure their astringency (τὴν στύψιν αὐτῶν)."[121] Isaiah worsened his condition by eating unhealthy but pleasurable foods that worsened his wounds. When the doctor sent him good food, his bad habits prevented him from accepting it.[122] Isaiah knew the struggle and pain that healing required. The imagery of illness and wounds empowered his discourse of illness as a spiritual teaching and the suffering patient characterized his view of the healing offered by the monastic life.

Health and Illness in Isaiah

Isaiah utilized Adam as a portrait of the healthy life. He called upon his monks to emulate Adam, who was "healthy from everything that is contrary to nature, to be worthy of becoming a bride for him. The soul recognizes his thoughts about conduct, for if it practices works, the Holy Spirit lives in it, because the works cause the soul to be reborn (ἀναγεννᾷ τὴν ψυχὴν ἀπαθῆ)."[123] Isaiah taught that the life of health was the practice of practical deeds that transformed of soul through the work of the Spirit.

Isaiah often depicted the healthy person as a person at creation, who was "according to nature (ἐν τῷ φυσικῷ),"[124] or a regenerated individual, a "new person (τό καινός ἀνθρώπος)."[125] The person whose state was according to nature eliminated those aspects of their humanity that are contrary to nature or even contrary to Adam's nature. Isaiah called these contrary aspects diseases. He taught that "Unless the senses have been alleviated of all disease (πρὸ τοῦ παύσωνται τῆς ἀσθενείας αἱ αἰσθήσεις), if the intellect wishes to ascend the cross, the wrath of God falls on it, for it has assumed something beyond its limitation, not having first cured its senses."[126] Acting in accordance with nature involved overcoming sin, removing the causes of sin, accepting punishment, weeping, and following one's teacher.[127]

Sin was, for Isaiah, an illness. He described the pursuit of health in the monastic life as surgery (ἰατρεῖον) to remove a disease.[128] The monk must attend to those parts of the body that are diseased. The health he described was conditional. He admitted that "some wounds are already healed (τραύματα ἤδη θεραπευθέντα), but when you eat something harmful, they return once again."[129] The sins of each should be addressed as the surgeon addressed one's body. The wise person "observes the precautions of his own doctor, taking care not to eat whatever harms his wound."[130] The metaphor of bodily illness played an important role in addressing the problem of sin.

For Isaiah, the monastic life was the rehabilitation of a person to avoid the disease of sin and live a new life as a new person. A person "who has reached these and eliminated the condition that is contrary to nature (ὅστις ἀφαιρέσας τὰς κακίας ταύτας, ταῦτα ἀσπασθῇ), shows that he is truly from Christ, and is the son of God and brother of Jesus."[131] Those who followed the way of Jesus acted according to nature. Quite simply, the new person "was made manifest in the Lord Jesus' holy body (οὗ ἐνεφάνισεν ἐν τῷ ἁγίῳ αὐτοῦ σώματι ὁ

Κύριος Ἰησοῦς)."[132] According to Isaiah, the old person cares about rest in this life, but loses his soul. The new person hunted down the desires of the flesh (ἤγρευσαν πᾶσι τοῖς θελήμασι τῆς σαρκὸς αὐτῶν) and was granted peace from God.[133] Elsewhere, he warned, "Blessed are those who acquire the New Person before meeting Christ."[134] Those individuals who neglected to cultivate the new person were in danger of punishment. Therefore he encouraged his monks to "do everything possible, with tears, gradually struggling (ἀγωνιζόμενοι κατὰ μικρὸν μικρόν) until the conduct of the Old Person is stripped away (ἕως οὗ ἐκδυθῶμεν τὴν πρᾶξιν τοῦ παλαιοῦ ἀνθρώπου)….We remove the earthly image and erect [Christ's] holy statue in our heart until we become worthy of him."[135] The notion of identifying oneself with Christ retained this element of struggle and suffering.

For Isaiah, the apostle Peter embodied the suffering and transformation necessary for the healthy life. As a representative of the need for the "the natural state of the Son of God (τὸ κατὰ φύσιν τοῦ υἱοῦ τοῦ Θεοῦ)," Peter was crucified upside down; revealing

> the mystery of the unnatural condition that dominates everyone (δηλῶν διὰ τοῦ τὸ μυστήριον τῆς παραφύσεως τῆς κατακυριευσάσης παντὸς ἀνθρώπου), for he was saying that each person who is baptized must crucify the wicked conditions contrary to nature (τὰς παραφύσεις τὰς πονηράς) which possessed Adam and drove him from his glory to an evil rebuke and eternal shame (αἰσχύνην αἰώνιον).[136]

The healthy life, as pictured in Peter's death, involved personal crucifixion. According to Isaiah, "Blessed, then, is the one who has been crucified, who has died, been buried, and arisen in newness (et resurrexit in notitate vitae) when he sees himself in the natural condition of Jesus, following his holy footprints which were made when he was incarnated for the sake of his holy saints."[137] The idea of individual crucifixion was a metaphor for the personal suffering this healthy life entailed.

Isaiah was quite clear that even in bodily sickness monks should rescind from medical care and endure that suffering as identification with acquiring the new person. For sick monks, he advised, "Should you be taken ill while silent in your cell, do not be discouraged but give thanks to the Lord. If you see your soul disturbed, say to it, 'Is not this illness better for you than the Hell that you will go to?' and you will again find inner peace (ἡσυχάσει ἐν σοί)."[138] He likened the suffering of bodily illness to the purifying suffering symbolized in one who ascended the cross, one who took up the nature of Christ, one who was healthy.

Barsanuphius and John

Despite the Old Men's role in establishing the monastery's infirmary, Barsanuphius and John maintained much of Isaiah's discourse on the healthy life, though often moderated. They also adopted Isaiah's notion of ascending the cross in imitation of Christ. For the Old Men of Gaza, Christ as physician would primarily prescribe suffering as a healing measure.

Christ and Physicians in Barsanuphius and John

Barsanuphius referred to Jesus in the context of healing on a number of occasions. To one respondent, Barsanuphius claimed, "Jesus is the Physician of souls and bodies (ὁ Ἰησοῦς ἰατρός ἐστι τῶν ψυχῶν καὶ τῶν σωμάτων). If you have a wound (τραῦμα), I shall lead you toward him and pray to him to heal you in both, that is, if you also desire this."[139] In another letter, Barsanuphius referred to brother Jesus as the physician who heals the passions.[140] By portraying Christ as physician, Barsanuphius was using an established metaphor.[141] Additionally, John referred to a local priest as a spiritual physician (ἰατρὸς πνευματικός) who "has been called to anoint with oil those who have been afflicted (τοὺς κακουμένους), and to heal (θεραπεύων) them from bodily illness; indeed, you also mix the anointing with the forgiveness of sins."[142] Barsanuphius and John identified Christ as the true healer of soul and body in their correspondence.

A nearby abba, Euthymius, wrote to Barsanuphius about an illness. Euthymius pled for Barsanuphius's advice, "Lord Jesus Christ, Physician of wounded souls (ὁ ἰατρὸς τῶν τετραυματισμένων ψυχῶν), we offer you prayers from your holy words, which [we ask] that you accept through your servant.... As for me, since I am lame and wounded, this is why I cry out, so that you may visit me....Still my illness swells."[143] The context of Euthymius' question pertained to a spiritual illness. He sought spiritual healing through Barsanuphius's prayers and guidance. The language he used, however, blurred the boundary between physical and spiritual disorder. The metaphor of healing pervaded his request especially as Euthymius alluded to Jesus's healing ministry in the gospels, saying,

> Since you said, Holy One [Barsanuphius in Letter 59], that anyone who visits a doctor and wants to be healed does whatever is prescribed by the physician, then send me, Master, whatever medicines, cauterizations, and plasters you want (ὅσα θέλεις φάρμακα, καυτῆρας, μαλάγματα); but please stop my stinking issue of blood, namely, my unclean thought.[144]

The matter became clear only at the end of his request; Euthymius was troubled by an unclean thought and he struggled against it as with a bodily illness.

Barsanuphius utilized the metaphor of medical healing to offer spiritual advice. He required that Euthymius follow the prescription of Christ as one would a human physician. Barsanuphius advised, "since you have spoken about also receiving other healing (ἰάματα) and medicines (φάρμακα), I am amazed by how your love does not comprehend the wisdom of our great Doctor in every art (τὴν πάντεχνον σοφίαν τοῦ μεγάλου ἡμῶν ἰατροῦ), how he has cut off all occasion [of sin] from every person who asks him."[145] Barsanuphius referred to a book of healing that was available to Euthymius, though Euthymius ignored its prescription. Barsanuphius mentioned the healing property of the Psalms from which Euthymius was unwilling to take counsel. Through scripture, the Physician had provided the necessary remedy and "he has demonstrated to us to be without excuse."[146] The exact context was that Euthymius had not been willing to characterize himself as the Psalmist, "I am a worm and not a man." (Ps. 21:6). Vainglory stood in the way of his healing. Barsanuphius explained that this admission is the medicine of God that undermines the old nature of humanity.[147] The "cauterization" of one's vainglory was the path of salvation in this instance. For Barsanuphius, the cure for Euthymius's illness was within reach. Euthymius, however, had rejected this cure. Barsanuphius questioned Euthymius's actions saying, the "great and heavenly Physician has granted us cures and plasters, through what else is the cause of our destruction to be found other than through the weakness of our own free will?"[148] Christ, as Physician, offered the cure. Barsanuphius adapted the language of physical healing and applied that mode of discourse to prescribe a course to spiritual health.

Barsanuphius and John advised their interlocutors who sought healing to invoke the care of Christ as Physician and also to consult doctors in many circumstances. An unnamed layperson consulted a physician for his illness. The doctor ordered him to bathe, but the layperson questioned John whether bathing was a sin. John responded that bathing was not forbidden when needed. However, bathing could lead to self-indulgence. Though not questioned about visiting a doctor, John stated,

> it belongs to the more perfect (τοῦ τελειοτέρου) to leave everything to God, even if this is a difficult thing to do; it is the weaker person (τοῦ ἀσθενεστέρου) who shows himself to the doctor. Indeed, not only is this sinful, but it is even humble; for being weaker, one needed to visit the doctor. One should, however, remember that, without God, not even a doctor can do anything. Rather, it is God who bestows health to the ill, whenever he so desires.[149]

The illness in question was not disclosed, but John's admonition against visiting doctors was clear. The humble and weaker person required doctors. The perfect need not visit a doctor but trust in God whose providence granted doctors their efficacy. In another letter, a monk asked John if those who despise medicine and food had reached perfection. John responded, "Those who have despised medicine and food have reached the measure of faith but not the measure of perfection (εἰς μέτρον ἔφθασαν πίστεως, ἀλλ᾽ οὐ τελειότητος)."[150] The Old Men's reaction to using doctors was mixed.

In Letter 508, Barsanuphius confronted a monk about both those who use doctors and those who merely hope in God to provide healing. He advised that one can use doctors but must also trust in the will of God. Those who do not use doctors run the risk of arrogance.[151] In Letter 532, another monk asked John, with reference to Barsanuphius's allowance of using doctors, if it is better to trust in the holy water of the saints rather than the physicians care. John cautioned the monk's concern for bodily illnesses. He chided this monk explaining that the fathers were not preoccupied with these cares. The overriding concern for John was that one have faith in God and patience in testing. These two methods of treatment are characterized as leading to the kingdom of heaven or Gehenna, planting sorrow in the heart or placing thanksgiving in the heart that "intercedes well for the salvation of all people before the great Doctor, who bears our sicknesses."[152] John then confided that

> As for me, my genuine brother, although I am completely reluctant, I have never shown myself to a doctor; nor have I taken any medicine for my wounds. I have done this not out of virtue (οὐ κατὰ ἀρετὴν), but out of reluctance, refusing to travel to cities and towns in order not to burden anyone…Whoever is able to endure this out of virtue is blessed; for such a one becomes a sharer in the patience of the holy Job.[153]

John was not against seeing a doctor for treatment. To a brother who asked about seeing a doctor because of his eye, John responded, "As for your eye, do not be afraid, because you have God as the one who illumines you. If, however, you happen to come across some skilled physician and show yourself to him, you are not sinning because this, too, is a cause for your humility."[154] Again, in the case of a brother who needed a surgery, John replied, "It is certainly necessary, child, for anyone who has any illness to ask one of the fathers about this and to do everything in accordance with his opinion. For there are times when the elder will have the gift of healing and may secretly work this healing; so it is not always necessary to seek doctors of the body."[155] The important factor was he had consulted a father of the monastery who had agreed that seeing the doctor was necessary. Only in an act of obedience and faith should monks consult a doctor.

Barsanuphius corresponded with a monk named Theodore who wished for healing of his weak eyes. This request for healing was among other inquiries about the proper monastic diet and prayer. Barsanuphius responded, "As for your eyes, the One who created them is also able to illumine them with the eyes of the soul. If, according to the words of the Savior, we understand by means of the inner eyes (τοῖς ἔσω ὀφθαλμοῖς), then we do not need the [outer] eyes that behold the vanity of the world (τούτων τῶν βλέποντων τὴν τοῦ κόσμου ματαιότητα)."[156] From Barsanuphius's response, the need for sight was a matter of seeing through the soul by means of inner eyes. True sight, according to Barsanuphius, was not the ability to view the world but to perceive God. Barsanuphius reinterpreted Theodore's understanding of health, displacing the emphasis of ocular function. Theodore should, as Barsanuphius advised, appreciate the healing God offered to his inner eyes and cultivate resignation in regard to his outer eyes.

These examples showed how Barsanuphius and John conceived of God as the source of all healing. They were able to address Christ as Physician, the healer of physical and spiritual illnesses. As in Theodore's case, the healing sought might not be the healing that Christ would provide. Their position concerning recourse to a human physician was not consistent. The individual instruction preserved in the *Correspondence* indicated that on some occasions visiting a human doctor was not permitted. Any instance of visiting a doctor was under the strict guidance of one's spiritual father. The inconsistent position of the Old Men's guidance on this subject matter may issue from the individual basis and intimacy with their interlocutors, something not clearly discerned from the preserved letters. It was clear that, for these Old Men, physical illness was a path toward spiritual healing, even if a complete state of health was not achieved.

Health and Illness in Barsanuphius and John

A large portion of Barsanuphius and John's correspondence dealt with illnesses of various sorts. Illness became a mode of discourse through which Barsanuphius and John could offer spiritual counsel. When they addressed sick individuals, Barsanuphius and John portrayed illness as a means to conceive spiritual healing. They allayed a focus on bodily healing and insisted that the health of the soul was a monk's main concern. Illness was a time for a monk to evaluate and discern the disposition of the soul through attention to the body. One should attend to the body to determine the source of the illness and the proper treatment of the illness from a spiritual perspective. Under the care of a spiritual father, monks must perceive illness as an opportunity to mature. Ultimately, illness was instructive. Illness was preparation and proof of the monk's fidelity to God, whose final provision of health awaited an individual after death. Health, for Barsanuphius and John, could only be described in terms of resignation and endurance in the face of illness, rather than any therapeutic or restorative notion.

Illness could be seen as a correction. A "father living in stillness" wrote twenty-one letters to Barsanuphius and John concerning a lasting illness. This father admitted to being a sinner in need of cleansing who could not bear his sickness with joy. Barsanuphius explained, "Now, you have said that you have an illness; and illness is a confessed correction (ἡ ἀσθένεια παιδεία ἐστὶν ὡμολογημένη). Therefore, the correction has been sent to a bad servant. If you grow despondent in accepting your correction, then cease from being bad. For if you rejoice at being corrected, you are not bad."[157] From his perspective, Barsanuphius viewed this man's illness as a corrective that he should enjoy. Barsanuphius reminded the monk of the Proverb, "the Lord reproves the one he loves" (Prov. 3:12).

Another monk asked if illness could come from God. John answered: "It can indeed."[158] When one had an illness unaccompanied by a troubling passion, then the illness was from God. Therefore, when one perceived an illness and observed that no troubling passion was present, then this illness came from God and would dispel the warfare. During these times, a monk should "condescend a little to the body (τῷ σώματι μικρᾶς συγκαταβάσεως)."[159] However, if a passion accompanied an illness, condescending to the body only strengthened the power of the demon. Discerning the cause of illness was important because mistakenly condescending to the body would put the soul in jeopardy. John explained that, "one should not cast the soul into illness in order to support the body."[160]

Barsanuphius also attributed some illnesses to demonic activity. One monk had been healed of an infirmity through prayer, recitation of Psalms and scripture, examination of thoughts, and regulation of diet. He wrote to Barsanuphius about an illness in his stomach. Barsanuphius perceived that this illness was due to the activity of the demons. He advised the monk to "despise both of them [his stomach and the demons]. For it is said: 'Those who belong to Christ Jesus have crucified the flesh with its passions and desires' (Gal. 5:24)."[161]

For Barsanuphius and John, attending to illness was an important facet of monastic life. Illness required introspection and discernment as well as seeking advice from spiritual guides and hoping in God's care. The sick monk should address the illness appropriately. Barsanuphius advised that illness prompted an invocation of God as well as certain bodily accommodations. When correctly attended, a sick monk "is not condemned for giving the body whatever it needs, if indeed it truly needs this, while also giving thanks for one's illness."[162]

Treating the body included an understanding of how illness and diet interacted. Diet was important for the healthy and the sick. John explained the importance of individual dispositions, "From daily experience, it is possible to observe what the body can accept in terms of food and drink….For not all human dispositions are the same (οὐ γάρ εἰσιν ἴσαι αἱ ἕξεις τῶν ἀνθρώπων)."[163] The discerning monk would know what his body required. The emphasis on diet was a precedent observed in the monastic heritage. John referred to the Fathers who, when they "adopted a very strict diet (ἐχρήσαντο σκληροτάτῃ διαίτῃ), they found that their bodies were obedient (ὑπακούοντα). Therefore, those who control themselves well and with discernment (οἱ καλῶς κυβερνῶντες ἑαυτοὺς καὶ μετὰ διακρίσεως) conform their routine to their body (πρὸς τὸ σῶμα καὶ τὴν ἕξιν ποιοῦσιν)."[164] The attentiveness one gave to the body was elevated for the sick. Barsanuphius elucidated the concern for food. He wrote to a sick monk, "If one does not eat for the sake of pleasure but for the sake of the body's weakness, God will not condemn that person. For foods are controlled in order to avoid excessive eating (τὴν πλησμονὴν) and bodily arousal (τὰ σκιρτήματα τοῦ σώματος)."[165] In times of illness, Barsanuphius advised modification according to the illness of each individual monk. He explained, "For when the body, too, is unwell, it does not receive food normally. Thus a rule would prove worthless in this case."[166] In some cases, the ability to digest food was an indicator of the source of illness. According to Barsanuphius, "if your body can accept daily food and is still slack, then this [illness] comes from the demons; otherwise, it is from the illness (ἀσθένεια) itself."[167]

Bodily illness and demonic attacks often affect the body in a similar manner. Discerning between the two was the responsibility of the monastic fathers. Often illness prevented the monks from performing their practical and spiritual regimen. Barsanuphius prescribed that, "The matter of illness is quite clear. For if the body cannot tolerate regular food, it is evident that it is unwell and one should relax one's ministry. If, however, the body accepts the customary food and does not rise for liturgy, it is evident that this comes from the demons."[168] Bodily illness often accompanied demonic afflictions. The body was rendered ill when the thoughts of a monk were full of turmoil.[169]

Illness was a means to refocus the monk's attention on God and place one's trust in God alone. Barsanuphius compared invoking God's name to a "medicine that dispels not only all of the passions but even the [sinful] act itself."[170] When a doctor prescribed medication, "this acts within the patient without one even realizing how this occurs, so also the mane of God dispels all of the passions when it is invoked, even without us knowing how this actually occurs."[171] Similarly, he described illness as a form of asceticism. Barsanuphius compared fasting to illness:

> What else is fasting but discipline of the body (τί γάρ ἐστι νηστεία, ἀλλ᾽ ἢ παιδεία τῷ σώματι), in order to enslave a healthy body (ἵνα δουλαγωγήσῃ τὸ ὑγιὲς σῶμα) and weaken it on account of the passions?... Illness, however is greater than mere

discipline, being reckoned as a substitute for the regular [ascetic] way (πολιτείας); and it is even of greater value [than asceticism] for the person who endures it with patience and gives thanks to God. That person reaps the fruit of salvation from such patience. Therefore, instead of the body being weakened through fasting, it is weakened in and of itself. Give thanks that you have been exempted from the toil of regular [ascetic] behavior.[172]

To an elderly monk named Andrew, Barsanuphius addressed the monastic perspective on bodily health and the passions of the soul. The monk was to give his body to God. In the event of bodily illness, some monks indicated that if they had treated their bodies better, the illness would not have burdened them. Barsanuphius rejoined that monks should give themselves to God unto death. God, who knows what is good for body and soul, will allow monks to be afflicted in body. When this occurred, the burden of the soul would be lightened.[173]

Illness provided benefits to the monks. Barsanuphius responded to a novice in the coenobium who claimed he could no longer bear his illness. Barsanuphius could only encourage the young monk to endure his illness gladly "in order that God's mercy may richly come upon us."[174] This illness was, according to Barsanuphius, a temptation to despair, but could also be seen as a trial to bring one hope. This young monk needed to understand that illness is the chastisement of God to a son. Barsanuphius advised him, "If you bear the affliction gratefully, then you have become a son (ἐγένου υἱός). If you break down, then you are an illegitimate child (ἐγένου νόθος)."[175] This illness was proof of God's acceptance of the monk and, yet, a testing of that adoption.

Barsanuphius's own brother entered the coenobium of Seridos. He soon fell ill with dropsy and wrote to Barsanuphius about this suffering. Barsanuphius responded to his elderly brother that his illness had come upon him only that he "may not depart fruitless (ἀπέλθῃς ἄκαρπος) toward God."[176] His brother had entered the monastic life at a late age. Barsanuphius considered that "if you endure it and give thanks, it will be reckoned for you as your ascetic life (ἀντὶ πολιτείας λογίζεταί σοι), especially since you have not long been in the monastic habit."[177] This illness was a teaching his brother not to see himself as being related to a great man, but that "we are all children of Adam's transgression (τέκνα ἐσμὲν τῆς παραβάσεως Ἀδάμ)? Do you not know that we are earth and ashes? Therefore, give thanks to God, who brought you to such a condition. If we had the humility of Jesus, we would say: 'Who is my mother, and who are my brothers?' (Matt. 12:48) and so on."[178]

When Abba Seridos died, the monks of the monastery questioned John about Seridos's continual struggle with stomach ulcers. John replied that God sent the ulcers (ἀνθρακιά) because Seridos had received glory among people. God proved

Seridos's humanity through this illness, so that people would not deify Seridos. This did not diminish the reputation of Seridos. John explained, "For truly, he was deemed worthy of receiving the Holy Spirit and perfection (τελειότητος); yet God extinguished the glory of the people by means of this pretext, so that the glory of God might perfectly abound."[179] For John, Seridos's illness was to the benefit of those around him, preventing them from thinking too highly of him.

Illness was also the path from this life to the next. To a monk in danger of death, Barsanuphius replied that death was not a reason to be sad, for death is a "transferal from affliction to repose (μετάβασις ἀπὸ θλίψεως εἰς ἀνάπαυσιν)."[180] When Dositheos, Dorotheos's disciple, had contracted typhoid, Barsanuphius commended him to rejoice and be glad.[181] This response "crushed" Dositheos, so he wrote to John making sure Barsanuphius was speaking about impending death.[182] This saying troubled not only Dositheos but his associates as well. Other brothers entreated Barsanuphius to pray that Dositheos might live, but Barsanuphius simply replied that Dositheos would soon be worthy of riches and freedom from slavery, "transferred from death to life and from affliction to repose."[183] The Great Old Man wrote this to the brothers confidentially so that Dositheos would not be grieved by his approaching death. After some time of suffering, Dositheos did die, and Barsanuphius indicated that his suffering was cut short on account of the care of the brothers.[184]

Barsanuphius and John were ambivalent in regard to physical health. In their estimation, monks were caught between illness of their own responsibility, demonic disruption, and even God's allowance. They instructed their correspondents to attend primarily to their spiritual response to illness. The Old Men supported the monastery's addition of an infirmary and encouraged Dorotheos in his work there, but they also advised the monks of the coenobium to avoid seeking medical attention on many occasions. Perhaps their negative attitudes toward medical care reflect a time before the monastery had its own infirmary and, thus, monks seeking care would be forced to visit an outside institution. Though chronological assessments of these occasions cannot be ascertained, their influence upon Dorotheos in both the construction and operation of the infirmary is without doubt. The discourse of healing in Barsanuphius and John appropriated the occasion of bodily illness to speak of spiritual growth. These categories ranged from correction for sin to divine, demonic, or dietary disruption to preparation for death. For the Old Men, illness was something to interpret; it carried meaning. Understanding one's illness did not necessarily lead to physical well-being and often relegated the desire for physical healing. Dorotheos agreed that bodily illness could be instructive. He departed from the Old Men when he employed the metaphor of healing, because, for Dorotheos, healing was more than a spiritual response to a bodily disease.

Healing was the work of God to bring humanity back to its intended, created state, a state of harmony between body and soul. Likewise, Zosimas's influence on Dorotheos was most evident in Dorotheos's conception of healing and provided a conception of the monastic community as a place of healing.

Zosimas

The short collection of reflections from Zosimas contain a number of key concepts that Dorotheos later developed. Central to Zosimas's teaching was that the monastic community functioned as a body that worked to keep each of its members in good health. With Christ as the head of the body, the members work to uphold one another and follow the commandments of Christ.[185]

Christ as physician enabled the therapy of communal life. Zosimas taught that when one interacted with others in the monastery, "you should think of that person as a healer, sent to you by Christ."[186] He also stated that when a brother illumined an evil thought, "you should accept whatever [the brother] offers you, as if it were healing medicine (ὡς φάρμακα ἰαματικὰ) sent to you by Jesus."[187] For Zosimas, the Lord was good and "gave us His holy commandments in order to purge our evils (καθαιρούσας), by cauterizing and cleansing them (δίκην καυτήρων καὶ καθαρσίων)."[188] Just as one who visited a physician was obliged to endure the prescribed treatment, so, too, one must surrender "to the doctor, knowing that, in return for a small amount of disgust (τῆς μικρᾶς ἀηδίας), a great deal of healing will result for an unhealthy and chronic illness (πολλῆς κακοχυμίας)."[189] Certain cures, like the "burning medicine of Jesus (καυτὴρ τοῦ Ἰησοῦ)," may cause a bit of harm, but they also brought healing. If that healing comes from a brother in community, then one should not blame him, but blame one's self and welcome the "medicine of Christ (τὸ φάρμακον τοῦ Χριστοῦ)."[190]

Zosimas cited Evagrius who called accusers his benefactors. Evagrius stated that he did "not despise the spiritual doctor (τὸν ἰατρὸν τῶν ψυχῶν), who brings the medicine of dishonour (φάρμακον ἀτιμίας) to the vainglorious soul (κενοδόξῳ ψυχῇ)."[191] In Zosimas's interpretation, Evagrius' fear was that Christ might tell him, "Evagrius, you were ill from vainglory, and I administered unto you the medicine of dishonour in order that you might be healed (Εὐάγριε, ἐνόσεις κενοδοξίαν, καὶ ἐπήγαγόν σοι φάρμακον ἀτιμίας, ἵνα δι᾽ αὐτοῦ καθαρισθῇς). Yet you were not healed."[192] The monastic community revealed to each person his own illness.[193] Zosimas understood the monastic community as one body whose members often became sick. One did not cut out an eye or cut off a hand when it was afflicted but sought to restore it to health. The "rejection (ἀποβολήν) of each of these [was] a very serious matter."[194] Instead of casting out sick members from the monastic community, Zosimas recommended placing the sign of Christ (τὴν σφραγίδα Χριστοῦ) on them and praying. Then medication and plasters were applied just as sore bodily members were treated.[195]

Dorotheos claimed to have met and interacted with Zosimas on at least one occasion and referred to him frequently.[196] Zosimas's example emphasized the importance of care for the health of others in the monastery. Dorotheos would emulate a similar discourse of healing in his own teaching.

Dorotheos

As a spiritual father of his own monastery, Dorotheos was able to reflect upon his experiences in the infirmary of Seridos's coenobium. His *Discourses* related a spiritual healing that was deeply connected to his interaction with physical healing. While the correspondence of Barsanuphius and John revealed particular interactions between monks and the Old Men on a wide variety of topics, Dorotheos's *Discourses* addressed more generally the needs of his monastery. The particularity of his work with the sick in the infirmary informed his comprehensive monastic vision. The role of Christ as Physician became a central trope through which Dorotheos was able to characterize the monastic life as a life of healing for soul and body.

Christ as Physician in Dorotheos

Christ, for Dorotheos, represented both the antidote for sin and the prescription for the health of the soul. Whereas a physician, bound by human limitations, may misdiagnose or apply inadequate medicines, Christ, as the true physician, always had the appropriate medicine and skill for the unruliness that plagues the soul.[197] Through baptism, Christ freed one from sin and offered forgiveness.[198] Then Christ taught by his holy precepts how to be cleansed from passions so that one does not fall back into sin.[199] Lastly, Christ explained how humanity first began to despise and disobey God's commandments and prescribes the "treatment (τὴν ἰατρείαν)" to obey God's commandments.[200] Citing Matthew's Gospel, Dorotheos presented this medicine as humility: "Learn from me, that I am gentle and lowly in heart and you will find rest for your souls" (Matt. 11:29).[201] Only through humility of heart could one correctly attend to and apply Christ's "holy precepts" and thus find rest for the soul. As physician and teacher, Christ supplied "the cure for the cause (ταύτης τὴν ἰατρείαν), so that we shall be able to obey and be saved."[202] Interestingly, Dorotheos never referred to himself as a physician (ὁ ἰατρός) but retained that title for Christ.

Christ the physician was the key to Dorotheos's monastic vision. This aspect of Dorotheos's teaching will be explored further in the following chapter.

Health and Illness in Dorotheos

Dorotheos based his portrayal of Christ and his discourse of healing and illness on his understanding of cultivating health within the body. As spiritual discourses, his teaching treated the condition of the soul as analogous to the condition of a sick physical body. This does not mean that Dorotheos disregarded the health of the body; rather, he was able to integrate his knowledge of the physical aspect of health in humanity with the accompanying spiritual aspect. Dorotheos was able to fortify the metaphor of healing and the discourse of illness that were already prevalent in Gazan monasticism with his infirmarian experience.

For Dorotheos, the goal of the monastic life, indeed of the Christian life, was a return to humanity's natural state at creation, a return to health. Dorotheos characterized the state of humanity at creation as continual prayer and contemplation accompanied by healthy emotions and sense perceptions: a state where the soul is neither encumbered by sin nor distracted by the passions.[203] His monastic teaching incorporated anecdotes of physical illness and healing to conceptualize the spiritual healing provided by his guidance. In Dorotheos's conception, humanity's fallen state is one that continues to fall "prey to sin, to ambition, to a love of the pleasures of this life and the other passions."[204] Meanwhile, the state of health for the soul is comparable to when "a person that had a problem with his eyes and recovers his normal sight or the person that suffered from any other sickness [...] regains his natural health (κατὰ φύσιν ὑγείαν)."[205] The endeavor of the soul, then, is a constant struggle to approach and maintain its state at creation. In accordance with Dorotheos's own mode of discourse, this section will move from a depiction of the sickly state of soul and body to the healthy state of soul and body.

Dorotheos was concerned with the state of a sickly soul. A sickly soul resulted from self-inflicted injury. Dorotheos explained, "if the soul digresses from the virtues it becomes a subject of passions and in this way evil is given existence. Through this the soul is punished (κολάζεται) and finds no natural comfort."[206] Although evil had no substance in itself, the soul generated evil by deviating from virtue. Just as wood produced worms, copper produced rust, and cloth produced moths: "In just the same way, the soul produces evil which, as I said, is nothing in itself as it has no essence or substance (μηδὲν πρὸ τούτου οὖσαν, μηδὲ ἔχουσαν… ὑπόστασιν) and the soul will then be punished (κολάζεται) through the evil."[207] Evil in the soul was analogous to sickness of the body. Dorotheos expounded upon his infirmary experience and stated,

The same thing happens with sickly bodies (τῶν ἀρρωστούντων σωμάτων). When someone lives to excess (ἀτακτήσῃ τις) and takes no care of his health (μὴ διοικήσῃ ἑαυτὸν ἐν τῇ ὑγείᾳ) either an excess (πλεονασμὸς) of something or a deficiency (ἔλλειψις) will be produced and thus he will lose his health. Before that the sickness did not exist and there was no other problem. When the body is healed again (οὗ ὑγιαίνει τὸ σῶμα), the sickness disappears completely (οὐδαμοῦ εὑρίσκεται ἡ ἀρρωστία)."[208]

Dorotheos argued that the sickness of the soul is self-generated. The habituation of vice impairs the activity and health of the soul through neglect and ill-use. Evil arises from within the soul as a self-generated disease.

Evil habits began in the soul as small, simple thoughts. When these thoughts were allowed to persist, they metastasized into large sores. What might seem insignificant, taught Dorotheos, could fester and become harmful. He warned his monks, "be careful not to neglect the small things, take care not to despise them as something insignificant. They are not insignificant; they are a sore for the soul (νομή ἐστι), a bad habit (κακὴ συνήθειά)."[209] While living in Seridos's coenobium, Dorotheos interacted with a monk who constantly stole food. The monk confessed his actions to Dorotheos. Dorotheos gave this monk permission to eat as much as he liked, but the monk still absconded with extra food. Stealing more than he could possibly eat, the monk admitted that he had been giving the food to the donkeys. Dorotheos explained that this monk made a habit of stealing, "He knew very well that it was bad, he knew that he did wrong. He was troubled and in tears and in spite of that he was drawn to his bad habit the poor wretch, which he had established in himself through his previous negligence."[210] Evil habits became ingrained in the monks so that they could not escape the influence, but health could be restored slowly and with great exercise. By searching oneself and repenting, the evil would diminish. With the help of God, one could progress. But if the passions were rooted in the soul as a habit, "even if that person wants it, he cannot deliver himself from the passions alone but he requires the help of some of the saints."[211] These examples were detrimental to the health of the individual monk, but other actions could endanger the health of the community.

In the coenobium, living with other monks was a constant threat of disruption. By provoking one's brother to evil actions, one allowed an infection to enter one's conscience.[212] This illness of the soul would have ramifications within the monastic community. Becoming angry with a brother could be detrimental. Dorotheos referred to anger over harsh words as "a little fire" that could consume the heart of a monk. Referring to Basil's *Asceticon*, Dorotheos taught that anger was the "seething of the blood around the heart (ζέσις τοῦ περικαρδίου αἵματος). The heart thus becomes angry and this is what is called irascible (ὀξυχολίαν)."[213] Dorotheos was sensitive to the small matters that could provoke illness and disruption within the soul.

Dorotheos told of a brother who lived with a fever for seven days. After the fever left him, he continued to be ill for another forty days. Dorotheos made the point that when one allowed a small disorder to persist, the recovery can be very long. Similarly with the soul, "if a person commits a small sin and spends so much time sweating blood (στάζων τὸ αἷμα αὐτοῦ), before it is put right."[214] In this example, the fever's disruption to the body was like a small sin that could easily be remedied. If allowed to persist, the sin could cause the soul's illness to extend for a lengthy period of time. For Dorotheos, the application of medicine to the body should relieve the disorder. Likewise, the application of a spiritual remedy would offer spiritual relief. However, with physical remedies, one was not assured of relief. Dorotheos noted that old medicine, an inexperienced doctor, or an undisciplined patient could negate the intended healing of the physician. Christ, "the doctor of our souls (ὁ ἰατρὸς τῶν ψυχῶν ἡμῶν)," treated the soul because, as the ideal physician, he "knows everything and gives the proper prescription (ἁρμόδιον...τὸ φάρμακον) for every passion."[215] Christ the physician is not inexperienced, nor is his medicine old. Because Christ is the physician of the soul, "there is no obstacle (τὸ ἐμποδίζον) to the soul's health, apart from its own disorder (ἡ ἀταξία αὐτῆς)."[216]

Dorotheos portrayed the vigilance against bad habits with a dietary metaphor. In his experience, sometimes after "eating something just once, [the body] will be irritated (ἐρεθίσαι) and produce more bile (ἐξάψαι κατ᾽ αὐτοῦ τὸν χυμόν)."[217] A disharmony of the bodily humors resulted in this uncomfortable situation. He explained that the habituation of vice results in a "pestilential sickness (λοιμώδης ἀρρωστία)" of the soul akin to a person that eats too many cabbages and lentils and has elevated bodily humors.[218] Just as a poor diet inundates such a body with melancholy and fever, so too, the soul that continues in sin develops a bad condition that "torments (κολάζουσα)" it.[219] This unnatural state is a continual detriment to the soul's health. One is no longer able to participate in the prayer and contemplation for which humanity was created, and one's soul is, conversely, continually disrupted and disturbed. The emotions and sense perceptions are no longer healthy but overtake the soul and lead it away from virtue.

Dorotheos did not hesitate to use himself as an example of poor vigilance. Dorotheos recalled an instance when he was afflicted with a foot ailment. He explained that he had allowed himself to indulge in gluttony and vainglory due to his, presumably, prestigious guests. The result was bodily malfunction and severe discomfort. While he was well aware that an "external cause (ἔξωθεν αἰτίαν)" for his bodily condition was available, he deferred to divine activity in the situation.[220] He acknowledged that, whatever the physical manifestation, the primary cause was a disturbance in his soul that led to his overindulgence. God permitted the physical ailment to take its course so that Dorotheos could reflect and repent of his soul's yielding to vice.[221] God also offered healing to Dorotheos in Seridos's coenobium. He recounted a time in the coenobium when he was so sorrowful, in pain and distress, that he was "almost ready to surrender his soul."[222] But the grace of God came to his aid. He had a vision of a bishop clothed in sheepskin. This man tapped his fingers to Dorotheos's chest and repeated three times: "I waited patiently for the Lord; and he inclined to me, and heard my cry. He also brought me up out of a horrible pit, out of the miry clay, and set my feet upon a rock, and established my steps. He has put a new song in my mouth, praise to our God (Ps. 40:1–3)."[223] Dorotheos admitted instantaneous healing at the vision's departure. This healing was a complete renewal for Dorotheos. In his description, "Suddenly light, joy, consolation, and sweetness entered my heart and I became a totally new man (εὑρίσκομαι ἄλλος ἐξ ἄλλου)....From that time on, through the mercy of God, I have never been bothered by sorrow or cowardice but the Lord has protected me up to now through the prayers of those holy elders."[224] This experience of healing, as Dorotheos recalled, was profound. His elaboration on healing was not as spectacular, though just as potent.

For Dorotheos, the healthy soul was well balanced and able to respond appropriately to any circumstance. It continually sought to retain its healthy state and habituated virtue. Like sophistry and medicine, virtue must become a habit so the soul can assume the skill through continual practice.[225] This state, while still susceptible to disruption, is able to maneuver through potentially harmful situations with great agility and even profit from the challenges faced therein. Dorotheos explains that,

> [A]ll those who have good habits are like the person who has a robust body (σῶμα εὔχυμον). Even if he eats something harmful, he transforms it into nourishing food according to his own condition (τρέπει αὐτὸ εἰς εὐχυμίαν πρὸς τὴν κρᾶσιν αὐτοῦ) and even this bad food does not harm him because, as I have said, his body is vigorous and transforms the food according to its condition...Thus, we too, if we have a good spiritual state and condition (καλὴν ἕξιν καὶ καλὴν κατάστασιν) we can, as I have said earlier, take profit from everything, even if, in itself, it is not profitable.[226]

The healthy soul had been trained and disciplined to retain its health even in the face of harmful situations. This training and discipline, as was observed earlier, was not due solely to the monk's own effort, but, primarily and initially, due to the actions of Christ that freed the soul from sin, and secondarily to the teachings of Christ and the example of the Fathers.

As seen above in Zosmias' *Reflections*, the monastery was a place where one found healing through the love of others. Dorotheos described healing within

community as the love of Christ exhibited through dedication and care for a sinning brother. He explained that a fellow monk trapped in sin was like a sick bodily
member. The proper comportment of the monastic community compelled others
not to "judge or dislike him but suffer with him, admonish him, offer him consolation and healing like a sick member. They do everything to save the sinner."[227]
The monastic community offered healing through its love, sympathy, and compassion. Dorotheos allowed correction of the sinful monk so that he would not harm
others, but this correction should come at the appropriate time and without hate.

Healing could also entail drastic measures. Dorotheos offered an example from
Abba Alonios in which a monk might be caught in the midst of a murder and
the murderer hid in his cell. Knowing the penalty for that murder was death, Alonios advised lying to the magistrate and abandoning this person to God.[228] This act
of lying would preserve the murderous person from the most extreme penalty and
enable healing of that individual. In Dorotheos's explanation, lying, in this case, was
like a drastic healing measure. He illustrated his point: "It is like an antidote (τῆς
θηριακῆς) for a poison or like the purgative (τοῦ καθαρσίου), which if taken continuously is harmful, but if taken once a year, when it is necessary, is beneficial."[229] In
this extreme case, one must take the utmost care, repent, and be in tears before God.
The preservation of the murderer for the purpose of healing involved struggle for the
monk but, like the body, was necessary for the hope of healing.

All healing came ultimately from God. Dorotheos spoke of a sick holy elder
who was attended by a brother. Honey was added to the elder's food as part of his
dietary treatment. The brother accidentally added linseed oil to his food instead,
and the elder knowingly ate his meal in silence, then a second plate as required.
Dorotheos emphasized the elder's humility by pointing out that linseed oil could
have devastating effects. When the brother realized his mistake and confronted the
elder, the old monk replied, "[I]f God wanted me to eat honey (μέλι), you would
have put honey in the food."[230] The elder was sick for many days after this incident.
Dorotheos extrapolated from the elder's reaction that though the brother made a
mistake, "if God wanted him to have honey, he could transform (μετέτρεπεν) the
stinking oil into honey."[231] Living in monastic community meant being subject to
injury from others. Yet, God could counteract those injuries. God could transform
the linseed oil into honey. The elder realized that healing and illness were in God's
control and beyond the effects of honey or linseed oil. He forwent the comfort of
honey to trust in God and humble himself before the young monk. Dorotheos
understood that the coenobitic life, while an avenue to health, required bodily
sacrifices. However, the body was to be trained, not tormented.

Dorotheos depicted Christ as the true physician and used medical metaphors
to exemplify how he understood both the sickened soul and its agent of healing

to be analogous to the way in which a patient would be treated by a physician. Dorotheos was also intently concerned with the physical health of his monks. For Dorotheos, the monastic life was not a life in which the soul thrived while the body suffered, but a life where health was afforded to both. The monastic life was the quintessential ground for achieving this integration of health.

Conclusion

The metaphor of healing in the monastic school of Gaza was a central motif used to describe the disposition of the soul. In the everyday activity of the monastic life, monks were either approaching health or retreating into sickness. Isaiah, Barsanuphius, John, and Dorotheos held this concept in common. Their approaches to illness in the monastic life reflected their distinctive positions. Isaiah emphasized the suffering of illness as identifying with Christ's sufferings. Barsanuphius and John maintained that illness was instructive for spiritual maturity. Dorotheos, however, conceived of illness as primarily the place where monks were open to God's healing. The difference, for Dorotheos, was that illness was the point at which God acted on a person's behalf to restore wholeness. This restorative process was the basis for his understanding of Christ's work as physician. As a monastic teacher, Dorotheos emphasized rehabilitating the sick and helping them return to a state in which their bodies could function according to their capacity. Dorotheos was conscious of the spiritual implications of disease in the monastic life. Even in his own life, he understood that certain illnesses could be instructive and remedy sickness within the soul by the temporary discomfort of the body. In the case of Dositheos, who died under his direct care, Dorotheos withheld the potential benefit of eggs for the sake of Dositheos conscience. Dorotheos displayed a balance in his teaching between the health of the body and the health of the soul.

True health was a harmony within the person, both in body and soul. Dorotheos's discourse of health and illness posited that the true physician was Christ who came to reinstate the health of humanity as it stood at creation. This was a health in which body and soul were an integrated whole that allowed humanity to worship and contemplate God without interruption. The monastic life, as Dorotheos understood, was a life that sought equilibrium. Dorotheos was not prescribing a mode of life that was itself efficacious for healing; rather, the monastic life was a prescription for the soul founded upon the work of Christ for humanity's salvation. Dorotheos's conception of health was most fecund when apprehended through his account of God's healing activity in the work of Christ and the drama of salvation.

CHAPTER FOUR

Healing in the Drama of Salvation

The discourse of healing was pervasive in the Gazan monastic literature, and Dorotheos stood well within this tradition. He was concerned with distinguishing the sources of humanity's illness and its cure. The metaphor of healing allowed Dorotheos to develop a rich explanation of the drama of salvation through which Christ the Physician offered the cure for humanity's ills and Christ the Teacher provided the prescription for continuing in this life of health.[1] Dorotheos's vision of humanity's health benefited from this broader approach. Additionally, this matrix earned Dorotheos a distinctive position within the monastic school of Gaza because of its rich texture and sustained employment of the metaphor of healing.

According to Bitton-Ashkelony and Kofsky, "Dorotheos wished to integrate his ascetic teachings on sin into a patristic theology of salvation history."[2] In Dorotheos's explication, the salvation narrative moved from healthy creation to sickness incurred from sin, to the remedies provided by God and, finally, to Dorotheos's own justification for the monastic life. In this chapter, I will analyze Dorotheos's contemporaries in light of Dorotheos's own discussion of the creation, fall, and healing of humanity and justification of the monastic life.[3] This chapter concludes with a final comparison of each teacher's approach to the passions. The conclusions drawn in this chapter will provide the lens through which to ascertain Dorotheos's distinct vision of the Christian life of virtue and the interrelation of healing for body and soul for ascetics.

Creation in Dorotheos

In *Discourse* 1, Dorotheos provided a detailed explication of the creation, fall, and salvation of humanity. At the core of this discourse was the notion that humanity was created in a healthy state. Dorotheos commenced this discourse, "In the beginning, when God created man...," he was "adorned with every virtue."[4] He described the state of humanity at creation as "having sound perception and being in his natural state."[5] The attribution of virtue was important because it signified a relational status between God and humanity's creation "according to the image of God (κατ᾽ εἰκόνα Θεοῦ)."[6] The inclusion of virtue in humanity's created state was absent from Dorotheos's contemporaries. Dorotheos explained that being "adorned with every virtue" was an aspect of humanity's creation in the image of God, "For God created him after his own image (Gen. 1:27), that is to say, immortal, with free-will and adorned with every virtue."[7] At creation, humanity enjoyed a life of harmony and freedom; the extent of which would only become clear after the fall. The natural state was characterized as healthy in contrast to the state affected by the fall. In paradise, humanity persisted "in prayer and contemplation (ἐν εὐχῇ, ἐν θεωρίᾳ)."[8]

Isaiah

Isaiah also proposed a narrative of salvation in his second discourse. Isaiah explained that when Adam was created, "God place him in Paradise with healthy senses that were established according to nature."[9] Isaiah continually referred to the created state as either the natural state or the state of Adam.[10] For Isaiah, the natural state included the passions. Much like desire, which leads to love for God, the passions were naturally good.[11] Ambition, anger, hatred, and pride were all part of Adam's created nature. As Isaiah explained, "when Adam tasted disobedience, these were changed within him."[12]

Barsanuphius

In their *Letters*, Barsanuphius and John never offered an explicit explanation of the theological foundation for their teaching. They always directed their spiritual guidance toward the questions posed to them, and this guidance reflected the spiritual and practical nature of the petitions. Barsanuphius only rarely wrote concerning the creation of humanity. In a letter exclaiming the thanks one should give to God, he asserted the view that God created humanity "before all else (πρὸ μὲν πάντων δημιουργήσαντι ἡμᾶς), then offered us assistance against our enemies by giving us prudence of heart, health of body, light in our eyes, breath of life, and, above all, a place of repentance as well as the reception of his body and blood for the forgiveness of sins and the establishment of our heart."[13] Barsanuphius recognized God's act of creation that led to God's provision for humanity.

In one letter, Barsanuphius affirmed that humanity was created dispassionate (ἀπαθῆ), free from the negative influence of the passions that became real after the fall.[14] He affirmed the creation of "both the soul and the body dispassionate, but through disobedience people fell away to passions."[15] In its created state, humanity was free from the negative influence of the passions that were realized after the fall.[16] Such a description would seem to anticipate Dorotheos's assertion of the dispassionate created human nature.

However, Barsanuphius was very vague concerning this natural state and contradicted his own position when, on another occasion, he explained that

> [T]here is anger that is natural (θυμὸς φυσικὸς), and there is anger that is against nature (θυμὸς παρὰ φύσιν). So the natural anger struggles not to give rise to the urges of desire and does not require remedy; for it has already been cured. The unnatural anger, however, struggles not to fulfill the urges of desire, but this requires remedy even more so than desire itself.[17]

This statement was reminiscent of Isaiah who held that the natural state of humanity included several positive passions that lead to love for God. Barsanuphius, too, maintained the inclusion of natural anger in the original state of humanity. When Barsanuphius emphasized the "dispassionate state" of humanity at creation, he noted the transition from a dispassionate state to a passionate state as a result of disobedience. Thus, the created, dispassionate state would have included the positive passions, like natural anger, which was also an aspect of Isaiah's teaching.

John

John was much less explicit in discussing the drama of salvation. His spiritual direction maintained three tenets: human freedom, human responsibility for evil, and the necessity of suffering in this life for future glorification. Concerning the creation of humanity, John merely stated that God created humanity free in order that people could "incline toward the good (ῥέψαι εἰς τὸ ἀγαθόν)."[18] For John, human freedom also entailed the possibility that humans could choose evil rather than good.[19] John offered no other explanation of humanity's creation.

In contrast to Isaiah and Barsanuphius, Dorotheos insisted that the virtues were intrinsic to humanity and denied any attribution of the passions to humanity's created nature. Instead, Dorotheos held that the passions were the result of humanity's fall and likened the passions to an illness that could only be overcome by divine action. Alternatively, virtues were the signs of health for humanity.

The Fall in Dorotheos

Dorotheos depicted the fall as Adam's disobedience in eating "from the tree which God had forbidden him to eat from." Hence, humanity

> fell from [its] natural state into a state contrary to nature (Ἐξέπεσε γὰρ ἐκ τοῦ κατὰ φύσιν καὶ ἦν ἐν τῷ παρὰ φύσιν), that is to say into sin, into ambition and the love of the pleasures of this life and all the other passions and was dominated by them, and became subject to them because of his transgression. Thus, in turn, evil increased and 'death reigned' (Rom 5:14)."[20]

For Dorotheos, humanity fell from a wholly dispassionate, natural state into an unnatural state that was subject to the passions. Only after the fall did the passions infect humanity.

In this fallen state, the illness that resulted from the fall had infected every aspect of the human person despite God's provision of the law and the prophets. God sent the law as an aid and correction of evil, but "evil prevailed as Isaiah says: 'There is no soundness in it, but wounds and bruises and putrefying sores. They have not been closed or bound up, or soothed with ointment (ὕτε τραῦμα οὔτε μώλωψ οὔτε πληγὴ φλεγμαίνουσα. οὐκ ἔστι μάλαγμα ἐπιθεῖναι οὔτε ἔλαιον οὔτε καταδέσμους.)' (Isa. 1:6)."[21] Dorotheos reinforced the notion of sin as an illness by quoting Jeremiah, "We tried to heal (Ἰατρεύσαμεν) Babylon, but she was not healed (ἰάθη) (Jer. 28:9)."[22] God alone must become the cure and administer the remedy for the illness that was plaguing humanity. Dorotheos borrowed abba Isaiah's notion of the fall from a natural state to a state contrary to nature. Yet, Isaiah and Barsanuphius provided a notable contrast to Dorotheos's conception.

Isaiah

According to Isaiah, humanity's fallen state as "contrary to nature (τὴν παρὰ φύσιν)" characterized the fall.[23] Isaiah contrasted the state of humanity according to nature with the state of humanity contrary to nature. One aspect of this fallen state was transformation of the passions from promoting love of God to inducing destruction. This contrary nature was manifest, for Isaiah, in shameful desire and perverted passion. Isaiah reflected upon the description of Daniel as "a man of desires," (Dan. 9:23) and maintained that "desire is a natural state of the intellect because without desire for God there is no love."[24] Much like desire, which leads to love for God, the passions were naturally good: "Now these things are innate to humanity. But when Adam tasted disobedience, these were changed within him into shameful passions."[25] In their perverted state, ambition, anger, hatred, and pride are misdirected, primarily towards one's neighbor. These passions, which once promoted love and unity with God and neighbor, had become divisive and damaging.

Barsanuphius

Except for a single excerpt, an explanation of the fall was absent from Barsanuphius's letters. Barsanuphius wrote that, "For the one who envied Adam from the beginning, casting him out of paradise, envies also our concord in Christ."[26] Satan was later mentioned in this same letter as the adversary of humanity and the one responsible for humanity's banishment from paradise. The role of Satan was not further clarified elsewhere. Yet, Barsanuphius did not abolish responsibility for the fall from humans but concluded that humanity should "direct the blame upon ourselves."[27]

Isaiah and Barsanuphius only offered meager explanations of the fall. In contrast, Dorotheos expressed a precise conception of the fallen state of humanity as an infection of the passions, and humanity's need for healing illustrated his infirmarian's perspective. Christ would become, in Dorotheos's works, the cure for humanity's illness. Dorotheos borrowed Isaiah's notion of the fall from a natural state to a state contrary to nature and maintained that humanity fell from a wholly dispassionate, natural state into an unnatural state that was subject to the passions. Unlike Isaiah and Barsanuphius, Dorotheos did not include the passions as a part of humanity's natural state. Only after the fall was humanity infected by the passions. In this fallen state, humanity also incurred the proliferation of evil and death.

Healing in Dorotheos

Dorotheos understood David's pleas for divine deliverance in the Psalms to be calls for God to contravene the fallen state of humanity. "David clearly says, 'You dwell between the Cherubim shine forth … stir up your strength, and come and save us.' (Ps. 80:1–2) Elsewhere, 'Bow down your heavens, O Lord, and come down.' (Ps. 144:5)"[28] Indeed, God intervened and "sent His only-begotten Son (John 3:16), because only God could heal Man (Θεοῦ γὰρ ἦν μόνου τὸ ἰάσασθαι) and enable him to rise up from this kind of suffering."[29] Again, the imagery of restoration of health appeared in Dorotheos's discourse. Borrowing from Gregory Nanzianzen, Dorotheos claimed that Christ came "to heal like with like; the soul by the soul and the flesh by the flesh."[30] Whereas the effect of the fall distorted the entire body and the whole of the human person, Christ's actions healed both soul and body. Christ restored the natural state of humanity by becoming a new Adam, a "perfect man without sin."[31] Dorotheos explained, "He has assumed our essence, the first fruit of our nature and He became a new Adam 'according to the image of Him who created him.' (Col. 3:10) He renews human nature and makes our senses perfect again, as they were at the beginning. He renewed fallen man by becoming man." [32] Through Christ's incarnation, humanity was restored to the natural state of health, the state of humanity in paradise. Dorotheos's portrayal of Christ's work for the healing of humanity shared similarities with Isaiah and Barsanuphius.

Isaiah

Similarly, Isaiah described God's action as enabling humanity's return to the state according to nature. Upon following the advice of the deceiver in the garden, Adam's "senses were twisted toward that which is contrary to nature" and "he fell from his glory."[33] God became human out of love, "that he might, through his holy body, transform that which is contrary to nature to the state that is according to nature."[34] According to Isaiah, God intervened and "the Word became flesh," became completely human, in order to "transform (μεταλλάξῃ) that which is contrary to nature (τὴν παρὰ φύσιν) to the state that is according to nature (εἰς τὴν κατὰ φύσιν)."[35] Isaiah affirmed that "God returned [Adam] to Paradise, resurrecting those who followed his steps and the commandments... that we may stay in the natural state in which God created us."[36] Much of this discourse resounded in Dorotheos's teaching. Isaiah, however, established a teaching from which Dorotheos would deviate.

The role of Christ in this transformation was for healing the contrary nature of humanity and providing a model of personal crucifixion. Isaiah explained,

> If our Lord Jesus Christ had not first healed all the passions of humanity for which he came into the world, he would not have ascended the cross, for before the Lord came in flesh, humanity was blind, dumb, paralyzed, deaf, leprous, lame, and dead on account of everything that was contrary to nature. When, however, God had mercy on us and came into the world, he raised the dead, made the lame walk, the blind see, the dumb speak, the deaf hear, and resurrected a new person, free of all illness. Then he ascended the cross.[37]

Only after Christ healed and resurrected human nature did Christ "ascend the cross." In his crucifixion, Christ "has made himself a model for us who follow in his steps, profoundly and deeply humbling himself and taking the nature of a slave…. May we allow ourselves to be led like sheep to the slaughter."[38] Christ's example revealed, for Isaiah, a new person.[39] "This is why the Lord Jesus became human, in order that we may be concerned with endeavoring to behave as he did, searching ourselves as best we can in accordance with his example."[40] The transformation of one's nature also enabled one to become a bride of Christ[41] or even a dwelling for Christ.[42]

Barsanuphius

Barsanuphius was clear on the role of the Trinity in the healing and redemption of humanity. In one letter, he recounted the activity of the "Holy and consubstantial Trinity (τὴν ἁγίαν καὶ ὁμοούσιον Τριάδα)" in a doxological form.[43] According to Barsanuphius, each person of the Trinity was to be praised for the salvation of humanity. The Father was praised for sending the Son, "the Redeemer of our souls."[44] The Son was praised for his humility and obedience unto death. The Holy Spirit was praised as "the Giver of life, which spoke through the Law, the Prophets, and the Teachers."[45] His praise for Christ was more specific when he wrote, "The Son of God became human for your sake; you, too, should become god through him. For he wants this, especially when you also want it (Ἄνθρωπος γέγονε διὰ σὲ ὁ Υἱὸς τοῦ Θεοῦ, γενοῦ καὶ σύ, δι᾽ αὐτοῦ Θεός. Θέλει γάρ, ὅταν σὺ θέλῃς)."[46] Barsanuphius introduced the notion of deification as the consequence of human response to the incarnation. His focus was on the exemplary kenosis and suffering of Christ, but his main point was that one "would be liberated from the old self."[47] His notion of liberation from one's "old self" had important implications for his monastic instruction.[48]

Dorotheos adopted Isaiah's conception of nature and counter nature and interpreted the work of Christ from the perspective of restoring health to humanity. His portrayal of Christ's restoration of humanity's health also extended to the monastic life. Dorotheos's understanding of salvation was instrumental in his development of a unique monastic vision. The monastic life was the gift of a person to God over and above the commandments of Christ to his followers. First, however, Dorotheos discussed the cleansing of baptism, the teaching of Christ, and the Christian way of life.

Monastic Life in Dorotheos

For Dorotheos, the Christian life began with baptism. Holy baptism forgave and erased one's sins. Yet, God was "aware of our sickness (τὴν ἀσθένειαν ἡμῶν)" and knew that humanity would sin after baptism.[49] Therefore, Christ gave commandments to his followers to purify them from their sins and the passions. Dorotheos held that "Sins are one thing and passions another. The passions are anger, idleness, desire for pleasure, hate, evil desire, and others. Sins, on the other hand, are the acting out of passions, that is to say, someone puts them into practice, when [one] uses his body to enact everything dictated by the passions."[50] Dorotheos taught that everyone was subject to the passions, but they should not act upon them. Through Christ's commandments, humanity could discern the passions and be freed from sin. Christ's restitution of humanity involved the means for humanity to distinguish between good and evil; he showed humanity the causes of sin and enabled humanity to avoid sin.[51]

The monastic life was the gift of a person to God over and above the commandments of Christ to his followers. Christ the Physician[52] became Christ the Teacher. Dorotheos contended that "The aim (σκοπός) of our Master Christ is simply to teach (διδάξαι) us how we came into all these sins, how we fell (ἐνεπέσαμεν) into those evil days…In this way, He gives us the cure (τὴν ἰατρείαν) for the cause, so that we shall be able to obey and be saved (ἵνα δυνηθῶμεν ὑπακοῦσαι καὶ σωθῆναι)."[53] The teacher himself modeled this cure: "Learn from me, for I am gentle and lowly in heart, and you will find rest for your souls.' (Matt. 11:29) Here briefly, in one word, He has shown us the root and cause of every evil and the treatment for it and also the cause of every good."[54] The humility of Christ was the key to undermining the effects of sin and one's proclivity to exercise the passions. Christ's commandments and example in life were the embodiment of humility. Dorotheos encouraged his monks to pursue the humility of Christ in their monastic way of life.

The pursuit of humility was the motivation behind the monastic lives of "Saint Antony and Saint Pachomius and the other God-bearing fathers (οἱ λοιποὶ θεοφόροι Πατέρες)."[55] These saints attempted to unite themselves with God through a humble way of life. They not only removed the effect of the passions but rooted out the passions themselves to reach a state of apathy, the natural state. These monastic predecessors literally applied Christ's suggestion to the rich young man in Matthew 19:16–21 and Mark 10:17–20. Christ did not command the man to sell what he had and give to the poor but suggested that if the man wanted to be perfect he should follow Christ's advice. They knew that living in the world was not conducive to this way of life, so "they decided to seek a strange life (ξένον βίον), a strange way (ξένην τινὰ διαγωγήν). This was the monastic life (τοῦ μονήρους βίου)."[56] The monastic way of life was characterized by the pursuit of perfection, the attainment of virtue, and the presentation of gifts to God. These gifts were virginity and poverty, along with the virtues. Dorotheos mentioned living in the desert, fasting, sleeping on the ground, and keeping vigil, as well as renouncing one's former life, relatives, and possessions, as the practical elements of monastic living.[57]

The motivation for this monastic way of life was the advice of Christ, but Dorotheos did not depict the crucifixion of Christ as the way to understand monastic withdrawal. Instead, he pointed to Galatians 6:14 where "the Apostle says, 'The world has been crucified to me, and I to the world.'"[58] Entering into the monastic life was crucifying oneself to the world. This was not the end but only the beginning for the monk. Dorotheos taught his monks that one ought also to be crucified to the world. He meant that the monk must struggle against the pleasures themselves and mortify the passions.[59] He explained, "With the cutting out of one's own will, one reaches freedom from desires and having attained this, he comes close to God in perfect dispassion (εἰς τελείαν ἀπάθειαν)."[60] The monastic life meant, for Dorotheos, a return to the natural state of health and the pursuit of purity from the passions by cutting off the will inclined toward the passions.[61]

Isaiah

For Isaiah, the goal of the monk was to gradually strip away "the conduct of the old person"[62] and to "acquire the new person."[63] Isaiah described the perfection of the monastic life as imitation of Christ's sufferings, "to ascend the cross with him (μετ᾽ αὐτοῦ ἀναβῆναι ἐπὶ τὸν σταυρόν)."[64] Isaiah described the distinction between the new and the old person: "The one who loves his soul and does not want to lose it keeps the ways of the New Person. The person who wants to rest in this brief lifetime carries out and practices the ways of the Old Person but loses his soul."[65] The new person represented the person who had renounced the counter nature of humanity after the fall and practiced Christ's model of suffering. This new life resembled the state of humanity at its creation and also entailed preparation for unification with Christ as one who embraced and ascended the cross.

Barsanuphius

Barsanuphius also emphasized the "new person" as representative of the individual who had renounced the counter nature of humanity after the fall, embraced the spiritual healing from Christ, and practiced Christ's model for life. He linked putting away the old self with enduring suffering and, according to Christ's example, ascending the cross.[66] Barsanuphius wrote to John explaining that the whole of the monastic life was a movement, from A to Z (ἀπὸ τοῦ ἄλφα ἕως τοῦ ὠμέγα), from the beginner's stage to that of perfection (ἀπὸ ἀρχαρίου καταστάσεως μέχρι τοῦ τελείου), from the outset of the way to its very end, from the 'putting away of the old self with earthly desires (τὸν πλαιὸν ἄνθρωπον σὺν ταῖς ἐπιθυμίαις)' (Eph. 4:22, Col. 3:9) to the putting on of the new self 'created according to God (μέχρι τοῦ ἐνδύσασθαι τὸν νέον, "τὸν κατὰ Θεὸν κτισθέντα).' (Eph. 4:24, Col. 3:10)[67]

The entire monastic life was a movement from putting away the old self to putting on the new self. Barsanuphius explained the new self and distinguished his own teaching from that of Isaiah when he wrote:

> Therefore, for those who desire to be spiritual, he [Paul] advised the rejection of the flesh.... This is precisely why, knowing that [the Apostle] is speaking about natural desires, he advised that *one should deny oneself and not what is contrary to one's nature.* For if one were to renounce the desires that are contrary to nature, the one has in fact left behind nothing of one's own for the sake of God, since these are not properly one's own in the first place.[68]

According to Barsanuphius, one must reject precisely that which is natural to humanity. This stark devaluation of the nature of humanity influenced Barsanuphius's teaching on the role of suffering in life. The one who endured sufferings was assured that sufferings entail imitation of Christ's sacrifice of himself, as seen in Isaiah above. Only through self-abnegation and patiently enduring suffering in imitation of Christ could one expect the indwelling of God.

For Barsanuphius, suffering was a preparatory state for ascending the cross. He stated, "Anyone who wishes to ascend with Christ on the cross (συναναβῆναι εἰς τὸν σταυρὸν μετὰ τοῦ Χριστοῦ) must become a partaker of his sufferings (τῶν παθημάτων αὐτοῦ) in order always to have peace (τὴν εἰρήνην). I, too, say to you: 'Struggle to acquire thanksgiving in all circumstances, and "the power of the Most High will overshadow you," (Luke 1:35) and then you shall find rest (τὴν ἀνάπαυσιν).'"[69] The notions of suffering and ascending the cross often appeared together in Barsanuphius's spiritual direction, "Therefore, if you do not endure sufferings, you cannot reach the cross."[70] The one who endured sufferings was assured that sufferings entail imitation of Christ's sacrifice of himself, as seen in Isaiah above. Ascending the cross or embracing the new self gave way to rest in God and a life free of care. The new self was cleansed of the passions and prepared as a dwelling place for God. "For 'we are his temples,' (2 Cor. 6:16) and the divine does not dwell in a temple stained by passions."[71] Only through self-abnegation and patiently enduring suffering in imitation of Christ could one expect the indwelling of God.

In a rare reference to his own struggles, Barsanuphius declared, "Therefore, having heard these things, I mourn and moan, until his goodness is also compassionate toward me, and he delivers me from the terrible passions of the old self, so that I may follow the footsteps of the new self, and accept all things that come upon me with great patience."[72] This same language appeared in another letter where he told a monk to seek "liberation from the old self."[73] He entreated those under his spiritual care to endure the sufferings of this life and put away the old self while putting on the new self, which "was created according to the likeness of God (Eph. 4:22–24, Col. 3:9)."[74]

Whereas Isaiah portrayed the natural desires of humanity as that to which one seeks to return, Barsanuphius emphasized the rejection of one's whole being. For Barsanuphius, "Unless a person dies according to the flesh, that person cannot rise to life according to the Spirit. For just as natural desires no longer remain within a person who has died physically, so also they do not remain within a person who has died according to the flesh spiritually."[75] One who sought to put away the old self should consider oneself physically dead.

John

For John, human freedom also entailed the possibility that humans could choose evil rather than good. John explained that "people are themselves to blame for their own evils, [God] allowed them their freedom so that they may be without any excuse on the day of judgment, when each would accuse the other."[76] John also held that, because of humanity's free choice of evil rather than good, one should expect suffering in this life just as Christ suffered.[77] One could only achieve the future rest through suffering in this life.

Dorotheos rejected the negative portrayal of bodily life as seen in his contemporaries and centered his teaching on the notion of Christ the healer and teacher of the healthy life. He stressed the pursuit of peace and virtue that the life of heath afforded to his monks in the present life.

Thus, in contrast to Isaiah and Barsanuphius, Dorotheos insisted that the virtues were intrinsic to humanity and denied any attribution of the passions to humanity's created nature. Instead, Dorotheos held that the passions were the result of humanity's fall and likened the passions to an illness that should be overcome. Christ brought humanity the cure for the illness of sin, the teaching for uprooting the passions and for habituating virtue, and the hope for a life of freedom from the passions. The imagery used here did not refer explicitly to Christ's suffering and crucifixion but rather to the incarnation. Whereas the image of the suffering and crucified Christ was pronounced in Isaiah, Barsanuphius, and John, it is absent in Dorotheos's first discourse. Instead, Dorotheos turned to the idea of crucifixion in Galatians 6:14 as the motivation to pursue the monastic life. The crucifixion of oneself to the world and the world to oneself in Galatians was an amplification of the healing and prescription for life that Christ offered to all his followers.

Passions

Each monastic teacher emphasized the importance of rehabilitating a person in order to struggle against the passions. Larchet remarked that in the monastic literature, "All the passions arise from the disease of the three main powers of the soul, namely the perversion of their various functions, spiritual therapy should consist in a reordering of the fundamental faculties. It is giving back to them a use in accordance with their nature that man recovers his health."[78] As was observed above, Dorotheos alone attributed the existence of the passions to the sickness of humanity after the fall. The notion of the passions as wholly alien to the created human nature led Dorotheos to treat them differently from his contemporaries. Instead of advising his monks to negate the old self and ascend the cross, he advised a gradual uprooting of the passions through discernment and prayer. His intention was to slowly nurse the person back to a state of health through recognition and elimination of foreign intrusions. A detailed analysis of Dorotheos's position will follow Isaiah's, Barsanuphius's, and John's portrayals.

Isaiah

Isaiah insisted that the passions were a facet of humanity at creation. He enumerated many of the passions burdening humanity: fornication, covetousness, avarice, gossip, anger, envy, vainglory, and pride (πορνεία ἐπιθυμία, φιλαργυρία, καταλαλιά, ὀργή, ζῆλος, κενοδοξία, ὑπερηφανία).[79] Isaiah described the passions as heavy burdens, curses, old skins for new wine, foxes in the vineyard, and strips of cloth that bound Lazarus.[80] After humanity's fall, the passions were distorted from their created function and became troubling to humanity. The passions controlled one's perspective of oneself and others. Isaiah considered Peter's "sanctified heart (ἡγιάσθη αὐτοῦ ἡ καρδία)" that saw no one as "common or unclean (κοινὸν ἢ ἀκάθαρτον) (Acts 10:28)."[81] The one whose heart was full of the passions saw "everyone in accordance with the passions in his own heart (κατὰ τὰ πάθη τὰ ἐν τῇ καρδίᾳ αὐτοῦ)."[82] The passions tainted one's appreciation of others because of the disorder caused within. When an elder of the community asked Isaiah when the passions tend to strike, Isaiah replied that just as seeds grow in watered earth, so, too, the passions grow within a person. He encouraged the elder "to uproot that which is contrary to nature from his heart (ἀγωνίσηται ἐκβάλαι τὰς παραφύσεις ἐκ τῆς καρδίας αὐτοῦ)," and the passions would not disturb him.[83]

Acknowledging the passions connoted humility toward God and others.[84] The enlightened perception of the passions was a painful enterprise. Isaiah likened hatred of the passions to sharp twigs that sting a person who still desired worldly things.[85] Rejecting the passions involved suffering. Isaiah viewed the relationship between struggle and suffering as so connected that he advised his monks to "Learn to love all forms of suffering, and your passions will be humbled."[86] Love of suffering was not the only conception of love at work in Isaiah. He also advised his monks to follow love "that quenches all the passions of the soul and the body (τῇ σβεννυούσῃ πάντα τὰ πάθη τῆς σαρκος καὶ τοῦ σωματος)."[87] Love redirected attention away from the body's rest and toward God. The self-concerned person was like an imprisoned soul that sought only its own bodily rest and comfort. This person was unable even to consider the passions that raged within. Isaiah discerned this imprisoning of the soul:

> There are two things that imprison the soul (συνέχουσαι τὴν ψυχήν). The external one cares for bodily rest in this world but the internal one considers which of the passions hinder the virtues. The soul, however, does not see the interior one regarding the passions unless it is freed from the exterior one.[88]

Only once a person was able to understand the benefit of the struggle against the passions could one then understand the difference between the fruits of virtue and the fruits of the passions: "The end of the virtues is love, and the end of the passions is self-justification."[89]

Isaiah recognized that the struggle against the passions was not a human struggle bereft of divine aid: "If you are struggling against a passion (ἀγωνίζῃ πρὸς πάθος), do not lose heart, but surrender yourself (παράρριψον σεαυτὸν) to God, saying, 'I cannot do this; help me, the wretched one'. Say this with all your heart and you will find rest (ἀναπαύῃ)."[90] God's salvific activity "changed our hardened nature (μεταβάλῃ τὴν φύσιν ἡμῶν τὴν σκληράν)" so that humanity could "cut off our willfulness (κόψῃ τὰ θελήματα ἡμῶν) and the false knowledge (τὴν ψευδῆ γνῶσιν) that dominated our soul."[91] In his salvific work, Christ initiated relief from the passions. Isaiah reconfigured the struggle against the passions as a transferal of struggle. Relief from the passions was initiated in Christ's salvific work. The struggle against the passions was reconfigured as a transferal of struggle. Isaiah built upon scriptural images, saying

Christ's burden is light; it is purity, the absence of anger, kindness, gentleness, the joy of the spirit, continence of passions, love toward all, discernment, holiness, steadfast faith, patience in tribulations, comes to be regarded like a stranger in the world, and desires to leave its body and meet Christ. These are the light burdens which Christ prescribes us to carry.[92]

Christ defeated sin so that humanity might be relieved of the burden.

Isaiah connected Christ's death to salvation, claiming, "[Christ's] death has become our salvation (ἡμῖν ἐγένετο σωτηρία), because through his death sin has died, once for all, and his resurrection is life (ἡ ἀνάστασις αὐτοῦ ζωὴ ἐγένετο) for all those who firmly believe in him and who have cured their own passions, in order that they live in God and produce the fruit of justice."[93] Additionally, quoting Paul, Isaiah could point to the spiritual fruits that a life free of the passions could produce. He explained that "[T]he apostle, seeing that those who merit to be raised up from the dead passions, no longer having an opponent, points out to them the fruit of the Spirit: 'Love, joy, peace, long-suffering, kindness, goodness, faithfulness, meekness, self-control. Against such things I say there is no law'. (Gal. 5:22–23)"[94] The life of virtue was a life prepared for spiritual fruit. Only by struggling against the passions and trusting in God to intervene could one hope to become fruitful.

Barsanuphius

Barsanuphius vacillated in his position on the origin of the passions. At one point he affirmed that humanity was created dispassionate.[95] At another point he followed Isaiah and stated that there were good passions at creation that were distorted in the fall.[96] The passions were a sign of the old self that was to be renewed. As long as these passions "trouble your heart (κινεῖται ἡ καρδία σου), wisdom will not enter it."[97] The passions prevented spiritual maturity and growth in wisdom. They disrupted the cultivation of a new person.

The passions could also result from demonic influence. Barsanuphius referred to a "throng of demonic passions and fantasies" that could break a monk down.[98] On another occasion Barsanuphius referred to the passions as the work of the demons and their captain, the devil.[99] Resisting the demons' arousal of passion was an opportunity to exercise virtue, maintain one's attention, and practice patience.[100]

A monk could also suffer from the passions through the work of God. To a deacon monk who was ill and suffering from passions, Barsanuphius advised, "endure passions and afflictions thankfully (βάσταξον οὖν τὰ πάθη καὶ τὰς θλίψεις εὐχαρίστως); for they are a discipline (παιδεία) from God, and he will have mercy on you, and they shall be for the salvation of your soul."[101] The passions were a means of God's discipline and testing of the monks. Brother Andrew faced many fantasies and questioned Barsanuphius about them. Barsanuphius explained that this testing was from God so that he might not hope in himself, but hope in God. Fantasies and other passions illustrated one's "weakness and where we still are."[102] This type of suffering would "bring us to humility, which leads to our salvation."[103]

The movement from enduring passions to humility was integral to Barsanuphius's teaching. It involved the total surrender of a person to God's will. When bodily illness was combined with passions of the soul, one might consider that taking better care of one's body could have prevented the illness. Barsanuphius declared that such a thought was duplicitous because it did not acknowledge that "God knows, far more than we do, what is good for our soul and body."[104] Salvation from the passions came from God, but it also required "labor of heart and contrition (κόπου καρδίας καὶ συντριβῆς)."[105] Fasting was an important method for stalling the activity of the passions. In one letter, Barsanuphius warned about "consuming food with passion, since this is harmful (βλάπτεται) for both soul and body."[106] In another letter on fasting, he elaborated, "What else is fasting (νηστεία) but discipline of the body (παιδεία τῷ σώματι), in order to enslave a healthy body (δουλαγωγήσῃ τὸ ὑγιὲς σῶμα) and weaken (ἀσθενοποιήσῃ) it on account of the passions?"[107] Through fasting, one could counter the activity of the passions and preserve the health of the soul through discipline of the body.

Fasting was just one of many treatments for the passions. Barsanuphius declared that "for every passion there is a medicine (παντὶ πάθει ἔνι φάρμακον)."[108] He championed God as the physician who heals the passions. In one letter to Euthymius, he exclaimed, "Those who approach the great doctor are illumined by him; and he heals all their spiritual passions (ἰατρεύει αὐτῶν ὅλα τὰ νοητὰ πάθη)."[109] Simply naming God was a means of administering this healing medicine. He attested to the inexplicable efficacy of naming God: "we learn that unceasingly naming God (τὸ ἀδιαλείπτως ὀνομάζειν τὸν Θεόν) is like a medicine that dispels not only all of the passions but even the [sinful] act itself."[110] The name of God was capable of dispelling the passions, "even without us knowing how this actually occurs."[111] Disrupting passions should drive the attention of the monk to God.

John

Only a person who had acquired stillness from the passions could be considered a dwelling-place of God. John responded to a monk about Barsanuphius referring to his own cell as a cemetery. John instructed this monk that Barsanuphius "has found rest from all passions there (ἀνεπαύσατο ἀπὸ τῶν παθῶν ὅλων)."[112] John explained that Barsanuphius had "died completely to sin, and his cell, wherein he is enclosed as if in a tomb for the sake of Jesus' name, is the place of rest, where neither demon nor the devil, the chief of demons, treads. Indeed, it has become a sanctuary inasmuch as it contains the dwelling-place of God (τὸ κατοικητήριον τοῦ Θεοῦ)."[113] According to John, Barsanuphius had given himself completely to God such that the passions no longer disturbed him in his rest.

Barsanuphius's repose was representative of one who had overcome the passions. John understood the passions as undistinguished from affliction in general, saying, "the passions are afflictions (τὰ πάθη θλίψεις εἰσὶ). And the Lord did not distinguish between them, but rather said: 'Call upon me in the day of your affliction; I shall deliver you, and you shall glorify me' (Ps. 49:15)."[114] He urged his audience to call upon God's name when battling the passions, recognizing that not every person was capable of contradicting the passions. When a weak person attempted to contradict the passions, "the demons ridicule (ἐκμυκτηρίζουσιν αὐτὸν οἱ δαίμονες) that person for being inferior to them and yet still trying to contradict them."[115] For John, "the passions are demons (οἱ δαίμονες... εἰσι τὰ πάθη)."[116] John referred to the archangel Michael, who rebuked the devil in Jude 9–10, and contrasted the weakness of monks to the strength of Michael. In battling the passions, monks should rely on the name of Jesus as their refuge.[117]

The influence of the passions, for John, resided in the will of a person. By cutting off one's will, the passions would lose their main area of attack. However, John also advised his respondent that, in addition to cutting off one's will, one should torment the senses (βασανίσειν τὰ αἰσθήρια) "in order to keep them disciplined (τὴν τάξιν), so that they may not be wrongly exercised (χρήσασθαι κακῶς). This is how you should cut off the root of these things and everything else."[118] His goal for the monks was to eliminate every avenue for the passions to gain influence. By rooting out the vestiges of the passions in the will and the senses, one could buttress against further disturbance.

The intentionality involved in John's approach against the passions included knowledge of how the devil attacks a person through the passions. A brother asked John if it was better to remain in ignorance with regard to certain passions. John responded that knowingly sinning would incur condemnation on a person. However, "If one has not learned anything and still sins, the one will never incur condemnation (οὐδέποτε καταγινώσκει ἑαυτοῦ); in this way, one's passions will continue to be unhealed."[119] The monk's priority was not to avoid condemnation through ignorance but to achieve a state in which the passions no longer afflict him. John suggested that the improper approach of ignorance was a suggestion from the devil, "in order that our passions may remain unhealed (τὸ μεῖναι ἀνίατα)."[120]

The passions were a proving ground for the monks. John quoted a monastic maxim that "the untempted is also untested."[121] John understood that the passions were not permitted to afflict the monks except as a means to test them. In another context, John explained that the passions were beneficial because God desired them to cultivate patience. He placed the care of the monk in God's hands, saying, "If it is beneficial for him to be delivered of the passion, then he allows him to be delivered. And we attribute all of this to God's foresight (προγνώσει... τοῦ Θεοῦ)."[122] His approach to the passions acknowledged that God was ultimately in control of one's afflictions and that rest from the passions was possible for some.

Dorotheos

Dorotheos's teaching on conquering the passions reflected much of his monastic heritage. Confronting the passions was certainly a struggle. Dorotheos held that "When someone struggles against the exercise of sin and begins to fight against his passionate thoughts, he humiliates himself, crushes himself, struggles and through the accompanying affliction, he is gradually purified and returns to his natural condition."[123] The battle against the passions was hard fought and central to the monastic life. His particular position on the origin of the passions at the fall of humanity was highlighted above, in contrast to his contemporaries. Consequently, Dorotheos developed a more nuanced stance on the passions than his contemporaries. For instance, Dorotheos demonstrated three situations of humanity. There are those who allow the passions to operate those, who do not allow the passions to act, and those who root out the passions. The last type struggled against the passions and always opposed them. From these three situations, Dorotheos felt he had provided and a paradigm from which his monks could analyze any passion within themselves to discover their own particular situation. He used vanity as an example. For the first situation, one adjusts oneself to accommodate the passions. If someone said a word against this person, he would say five or ten words in response and still ache for more retorts. For the second situation, the person may entertain the passions and fire back some words of response, but eventually this person would repent. The last person might respond harshly, but immediately changes his mind and repents.[124] A person in this third situation understood that the passions were at work and consciously uproots that passion. Additionally, this person considers himself to be the cause of the insult. Through this method of reconsideration, a person in the third situation took responsibility for the insult and the passion. His own sin humbled him, and he roots out the passion that caused him to lash out.[125] The danger of the passions for Dorotheos was the tendency to make succumbing to a passion a habit.

Dorotheos recommended constant vigilance and examination of the passions so that they could not become a habit. He encouraged each monk to regularly "learn what state he is in (, as I have already said.... Let each person learn where he is and what milestone (εἰς ποῖον μίλιον) he has reached."[126] These intervals of introspection were recommended at different times each day, each week, and each month. The monk should gauge himself to determine how well he had battled the passions at each interval: "we must discipline ourselves (γυμνάζειν ἑαυτούς) every day to see if we have made a little progress, or if we are in the same state, or whether we have become worse."[127] He explained that the first situation was like a person who catches the arrows of the enemy and thrusts them into his own heart. The second situation was like a person protected from the arrows with a breastplate. The third situation was like a person who takes the arrows of the enemy and fires them back![128]

Habitually acting upon the prompts of the passions was extremely detrimental to the monastic life. Dorotheos referred to the monk who stole food only to give it to the donkeys as one who had allowed the passions to become habituated in his soul. That particular passion affected him because of his sensitivity to it, like someone with sensitivity to a certain kind of food.[129] Removing the passions by the root was important because they grew like weeds, "If the roots (αἱ ῥίζαι) are not removed, the thorns (τὰς ἀκάνθας) inevitably grow up again."[130]

It was important to uproot the passions early in the monastic life. Once they became rooted and habituated, they caused deeper distress.[131] In describing an attempt to uproot a tree, Dorotheos granted more detail to the metaphor of uprooting the passions. An elder once told a monk to pull a weed from the ground, which he did easily. Then the elder slowly increased the difficulty of uprooting plants until the monk was faced with a tree which he was unable to dislodge. This elder, in Dorotheos's story, explained that "If [the passions] become rooted in us then we cannot dig them out, even with great effort, unless we have the aid of certain saints who will help us, after God."[132] Passions must be removed while they are young. The concept of uprooting the passions was often accompanied by the searching of self. Dorotheos articulated the progress of a monk:

> If one searches himself (ἐρευνᾷ τις ἑαυτὸν) thus every day and tries to repent (μετανοεῖν) for his sins and correct himself, he will begin to diminish the evil (ἄρχεται μειοῦν τὴν κακίαν) and if he used to commit nine faults, now he makes eight. Thus, with the help of God, he gradually progresses and he does not allow the passions to become rooted (στερεωθῆναι) in himself. There is a great danger of passions becoming habitual, since, as we have said, even if that person wants it, he cannot deliver himself from the passions alone but he requires the help of some of the saints.[133]

Removing the passions early was essential to the promise of rest from the struggle against the passions.

Gradual progress in the struggle was possible. As a soul advances, "it becomes stronger and powerful enough to withstand anything."[134] The slow growth in strength against the passions alleviated the burden of the accompanying distress; the passions became easier to bear. Dorotheos expressed this gradual progress as comfort and acknowledgement that everything one endured was under the providence of God.[135] In instances when divine aid assisted a monk against the passions, the devil (ὁ διάβολος) increased the attack, making "the soul's burdens heavier (αὐτὸς πλεῖον βαρεῖ) with the passions and its struggle more violent (σφοδροτέρως πολεμεῖ αὐτήν)."[136] At other times, the rejection of passion might merely pave the way for subsequent demonic attacks. Like the parable from Luke 11:24–27, the demon returned to its former abode and found it swept and clean and brought worse demons to accompany him.[137] Amid the struggle against the passions, one must also cultivate virtue to prevent the passions from returning.

Once the soul was cleansed of the roots of the passions, Dorotheos emphasized the importance of sowing the seeds of virtue: "one must not only cut off the passions but also their causes and thus perfect his entire way of life through repentance and tears. He must then start to sow the good seed, which are good works."[138] Uprooting the passions was only part of the monastic task. For Dorotheos, the soul was always in a state of flux. It fluctuated between better and worse states because "it is impossible for the soul to remain in the same condition."[139] The activity of the soul with regard to virtue or passion determined its trajectory. For Dorotheos, each passion had an opposing virtue.[140] Uprooting a passion also required practicing its opposing virtue.[141]

Dorotheos envisioned a process of rejuvenation to the healthy state, a return to a life of virtue. He explained that "We have lost the virtues and put the passions inside us instead, so we must struggle not only to be rid of the passions, but also, to regain the virtues and re-establish them in their own place."[142] For Dorotheos, the virtues were natural and inherent in humanity at creation, "When God created Man, he implanted in him the virtues (ἐνέσπειρεν αὐτῷ τὰς ἀρετάς)."[143] The passions are, however, unnatural, having no essence or substance. Through a desire for pleasure, humanity has turned away from the virtues (the healthy life) and the soul "created the passions and established them against itself (κατεσκεύασε τὰ πάθη καὶ ἐστερέωσεν αὐτὰ καθ᾽ ἑαυτῆς)."[144] The rest, peace, and health Dorotheos described as characteristic of humanity in Eden were disrupted by sin and continually inhibited by the passions. Yet, Dorotheos was cognizant that the healthy life could be restored. Much like the witness of

John concerning Barsanuphius's rest in his cell, Dorotheos believed that "if we want to be totally released and freed from our passions we have to learn to cut off our will (κόπτειν τὰ θελήματα ἡμῶν) and so, with God's help, we gradually progress until we reach freedom from desire (τὴν ἀπροσπάθειαν)."[145] Through the cutting of the will, one could begin the slow progress back toward a life of virtue. Cutting the will was even reckoned as a virtue, because "Man progresses from [cutting the will] more than by exercising any other virtue."[146] After having cut out one's will, "one reaches freedom from desires and having attained this, he comes close to God in perfect dispassion (εἰς τελείαν ἀπάθειαν)."[147]

Dorotheos was certainly within his monastic tradition by emphasizing the role of the will in the passions and the need to struggle against passion. He, however, moved beyond his contemporaries by taking Barsanuphius's example of rest from the passions and applying it more generally in his teaching. His conception of the passions and virtue reflected the way he described the health of humanity at creation and the subsequent illness after the fall. His contemporaries also utilized the metaphor of healing in their instructions to emphasize the need for struggle and endurance. Alternatively, Dorotheos employed the metaphor of healing to distinguish a discourse in which healing and restoration were the central themes. The life of virtue, as characteristic of the healthy life, was a real possibility for Dorotheos's audience.

Conclusion

Dorotheos stood apart from his contemporaries because he conceived the creation, fall, and salvation of humanity through his discourse of healing. This mode of discourse offered his monks justification for the monastic life and an interpretive framework to comprehend its struggles and goals. Analysis of Dorotheos's conception of the drama of salvation reflected what Nicholas Engender described as "an optimistic vision of humankind in that the 'image of God'; is not disfigured, only the 'likeness.' For Dorotheos the image is the immortality and the freedom; the likeness is the virtues. By disobedience and pride humankind lost the likeness to God."[148] An explication of Dorotheos's salvation narrative, in contrast to the relevant discussions of his contemporaries, made clear how his conceptual framework and emphasis on the health of the soul set Dorotheos apart from his spiritual guides.

This larger framework situates Dorotheos's achievement as a reformulation of his predecessors' teaching and inaugurates a new monastic emphasis on the discourse of healing. Isaiah and Barsanuphius admitted the presence of good passions in the original state of creation. Dorotheos, however, rescinded the notion of the natural passions in the healthy human person. For Dorotheos, the passions were an abiding consequence of humanity's fall. Whereas Barsanuphius and John focused on the suffering and crucifixion of Christ as an example of the monastic life and encouragement for enduring trials, Dorotheos founded his teaching on the role of Christ's incarnation as a healing measure to reinstate the natural state of humanity. While Isaiah and Barsanuphius continually belabored the rejection of the natural, old self in hope for the future indwelling of God, Dorotheos emphasized the transformation of humanity from a state of sickness to a state of health.

Dorotheos taught that Christ brought humanity the cure for the illness of sin, the teaching for uprooting the passions and habituation of virtue, and the hope for a life free from the passions. The imagery used here did not refer explicitly to Christ's suffering and crucifixion but rather to the incarnation.[149] Dorotheos founded his teaching on the role of Christ's incarnation as a healing measure to reinstate the natural state of humanity. The monastic life was therapeutic rather than punitive; the pursuit of the healthy life that is made available through Christ's instruction. The healthy life was founded upon virtue, and Dorotheos literally built his spiritual guidance upon the notion of virtue as a protective abode for the soul.

CHAPTER FIVE

Virtue in the Monastic Life

This chapter explores Dorotheos's robust account of the essential dimension of virtue in spiritual health, which contrasts with his contemporaries in the monastic school of Gaza. Each monastic teacher contrasted the passions by emphasizing the virtues. In this chapter, I will show how Isaiah's teachings failed to adequately explain the integration of the virtues into the monastic life, while Barsanuphius and John often reprimanded monks for speaking of virtue with one another. Dorotheos, however, saw virtue as an integral part of humanity's created nature as well as an inherent link to the divine nature.[1] Dorotheos offered the metaphor of a house built for the soul with bricks of virtue. The virtues were also symptoms of a person who lived the healthy life.

William Harmless explored the contours of early Christian monasticism in his contribution to the *Oxford Handbook of Early Christian Studies*. He directed attention to the fact that contemporary scholarship on asceticism has been focused on the body and neglected the role of struggles "with the heart." According to Harmless,

> Early monks worried much about the slow, unswerving, unspectacular routine of cultivating virtues—charity, forgiveness, peace-making. Cultivating virtue may not sound very monastic; it may sound too much like ordinary Christian living. But early Christian monks were in the business of doing ordinary Christianity extraordinarily well. If we do not see this, we do not see them.[2]

Early Christian monastics proffered diverse perspectives on the role of virtue in the monastic life. Larchet remarked on the fundamental role of virtue in the reordering of human life, "This reordering is done by acquiring all virtues, but primarily in the virtues called principal or not generic in the sense that they would generate all the others, but they are the conditions of acquisition and are somehow the basis of the whole spiritual edifice that must form."[3] Larchet rightly pointed to the importance of a unified understanding of virtue, an understanding in which virtue was a constitutive reality rather than individual actions.[4] For Dorotheos, virtue (ἀρετή) played a central role in the healthy life that he advocated and stood at the forefront of his monastic instruction.

House for the Soul: A Shared Metaphor

As an initial point of comparison, Isaiah, Barsanuphius, and Dorotheos referred to a structure in which the soul should dwell.[5] 1 Peter 2:5 commended readers, "like living stones, let your selves be built into a spiritual house (οἰκοδομεῖσθε οἶκος πνευματικὸς), to be a holy priesthood, to offer spiritual sacrifices acceptable to God through Jesus Christ."[6] The metaphor "structure for the soul" offered each monastic teacher the opportunity to conceptually concretize the spiritual advancement of his monks. This comparison serves as an initial foray into the shared use of the metaphor and the more complex problem of distinguishing each author's instruction on virtue more generally. Dorotheos's conception of the house for the soul expanded this shared metaphor to explain how virtue provided safety and security for the soul and showed how care for the sick was the exemplary mode of virtue acquisition.

Isaiah

Among Isaiah's corpus, the idea of a structure for the soul was most fully explicated in a single monastic discourse, though he used the metaphor at other times.[7] The concept of a structure served as a means to conceive of both the goal of the monastic life and the means by which to attain it. Isaiah utilized the Exodus story to draw an analogy between the understanding (ἡ αἴσθησις) of the monk as a tent and the tabernacle where God dwelt among the Hebrew people: "If the cloud has enveloped the tent (τὴν σκηνήν), then *the sun does not burn you by day nor the moon by night* (Ps. 121:6)."[8] Isaiah did not mention who constructed the tent, but he implied that the tent had already been erected and the monk must prepare and inhabit the tent, saying, "If you have found everything in readiness for the tent, and you keep it according to the will of God, then the victory comes to you from

God."[9] God intended the monk to dwell within the tent, within his understanding, in a certain manner. This intentional manner of living signified the opening of the monk to God's direction: "All the rest (τότε λοιπὸν) from now on will overshadow the tent because it is his will and he will walk in front of it and prepare, beforehand, his place of rest, for unless he appoints a place for it as he wills, you will not be able to rest (καταπαῦσαι), as it says in the Scriptures."[10] God's presence offered protection from the destructive exterior elements as well as guidance and deliverance to the promised end. The monk was responsible for the preparation of his understanding that he might be encompassed and led by God to a place of rest.

Further in the same discourse, Isaiah claimed, "The person who searches for quietness (ἡσυχίαν), but does not take care to remove the passions, is blind to the holy building of the virtues (τῆς ἁγίας οἰκοδομῆς τῶν ἀρετῶν)."[11] Isaiah suggested that monastic living was directed toward the goal of quietness. One could only achieve this quietness through removal of the passions and recognition of the restructuring of humanity that occurred when the virtues were practiced. The virtues were the materials out of which the holy building was constructed, but perceiving this building required a special mode of sight. The construction was later interpreted as self-knowledge that can only be obtained through mourning the realization that one was an "enemy of God." The monk could only perceive his status in relation to God through "spiritual eyes (ὀφθαλμοὺς νοεροὺς)."[12] The mourning produced by this recognition served as the foundation of the building (τὴν οἰκοδομήν).[13]

Isaiah's use of a tent or building to describe the spiritual dimensions of the monastic life illustrated the role of the virtues in his monastic teaching. For Isaiah, virtue was an essential aspect of the new person. He taught his monks to strive to put away those activities that are against nature and to acquire those activities that are in accordance with nature. The re-building of the individual began with mourning one's situation in light of God's glory. Upon this foundation of mourning, God constructed the building of virtue which was able to lead and protect. The monk who inhabited the building of virtue, "[w]hen he becomes perfect,... when those who dwell in heaven testify that he has escaped from the princes of the Left, he will be remembered by those heavenly inhabitants."[14] God finally called upon the monk to "dwell" within this habitation. The monastic life was a life of re-structuring and re-building in preparation for a literal final resting place.

Barsanuphius

Barsanuphius also referred to the monastic life as the building of a house. In Letter 32, he referred to Matthew 7:24 in which the wise man built his house on the rock. Barsanuphius exhorted:

And pay attention to how you practice your sitting, in humility and fear of God and unfeigned love toward all; then you 'are building your house (τὴν οἰκίαν σου) on' firm and unshakable 'rock.' For it is said: 'And the rock is Christ.' (1 Cor. 10:4) As for certain other commandments, this is not necessarily the right time. I have written quite enough to you. Indeed, these words are sufficient to lead a person from the stage of a beginner to [that of] perfection (ἀπὸ ἀρχαρίου ἄνθρωπον εἰς τέλιον). Study and remember them in order not to forget them. For they contain an entire library.[15]

In other letters, Barsanuphius continued to explain the monastic life as the preparation of a house. He urged a brother named Andrew to "prepare your house with much cleanliness in order to receive these gifts. For they are stored in a house that has been much cleansed, and they offer their sweet fragrance where there is no stench."[16] The house was a metaphor for an alternative dwelling place in which the gifts of God could be stored. The "old self" was inadmissible for such a task. The gifts of God encouraged the monk to "become a stranger to the old self (ξένος γίνεται τοῦ παλαιοῦ ἀνθρώπου), being crucified to the world and having the world crucified to that self (σταυρούμενος τῷ κόσμῳ καὶ ὁ κόσμος αὐτῷ)."[17] The sense was that the monk should become estranged to the old person and abide in a new abode.

In Letter 208, Barsanuphius offered his most extensive discussion on constructing one's home. The impetus for this instruction was a brother who wanted to reach the state of stillness. While Barsanuphius encouraged patience, he redirected the attention of the brother from the higher gift of stillness to the preparatory stage of building one's home. The nature of this construction project was a cooperative effort between the monk and another entity: "Therefore, if you wish to construct your home, first prepare the material and all other necessary things. And then, it is up to the professional builder (τοῦ τεχνίτου) to come and build the house (οἰκοδομῆσαι)."[18] Barsanuphius was clear that the monk provided the raw materials from which the house was to be built, but the "professional builder" constructed the house. The walls were faith, the wooden windows were the five senses "affirmed in the precious cross of Christ that allow in the light of the spiritual Sun of righteousness, and do not permit any darkness to appear inside the house," and the roof was "symbolical of love for God, 'which never ends,' (1 Cor. 13:8)."[19] Interestingly, Barsanuphius referred to the same pericope that Isaiah used to describe God's protection of the tent, "Furthermore, you need the house to be covered by a roof, 'so that the sun does not strike you by day, nor the moon by night' (Ps. 120:6)."[20] However, Barsanuphius gave an interpretation of the role the sun and moon play in this context. The roof "covered the house and does not allow the sun to set upon our anger, so that we may not find the sun accusing us on the day of judgment, consuming us in the fire of Gehenna, nor again the moon bearing witness to our slackness and laziness by night, consuming us in eternal hell."[21]

Only when Barsanuphius discusses the door of the house does he explain the spiritual nature of the house, saying, "When I speak of a door, brother, you should understand the spiritual door, namely, the Son of God, who says: 'I am the door' (John 10:9)."[22] This spiritual abode was intended as a place of safety and security for the monk. With Jesus serving as the "door," the monk was assured that he could dwell in this house safely. However, the monk could also fill his house with whatever items he brought into it. Barsanuphius warned that a house of proper preparation could not include "any of those things which are hated by the Son of God."[23] Only when the house was properly constructed and the monk was safely housed could he achieve his desire, stillness. At that point, Jesus "will come with the blessed Father and the Holy Spirit, and will make a home with you, teaching you what stillness (ἡσυχία) is and enlightening your heart with ineffable joy."[24] For Barsanuphius, the house was not constructed by the monk but by the builder, presumably the abba or Christ. By distinguishing between the monk who provided the materials and the builder who oversaw the construction, Barsanuphius ensured that the monk did not see the finished house as his own but a residence provided for him by the builder. This ensured that such an achievement would not imperil the monk's humility

Dorotheos

Dorotheos followed his monastic tradition and offered an analysis of the house for the soul. His discourse echoed much of the emphasis already given by Isaiah and Barsanuphius, but Dorotheos utilized virtue in a profound manner. The monk himself built the house for the soul out of the practice of virtue. Dorotheos's conception of the monastic pursuit emphasized the role of the monk to construct for himself the house of the soul through faith and virtue. Virtue, as a symptom of the healthy life, was the key element in Dorotheos's portrayal of the re-constructed person in the paradisiacal mode.

Dorotheos commenced his teaching on the house of the soul by distinguishing between a physical building and the spiritual abode of the soul. He referred to Exodus where "Holy Scripture says of the midwives who gave life to the sons of the Israelites that, through their fear of God they built themselves houses. (Exod. 1:21) Do they mean material houses (αἰσθητῶν οἰκιῶν)?"[25] In Exodus, the Israelites built homes through fear of God. But, Dorotheos's monks would have understood fear of God as prompting them to leave their homes in pursuit of the monastic life. Dorotheos explained that scripture "does not mean material houses but the house of the soul (τοῦ οἴκου τῆς ψυχῆς) which a person builds for himself when he keeps the commandments of God (Matt. 19:29).... The fear of God prepares the soul to keep the commandments. Through the commandments, the house of the soul is built."[26] Dorotheos emphasized the role of the monk in the construction of this abode. The monk was responsible for both its material and its assembly. This variation from the teaching of Isaiah and Barsanuphius was apparent later in the discourse when Dorotheos concluded, "Briefly, we must practice each virtue in such a way that we reach it and it becomes a habit for us. Thus, as we have said, we are a good and skilled builder (καλὸς καὶ τεχνίτης οἰκοδόμος), able to build our house securely."[27] The skilled builder had honed these skills through pursuing virtue and following the commandments of Christ.

The monk built the house of the soul analogously to the construction of a physical house. Dorotheos asked, "How is the house of the soul built? We can learn about this precisely, with the example a visible house."[28] As the walls of a physical house were erected at the same time so too must the walls of the soul's house be built simultaneously.[29] Dorotheos explained that in the case of the soul, "It is crucial that no part of the building should be neglected but it must be built simultaneously and correctly."[30] This explanation of building method ensured balance, stability, and the integration of all the virtues in the monastic life. Dorotheos appealed to his monks that the walls of the house were the virtues and, as such, must be added in a prescribed manner. Dorotheos quoted John the Dwarf's recommendation that monks achieve all the virtues, rather than practice a few while neglecting the others.[31] Asymmetrical monks, who focused on a single virtue, were susceptible to the winds of passion that could damage their houses because of their insecurity. In contrast, his monks were advised to habituate all the virtues in harmony so that the house of the soul would remain steady and balanced. The house for the soul represented a unity of virtue. Only through this unity could the monk achieve the safety and security that the healthy life ensured.

The construction of the house of the soul began with a firm foundation. Dorotheos designated the foundation stone (τὸν θεμέλιον) "faith (ἡ πίστις)," because "'Without faith,' as the Apostle says, 'it is impossible to please God' (Hebr. 11:6) and thus, on this foundation he must build his houses symmetrically."[32] Faith served as the secure footing upon which to lay the stones of virtue. The monk acquired these stones through the practice of virtue. Many of the occasions for practicing virtue were interactions within the monastic community. Dorotheos proffered the laying of a stone of obedience (λίθον ὑπακοῆς) whenever obedience was exercised. The stone of patience (λίθον μακροθυμίας) could be added when one dealt with a brother who had become angry with him. Dorotheos utilized the immediate monastic context to illustrate the building of the house. Other virtues, like temperance (ἐγκράτεια), sympathy (συμπαθής), cutting out of the will (κοπῆς θελήματος), and gentleness (πραότητος), would be added as the occasion arose to practice them.[33] The laying of these stones required the addition of stones of endurance (ὑπομονή) and courage (ἀνδρεῖος), "because these are the corner stones (αἱ γωνίαι) and it is through them that the building is held together and each wall is joined to the others, so they do not stop and are not separated one from another. Without these virtues, one does not have the strength to fulfill any others."[34]

Dorotheos was also attentive to the finer details of construction. He noted that the builder "must also place mortar between the stones since without it, the stones rub against one another and the house will fall down."[35] Mortar served to bind the stones together and strengthen the entire structure. For Dorotheos, "Mortar (πηλός) represents humility (ἡ ταπείνωσις) because it comes from the earth and is under the feet of all. Therefore, the *Sayings of the Fathers* say, every virtue that is done without humility is not a virtue."[36] Humility was not the only binding element, the beams (τὰ ἱμαντώματα) were discretion (ἡ διάκρισις). Discretion added stability to the walls and provided space for the roof of love (ἡ ἀγάπη) to be added.[37] Love was the completion of virtue but not the completion of the house. Humility, as the retaining element, also served as the parapet for the roof. Dorotheos quoted Deuteronomy, "In the law it is written, 'When you build a new house, then you shall make a parapet for your roof, that your children do not fall from it' (Deut. 22:8)."[38] The stipulation of this law concerned protection for the children of the house. For Dorotheos, the children were "the thoughts (οἱ λογισμοί) which come to the soul and which we must keep in humility so that they do not fall from the roof, which as we have said, is the fulfillment of every virtue."[39] The parapet kept the thoughts safely contained within the security of the soul's house. Virtue's role in the monastic life was fulfilled in the securing of one's thoughts. Dorotheos ensured that "When the saints naturally advance in the virtue, they reach humility, as I always say to you, that the more a person approaches God, the more he sees himself as a sinner (ἁμαρτωλόν)."[40] The necessity of humility increased with the addition of virtue. This relationship ensured that the progress of the monks did not prompt the opportunity for pride.

Once Dorotheos had fully described the house of the soul, he returned to the builder. It was the responsibility of the builder to practice construction and be intentional in the assembly. Dorotheos warned his monks that "The workman is the person that acts with full knowledge of what he does since sometimes a person may work at the virtues and because he acts without full knowledge (γνῶσις) his work is destroyed or he may wander about aimlessly without being able to fulfill his work but he puts one stone and removes two."[41] Concentrated effort was required to ably construct this edifice. Dorotheos contended that keeping the construction of the house at the forefront of the mind was crucial to acting with knowledge. Acting with knowledge distinguished virtuous actions from non-virtuous actions because it ensured that the monk was intent on practicing virtue for the sake of the soul. Those who do good actions without full knowledge are culpable of taking away stones from their house. These actions might have been mixed with vanity, ignorance, indifference, or done for the sake of a reward.[42] Such actions actually took away stones from the monk's house.

Dorotheos's prime example of the monk that acted virtuously was one who served the sick (ἄρρωστος). The monk who served in the infirmary with full knowledge had acquired sympathy (συμπαθής) and inner mercy (σπλάγχνον οἰκτίρμων).[43] This monk "concentrates his aim and knows that the sick person is a greater source of benefit to him than he is to the sick person. Believe me that the person that serves a sick person in full knowledge is relieved even from the passions and the struggles."[44] Dorotheos realized that service to others, especially the sick, could impact the monk's own life. Care and dedication to the sick not only built virtue but also compassion and mercy that could protect the monk from various internal conflicts. Serving the sick was an important monastic occupation that Dorotheos well knew. His experience in the monastery's infirmary solidified his understanding of the practice and acquisition of virtue. Dorotheos also attested to the testimony of Evagrius on the benefit of serving the sick:

> Evagrius said about a certain great elder that he delivered a brother who was bothered during the night with that type of imaginations, when he ordered him to serve the sick with fasting. When he was asked why he did so, he answered, "Absolutely nothing extinguishes the passions more than compassion."[45]

The monastic duty of serving in the infirmary was the ideal venue for building the soul's house of virtue.

Conclusion

Dorotheos utilized a shared metaphor to explore the role of the virtues in the monastic life. This analogy of the house for the soul was not peculiar to Dorotheos but was also used by Isaiah and Barsanuphius in the monastic school of Gaza. Dorotheos, however, emphasized the house as the monk's own construction. Isaiah and Barsanuphius relegated the construction to one other than the monk. Isaiah and Barsanuphius did not clearly demonstrate the role of virtue in the construction project. Dorotheos, though, elaborated on both the function and role of virtue within this project, carefully weaving the notion of humility through his discourse to avoid pretense to pride. The virtues represented the symptoms of the healthy life.

The Role of Virtue in the Monastic Life

It was not a coincidence that the acquisition and practice of virtue was prevalent in providing health care to others, as seen in Galen and Basil above. The possession of virtue represented was a new life, a new reality. For Dorotheos, unlike his contemporaries, virtue was the restoration of humanity's created nature. His approach to virtue appropriated a unified understanding of virtue as the proper function of the healthy life. Humanity was created "adorned with virtue" and the habituation and acquisition of virtue would characterize humanity's return to that state. Habituating virtue resembled Rowan Williams's suggestion that "Monasticism's emphasis was always on the prosaic process of daily conversion, the decision for God made—joyfully or wearily—time and time again in the smallest matters of daily business with other human beings."[46] Graham Gould pointed to an important saying in the *Apophthegmata Patrum* by John the Dwarf. John said, "I think it best that a man should have a little bit of all the virtues. Therefore, get up early every day and acquire the beginning of every virtue and every commandment of God."[47] Thereafter, John was "expounding exactly this view, by listing all the virtues which a monk must have. The list covers humility, patience, penitence, not judging others, praying often, and a large number of other such virtues."[48] Gould explained that this saying was unlike many monastic sayings in that it was not addressed to an individual brother, but to an assembly of monks.[49] In addressing his monks, Dorotheos, too, emphasized the role of virtue as both individual actions and a unified state of being. A virtuous monk had a bit of all the virtues. Dorotheos incorporated this unified view of virtue into his monastic teaching because virtue was vitally important to his understanding of health.[50] This position moved well beyond the views his contemporaries disclosed.

Isaiah

Isaiah's discourses revealed a pronounced emphasis on the importance of virtue for the monastic life. However, virtue was not attributed to the created state of humanity in paradise. Isaiah's comments on virtue must be understood as pertaining to fallen humanity and in imitation of Christ's sufferings, "to ascend the cross with him (μετ᾽ αὐτοῦ ἀναβῆναι ἐπὶ τὸν σταυρόν)."[51] Only through suffering and self-abnegation are the virtues acquired. This hermeneutical key will help underscore the distinctive adaptation of virtue by Dorotheos.

Isaiah gave several accounts of the role of the virtues in the monastic life. The compiler of Isaiah's teachings provided summaries of what may have been more explicit accounts of the virtues. In Discourse 7, Isaiah offered lists of various virtues with emphasis as to their importance for the monastic life. The thematic lists implied the prominence of the virtues in Isaiah's spiritual guidance even if the explanation of his teaching remains lost. The varied arrangements and collection of virtues listed in this discourse attested to the important place Isaiah conferred to teaching on virtue. Isaiah admitted a progression of virtue that leads to dispassion. His ladder of eight virtues was: silence, ascesis, weeping, fear of God, humility, foresight, love, and dispassion.[52] The *telos* of monastic life, according to this construction, was a passionless state. Importantly, the associated implications of love were dispassion of the soul (τὴν ψυχὴν … ἀπαθῆ) and health of the soul or freedom from disease (τὴν ψυχὴν ἄνοσον). As explained above, Isaiah held that there were good passions in humanity's created state. These passions were distorted and turned toward evil after the fall. If this analysis holds, Isaiah was repudiating the perverted natural passions entirely, rejecting a part of created humanity. The achievement of dispassion was accompanied by recognition of one's separation from God and acceptance of death: "Then, and only after all this, a person knows that he is far from God. So one who wants to receive all these honorable virtues (πάσας τὰς τιμίας ταύτας τῶν ἀρετῶν) must not care about what all the other people think but must be prepared for death (ἑτοιμάσῃ ἑαθτὸν εἰς θάνατον·)."[53] Isaiah's entire monastic program was designed as a preparation for death. The soul acquired the virtues with the hope of being prepared to release the body in death.

Virtue and Monasticism

Virtue was the result of a long and arduous monastic pursuit. Isaiah warned his monks that "On the way of virtues is the fallen, enmity, change, variation, excess, measure, distribution, discouragement, joy, heartache, gloom, peace of heart, progress, and violence. That is a journey (ὁδοιπορία) you must undergo, until you attain rest (τὴν κατάπαυσιν)."[54] The way of virtue was fraught with peril and only the persistent, discerning monk could hope to endure. Beginner monks were advised to be cautious when contemplating the virtues and discussing the monastic lives of the Fathers. Isaiah warned,

> If you are a beginner (νεώτερος) and have not made a slave of the body (μήπω ποιήσας τὴν δουλείαν τοῦ σώματος), then, when you hear of the sublime virtues (ἀρετὰς

ὑψηλὰς) of the Fathers, do not pursue them, hoping to acquire these with ease, for they do not come to you unless you first cultivate the soil. If you cultivate the soil, they will come to you by themselves.[55]

For Isaiah, the virtues were the fruit of discipline and perseverance. Most importantly, the virtues, as exemplified by the Fathers, were not the result of human effort but were attained only through grace. Acquiring virtue was only possible through God who "is powerful enough to give each one of you the ability to carry out and keep these commandments."[56] Isaiah not only maintained a connection between the commandments of God and the acquisition of virtue but also addressed the activity of virtue in the inner life of the monk.

Virtue and the Monk

The role of virtue was manifest in the activity of the conscience (συνείδησις). Isaiah's emphasis on the role of virtue in the monastic life was that "the fear of God is the mother of all virtues (ὁ γὰρ φόβος τοῦ Θεοῦ μήτηρ ἐστὶ τῶν ἀρετῶν)."[57] He was clear that practice of the virtues was efficacious for maintaining proper relation to one's conscience. Isaiah commended his monks in "the practice of the virtues [and] not presenting any obstacles to our conscience."[58]

The conscience illuminated the path to obedience and virtue for Isaiah. By adhering to one's conscience, the monk was able to safely navigate through the desires of humanity's fallen nature. Neglecting one's conscience was viewed as opening oneself to the enemy. Isaiah recounted the words of Jesus in Matthew 5:25–26 concerning coming to terms with one's accuser. Expositing this passage, Isaiah interpreted the accuser as one's conscience "inasmuch as it opposes us whenever we want to fulfill our fleshly desires (τὰ θελήματα τῆς σαρκὸς αὐτοῦ), and, if we do not listen to it, our conscience hands us over to the enemy."[59] The monk's conscience was able to guide him toward virtue and also accuse him for wrongdoing.

Virtue symbolized the monk's adherence to the direction of conscience and life according to the new person. Isaiah illustrated the virtues as a garment that displayed the evidence of the new person. He wrote, "Let us do, then, what will enable us to put on the garment of virtues (τὸ ἔνδυμα τῶν ἀρετῶν), brothers, in order that we might not be thrown outside because on that day there will be no preference in his eyes."[60] Isaiah clarified the divine source of the garment. From the parable of the prodigal son, Isaiah indicated that the "father immediately arranges that the robe of purity and security of adoption (τὴν στολὴν τῆς ἁγνότητος, καὶ τὸν ἀρραβῶνα τῆς υἱοθεσίας) be given to [the returning son]."[61] Appealing to his monks to examine themselves, Isaiah asked if the monks have "put on Christ (ἐνεδυσάμεθα τὸν Χριστὸν)."[62] Putting on Christ was a call to maintain the purity exemplified in Christ. The monk also sought to adorn the garment with virtue as the fruit of the new person. Isaiah imparted the words of Paul, "That is why the apostle, seeing that those who merit to be raised up from the dead passions (ἐγερθῆναι ἐκ τῶν νεκρῶν παθῶν), no longer having an opponent, points out to them the fruit of the Spirit."[63] For Isaiah, virtue was an adornment to the monk's life that signified following one's conscience and the commandments of God. The fruit of the monastic life, as Isaiah interpreted Galatians, qualified the monk to anticipate being "raised up from the dead passions."[64] Isaiah intimated an eventual separation from humanity's subjection to the passions. In another passage he clarified this separation as "fear that in leaving our body we may not be found naked of virtues and fall to the serpent's power, for the enemy is full of deceit."[65] Attainment of virtue was incorporated into Isaiah's assertion that the monk's salvation from the struggles of this life was coterminous with leaving the body.

Barsanuphius and John

Barsanuphius and John did not overtly promote a unified vision of virtue in their correspondence. The Old Men did insist that practicing virtues like patience and obedience were important to combat the passions, but they did not emphasize the connection between being virtuous and being healthy. They even avoided the use of the term ἀρετή. On several occasions, different monks and a layperson inquire about virtue in their questions to the Great Old Men, but Barsanuphius and John do not respond by expounding on virtue or even using the term.[66] In fact, Barsanuphius and John both reacted quite negatively to discussing virtue with certain monks and laity. Barsanuphius and John's reluctance to offer guidance with respect to virtue set them apart from the tradition of Isaiah. The few instances in which they mentioned virtue accentuated Dorotheos's later heavy emphasis on virtue.

Virtue Privately

As the ancient prologue to their letters acknowledges, Barsanuphius and John corresponded with a variety of individuals from young monks and older monks to laypersons and bishops.[67] Their guidance was not intended for a general, but for a very particular audience. This individualized approach has not prohibited scholars from drawing out overarching principles or aspects of their spiritual guidance. Yet, the prologue promotes a view of Barsanuphius and John's intentions for spiritual growth in contrast to their own letters, namely the pursuit of virtue. The author of the preface understands that one category of recipients was "approaching the perfection of virtue (τελείωσιν τῆς ἀρετῆς ἐγγίζουσι)."[68] Teaching on the virtues was only for the advanced monk, one who had progressed in the spiritual life. Responding to a layperson that spoke openly about the *Lives of the Fathers* or the *Sayings*, John retorted,

> When you are speaking about the *Lives of the Fathers* or their *Sayings*, you should con-demn yourself (ὀφείλεις ἑαυτὸν κατακρίνειν), saying: 'Woe to me! How can I speak about the virtues of the fathers, when I have not acquired any of them? I have not even begun to make progress; yet I am sitting down and speaking with others for the sake of their benefit! If only the words of the Apostle had not been fulfilled in me: 'You then that teach others, you do not teach yourself.' [Rom. 2:21] And when you say this, your heart will burn, and you will find a way to speak with humility (μετὰ ταπεινώσεως).[69]

This layperson had not advanced to the point where he could even speak of the virtues of the fathers with humility, seeing himself diminished by the great deeds of the Fathers.

In Letter 469, a monk inquired whether is it good to tell others the stories from the Lives of the Fathers. John responded that

> since we have not reached the point of walking the way of the perfect (εἰς τὴν τῶν τελείων βαδίζειν ὁδόν), on account of weakness (διὰ τὴν ἡμετέραν ἀσθένειαν), let us speak about those things which contribute to edification, namely, from the Sayings of the Fathers, rather than risking our souls by using accounts from Scripture. For this matter contains a risk (κίνδυνον) for someone who does not understand (τῷ μὴ εἰδότι); [the scriptural words] have been spoken spiritually (πνευματικῶς), and a fleshly person (ὁ σαρκικὸς) will not be able to discern their spiritual truths (τὰ πνευματικὰ). It is written: 'The letter kills, while the spirit gives life.' (2 Cor. 3:6) Therefore, let us take refuge in the words of the fathers, and we shall benefit from them.[70]

Here the stories of the Fathers' great deeds are one step removed from Scripture. However, "Even if our thought tells us that the words or the stories are good, let us recall the fact that we do not practice what we speak; and so, if we suppose that we are edifying others by telling them these stories, then we are instead condemn-ing ourselves, inasmuch as we do not practice these words."[71] The stories of the Fathers were intended to encourage and condemn. The great deeds were edifying, but they also reflected the meager achievements of each monk by comparison.

On another occasion, Barsanuphius blessed some water that healed a man. The man told others, and Barsanuphius rebuked him for it.[72] Later, the same man noticed the abbot telling visitors about the wonders performed by Barsanuphius, and this man asked John why the abbot was able to speak of the virtues of the elders. John told the man that he had a sinful pretense to rights:

Therefore, the words of the abbot are for the benefit (ὠφέλειαν) of those who listen with fear, but for the condemnation (κατάκρισιν) of those who do not accept them with faith. Yet, for the time being, you are still unable to discern these things, because your heart is still in the process of being transformed (ἀκμὴν μεταβάλλεταί σου ἡ καρδία). For the Apostle says: 'We are the aroma of Christ to God, among those who are being saved and among those who are perishing; to the one a fragrance from death to death, to the other a fragrance of life to life. Who is sufficient in these things? For we are not peddlers of God's words like so many.' (2 Cor. 2:15–17)[73]

These two passages illustrated the approach of Barsanuphius and John concerning speaking of the virtues of the fathers. Such discussions were only for a select few who were able to understand the message. The layman was not transformed and, thus, was unable to understand.

Virtue Positively

There were several instances where Barsanuphius referred to virtue positively. These passages were all directed to monks. In Letter 241, Barsanuphius replied to a brother who asked about how one was to serve in the liturgy. Barsanuphius began by stating, "Brother, all of this is a spiritual allegory (ὅλα πνευματικῶς ἀλλεγορεῖται), but you understand it literally (σαρκικῶς ταῦτα νοεῖς)."[74] He continued to explain that the vestment of concern to the monk should be the garment of virtues: "The Lord ordered us to have one garment (ἑνὸς χιτῶνος), and that is the garment of virtues (τοῦτ᾽ ἔστι τοῦ ἐνδύματος τῶν ἀρετῶν), of which may God make all of us worthy to the ages. Amen."[75] The garment of virtues was also prevalent in Isaiah's discourses.[76]

Virtue was continually cast as the proving ground for monks. Barsanuphius twice mentioned virtue in conjunction with the perseverance of Job. In a series of letters to a monk named Andrew, Barsanuphius, wrote concerning Job, "how could such a person, who did not deserve to suffer anything evil, be given over to temptation for the testing of his virtue (παρέδωκε πειρασθῆναι πρὸς δοκιμὴν ἀρετῆς), until he brought shame upon his enemies and accusers, who could offer no defense against his charges?"[77] Job was an example of how one could be tested in an extreme manner. Job's constancy was proof of his virtue. In a later letter, Barsanuphius offered additional encouragement, "Do not let the throng of demonic passions and fantasies (ὁ τῶν δαιμονικῶν παθῶν καὶ φαντασιῶν ὄχλος) break you down, but trust that they accomplish nothing by their thronging and tempting except to multiply virtue, so long as we pay very close attention and try to retain a little patience (τοῦ κατασχεῖν μικρὰν ὑπομονήν)."[78] Enduring temptation was an opportunity to acquire virtue through faithfully following the example of Job.

In response to an inquiry about monastic diet and sleep, John offered a saying from an elder, "Giving rest to one's neighbor (τὸ ἀναπαῦσαι τὸν πλησίον) is a great virtue, especially when one does not do this under coercion or with wastefulness."[79] This unassigned quote may be John's own counsel to this monk. Otherwise, the context for its citation is unclear. On another occasion, a sickly monk wrote a series of letters to John. In Letter 532, John responded, "As for me, my genuine brother, although I am completely reluctant, I have never shown myself to a doctor (ἰατρῷ); nor have I taken any medicine for my wounds (οὐδὲ φάρμακον ἐπέθηκα τραύματι). I have done this not out of virtue but out of reluctance.... Whoever is able to endure this out of virtue is blessed; for such a person becomes a sharer in the patience of holy Job."[80] As in Barsanuphius, the attainment of virtue was reflected in imitating the perseverance of Job.

John also responded to inquiries about virtue. When a Christ-loving layperson asked, "Since each of the Beatitudes contains a single virtue, is this one virtue sufficient, father, for salvation, if a person should acquire it?"[81] John responded,

> Just as the body (τὸ σῶμα) is one but has many members (πολλὰ ἔχει μέλη), and if one member is missing, then the body is incomplete, you should understand the inner self (ἐν τῷ ἔσω ἀνθρώπῳ) in the same way, too. For the inner self has many members, namely, the virtues, and if one of these is missing, then a person cannot be perfected. This resembles a craftsman (τεχνίτης) who knows his profession well and who may also be able to handle other crafts on account of his skills; nevertheless, he is not called a craftsman except in his own profession. Likewise, one needs to have all the virtues, but will only be recognized by and renowned for one particular virtue, through which the grace of the Spirit especially shines.[82]

John followed the monastic example of Isaiah and other Fathers in conceiving of the virtuous monk as attaining all the virtues.[83] Yet, many monks were seen as being especially gifted in the practice of a particular virtue, hence the layperson's misunderstanding.

Finally, John responded to an inquiry about the interpretation of the soul as a city on a hill. John explained that, "The city is the soul, while the hill signifies the height of virtue (τῶν ἀρετῶν ὕψωμα), whereupon those who have ascended 'shine as stars in the world, holding fast to the word of life so that they might boast for themselves on the day of Christ' (Phil. 2:15–16)."[84]

Two final uses of virtue in the letters occur in the description of Abba Seridos and Abba Aelianos. Letter 570c was a hagiographical account of Abba Seridos's life in the monastery. Both Barsanuphius and John are mentioned in this letter indicating that an editor or compiler has added this account to the writings of Barsanuphius and John. This writer claimed that "About Abbot Seridos, I have many things to tell you, … yet I shall omit most of them for the sake of brevity and shall only recall enough information to present the man's virtue."[85] As the account of Seridos continued, the author noted that Barsanuphius

> entreated God to grant him the gift of discernment (τὸ χάρισμα τῆς διακρίσεως); once this was acquired, he was able to direct souls to life (ψυχὰς εἰς ζωὴν ὁδηγῆσαι) with the grace from above, as well as to heal the afflicted (τεθλιμμένους θεραπεῦσαι), to bring the healing medicine of the word of the Spirit (φάρμακον ἰαματικὸν εἰσενεγκεῖν τὸν ἐκ τοῦ Πνεθματος λόγον), and to negotiate a peace for those in conflict.[86]

The writer described the virtue of Seridos as enabling the healing and medication of others. The monk who composed this account acknowledged the healing power of virtue. Though hagiographical, the author admitted a wide perspective of Seridos's reputation. The author noted that, in the monastery, Seridos "was deeply loved by the brothers, gladdening their souls with the spiritual word of counsel, and encouraging them in virtue through his good example of conduct and virtuous practice (τῆς ἐναρέτου πράξεως)."[87] The account closes with the praise of Seridos by a layperson who, having asked forgiveness for his sins, "glorified God for the virtue of the fathers and departed."[88]

Abba Aelianos was selected to replace Seridos as abba of the monastery only after a number of other monks declined the position. He attested to the virtue and obedience of these monks but questioned his own worthiness. John encouraged Aelianos, saying, "Everything occurs in order that God's judgments, which are beyond us, may be accomplished and in order that the virtues (αἱ ἀρεταί) of the saints may be variously manifested."[89]

Among the 850 letters, Barsanuphius and John only mentioned virtue twelve times, though inquirers asked them specifically about virtue. Additionally, there were only eight instances in which they positively affirmed virtue. Of the positive affirmations, one was not a letter from Barsanuphius or John. None of the positive affirmations was directed toward the specific recipient's spiritual life and acquisition of virtue. The positive affirmations described the virtues of others as goals to be pursued. It is clear, then, that Barsanuphius and John very rarely offered spiritual guidance on virtue. They did not inherit this hesitation from Isaiah, nor did they pass it on to Dorotheos, whose discourses were laden throughout with the role of virtue in the monastic life.

Dorotheos

The centrality of virtue to Dorotheos's project and its significant scarcity in Barsanuphius and John demonstrated how far Dorotheos was willing to go beyond the monastic instruction of his spiritual elders. In contrast to Barsanuphius and John's reticence, Dorotheos returned to the tradition of Isaiah by expounding upon the role of virtue in the monastic life. Unlike the surviving works of Isaiah, Dorotheos provided detailed instructions on how virtue was conceived, practiced, and acquired, with particular attention given to the role of the body in virtue acquisition. Dorotheos depicted this new emphasis on virtue in his distinctive house of the soul, and it also resounded throughout his particular monastic vision.

Virtue Conceived

Dorotheos clearly held that the natural, created state of humanity included every virtue, "For God created him after his own image (Gen. 1:27), that is to say, immortal, with free-will and adorned with every virtue."[90] Dorotheos interpreted the words of Jesus from within his understanding of the image of God in humanity. Dorotheos quoted a saying of Jesus in Luke, "Be merciful (γίνεσθε οἰκτίρμονες) as your heavenly father is merciful (Luke 6:36)," to illustrate the regard he had for mercy. As Dorotheos included the virtues in his portrayal of the created state of humanity and identification of humanity with the image of God, so, too, "this virtue [of mercy] above all emulates God and is a characteristic of Him (ἡ ἀρετὴ αὕτη μιμεῖται Θεόν· χαρακτηρίζει αὐτόν)."[91] Virtue reflected the image of God and pointed to the spiritual health of the individual.

At no other point could the monastic display the signs of spiritual health and a return to the created nature than in practicing and acquiring virtue. This endeavor was not solely based upon the monk's own ability. Dorotheos conceded that divine aid was a necessary component of the monastic pursuit:

> Let us make a beginning and let us desire the good with all our heart. Because, even if we are not perfect, wanting to be is the beginning of our salvation. From wanting we come, with God's help, to struggling and from struggling one is helped in acquiring the virtues (τὸ κτήσασθαι τὰς ἀρετάς). This is why [Longinus] says, 'Give me blood and receive spirit,' that is to say, 'Struggle and you will become accustomed to virtue.'[92]

From creation to perfection, virtue was endemic to Dorotheos's monastic vision. Dorotheos depicted the monastic life as a continual striving after virtue, just as various predecessors witnessed to role of virtue in the monastic life.

Dorotheos bolstered his claim on the priority of virtue by pointing to monastic exemplars. The attainment of virtue was the motivation for Saint Antony and Saint Pachomius pursuing the monastic life,

They knew that, as we have already said, the soul is purified (καθαίρεται ἡ ψυχὴ) and it could be said that the nous is also purified (καθαίρεται ὁ νοῦς) and by the keeping the commandments it can see and arrive at its natural state (τὸ κατὰ φύσιν). This is because 'The commandment of the Lord is pure, enlightening the eyes.' (Ps. 19:8) They have realized that by living in this world they could not attain virtue easily. So they decided to seek a strange life (ξένον βίον), a strange way (ξένην τινὰ διαγωγήν). This is the monastic life.[93]

The pursuit of virtue characterized the monastic life precisely because virtue was identified as essential to the natural, created state of humanity. The great monastic precedents set by Antony and Pachomius were, for Dorotheos, the pursuit of virtue through the monastic life.

Recollecting his own disciple, Dorotheos referred to the miraculous event involving Dositheos. The *Life* of Dositheos described "a saintly man, a great elder," who saw the young Dositheos among the deceased saints of the monastic community.[94] Dorotheos reminded his later monks that, "we all know how God has glorified [Dositheos] and has not allowed his virtue to be forgotten, but revealed it to his spiritual father who saw him among all the saints enjoying the blissful life (ἀπολαύοντα τῆς μακαριότητος αὐτῶν)."[95] The acquisition of virtue for Dositheos was not outwardly evident. Dositheos's fellow monks were only able to apprehend his manifest failures. However, the obedience that Dositheos internalized was made evident only after his death. The elevation of Dorotheos's own disciple to such spiritual height was evidence of Dorotheos's invaluable monastic instruction.

Dorotheos's own compiler did not hesitate to employ the teachings of Dorotheos as a means to understand virtue. The *Introductory Letter* commended Dorotheos to follow a way of life similar to that Gregory the Great commended, for whom "appreciation leads to zeal; zeal to virtue and virtue to blissfulness (ἀρετὴ δέ, μακαριότητος)."[96] Reminiscent of Dorotheos's own account of humanity's created state, the *Introductory Letter* claimed that Dorotheos was adorned with all the virtues. "He learnt the most excellent and highest way, that is to say humility, and through his own personal efforts, he fulfilled the words of the holy elders 'be merciful and gentle', thus, adorning himself (πάσαις διὰ τοῦτο ἐνεκοσμήθη ταῖς ἀρεταῖς) with all the virtues."[97] The author of the letter appropriately connected Dorotheos's adherence to a saying of the elders, "The person that manages to cut off his own will has reached the resting place (τὸν τόπον τῆς ἀναπαύσεως),"[98] as a guiding principle for his monastic teaching. Accordingly, Dorotheos found, having asked God, that the root of all passion is self-love (πάντων μὲν ῥίζαν οὖσαν τῶν παθῶν τὴν φιλαυτίαν), whose basic element is our own bitter-sweet will. Therefore, he used this effective medicine (τῷ δραστηρίῳ τούτῳ φαρμάκῳ) and dried out both the root and the evil shoots, becoming an honest farmer of immortal plants and a cultivator of the true life (τὴν ὄντως ζωήν).[99]

This astute commentary on Dorotheos's monastic guidance appropriately connected the major themes to be drawn out here. Virtue, as symptomatic of the true life or healthy life, was the medicine that cured the passions by rooting out self-love through cutting off the will.

Virtue Practiced

The practice of virtue revolved around three interrelated concepts: cutting off the will, obedience, and humility. Barsanuphius and John also heavily emphasized these concepts, though Dorotheos imbued them with further significance by associating them with his understanding of virtue. If virtue was truly practiced and spiritual health sought, virtue must be understood within the context of cutting off the will, obedience, and humility. Additionally, a virtuous monk pursued virtue through these activities with knowledge.[100]

The most important virtue for Dorotheos was the ability to cut off one's own will. The negation of the will stimulated by the passions was itself a virtue: "Thus, if we want to be totally released and freed from our passions we have to learn to cut off our will…. For, nothing does men so much good as to cut out their own will. Indeed, Man progresses from that more than by exercising any other virtue."[101] Cutting off the will was a key symptom of the return to health, "Since, with the cutting out of one's own will, one reaches freedom from desires and having attained this, he comes close to God in perfect dispassion (εἰς τελείαν ἀπάθειαν)."[102] This dispassionate state was the healthy state of humanity at creation. Only once the will was completely cut off could the monk begin to see the signs of heath returning.

Dorotheos noted the miraculous power of obedience when a visiting monk survived swimming a raging river to remain obedient to his own monastic superior: "We stood there in admiration, surprised at the power of virtue, because we had faced the situation with fear, while he himself went without any danger because of his obedience (διὰ τὴν ὑπακοὴν αὐτοῦ)."[103] This monk, risking his life in obedience, was protected by the virtue of obedience. Virtue had permeated the monk, giving him the power to put himself at risk for the sake of his obedience.

In the monastic environment, a spiritual elder directed each monk. Dorotheos wrote in Letter 2 to supervisors of other monk, saying, "If you are in obedience, never trust your own heart, since it is blind from the many passionate inclinations."[104] Obedience opened the monks to virtuous living because through obedience a monk can begin to appreciate "things as they are (θέλεις ὡς γίνεται)" and "believe that all things, up to the smallest detail, are under God's providence (ὑπὸ πρόνοιαν Θεοῦ) and bear all that happens calmly."[105] Dorotheos recalled his early years as a monk and his struggles with certain thoughts in Discourse 1. He would often write to Abba John on his slate. The act of writing offered Dorotheos immense release from those struggles. He recounted,

> Before I finished writing I would feel relief and benefit so great was my freedom from worldly care and my rest (ἀμεριμνία καὶ ἡ ἀνάπαυσις). Since I did not know the power of virtue (τὴν δύναμιν τῆς ἀρετῆς) and often heard that we must "through much tribulation, enter into the Kingdom of God," I was afraid because I had no tribulation. When I mentioned this to my spiritual father, he answered, "Do not be sorrowful, you have no reason to be so because everyone who has put himself under the obedience of his fathers has this peacefulness and freedom from care."[106]

Dorotheos's own obedience to his spiritual elder ensured the peace to practice virtue in the same manner as the monk that braved the raging waters and was protected by his virtue.

Dorotheos composed an entire discourse to instruct his monks on humility. He began by quoting an elder who claimed that monks need humility more than anything else.[107] In agreement, Dorotheos responded to this statement by explaining that "The elder wants to show us that neither the fear of God, or almsgiving, or faith, or temperance (ἡ ἐγκράτεια) or any other virtue, can be achieved without humility."[108] Humility was the key to undermining "all the temptations of the enemy" and "is able to draw God's grace to the soul."[109] Humility, described in two variations, counteracted two kinds of pride. Humility towards one's brother counteracted the pride that led one to despise one's brother. Humility towards God, attributing all one's achievements to God, was the perfect humility of the saints. This later humility "grows naturally within in the soul, through the keeping of the commandments" and impeded the pride that sought glory for one's actions.[110] Through humility towards God, "the more they approach God, the more they see themselves as sinners (ἁμαρτωλούς)."[111] In describing this saintly humility, Dorotheos invoked the notion of a garment of virtues as seen in Isaiah and Barsanuphius. For the saints,

> Even when God sent them to help other people, they did not agree to this easily out of humility and to avoid glory (τὸ δοξασθῆναι). Like a man wearing an all-silk garment (ἐνδεδυμένος ὁλοσήρικον), if someone throws a dirty rag at him he leaves so as not to ruin his expensive clothes, it is with the saints, who are dressed in virtues (οἱ ἅγιοι ἐνδεδυμένοι τὰς ἀρετὰς), and avoid human glory in order not to be defiled. However, those who seek glory are like a naked man trying to find a small rag or anything else

to cover his indecency. The person who is naked of virtues (ὁ γυμνὸς ἀπὸ ἀρετῶν), seeks the glory of people.[112]

Human glory could defile the virtuous monk, and it also served as erroneous attire for the soul. Humility, like obedience, allowed the monk to see things as they truly were: monks as sinners before God and human glory as nakedness. Keeping the commandments of God provided the fertile soil in which humility could grow. To this point, Dorotheos appealed to the experience of the monks themselves. He attested that "Nobody can express what this humility is in words and how it grows within the soul, unless he learns about it through experience (ἀπὸ πείρας)."[113]

Through cutting off one's will through obedience and humility monks could truly practice virtue. Still, virtue was not simply a collection of random actions but a way of life, a unified, habituated activity that was internalized and acquired.

Virtue Acquired

The acquisition of virtue was closely associated with Dorotheos's emphasis on the restoration of health of the soul. Acquisition of virtue, for Dorotheos, was a method of habituating action. As envisioned in his house of the soul, Dorotheos elsewhere described the monk's intention to consciously act in accordance with the building program in terms of habituated activity. This habituation affected both the monk's relational status to God as well as his spiritual health. Interestingly, virtue acquisition was not solely a spiritual enterprise but was also closely connected to the body. Dorotheos's account of the body in virtue acquisition was only one aspect of his positive portrayal of the body.

The acquisition of virtue had relational ramifications. In a discourse on the fear of God, Dorotheos examined an excerpt from 1 John: "In his Catholic Epistle St. John says, 'perfect love casts out fear.' (1 John 4:15) What does the saint mean by this? What does he mean by 'love' and 'fear'?"[114] Dorotheos explained, "There are two kinds of fear—one is introductory and the other one is perfect. The first is for beginners in the Christian life, whilst the other one is of the saints, of those who have been made perfect and have reached the point of divine love (τῶν φθασάντων εἰς τὸ μέτρον τῆς ἁγίας ἀγάπης)."[115] Dorotheos understood spiritual progress as the movement through the fear of punishment and into the second kind of fear that is identified with love. The person with perfect fear "follows God's will because he loves God himself and specifically because he wants to please Him."[116] This person "has tasted the sweetness of being with God. He is afraid of falling away and being deprived of this sweetness."[117] Dorotheos explained the stage at which true love has cast out fear as the adopted state of sonship. Basil of Caesarea wrote that the slave fulfilled God's commands because of fear of punishment. The hired hand fulfilled God's commandments because of a desire for payment. A son, however, fulfilled God's commandments because of love for God.[118] Simply put,

> When a son matures (εἰς φρόνησιν) he does his father's will not because he is afraid of being beaten nor because he expects a reward from him, but because he loves him, he respects him especially and he is convinced that everything belonging to his father is his own. This son becomes worthy to hear, 'You are no longer a slave but a son, and if a son, then a heir (κληρονόμος) of God through Christ' (Gal. 4:7).[119]

Dorotheos agreed with "the order (τὴν ἀκολουθίαν) of the three states.... We can see how, through the fear of God, we are led to avoid evil (τὸ ἐκκλῖναι ἀπὸ κακοῦ) and are thus urged to ascend toward good (προτρέπεται ἐπιβῆναι καὶ τοῦ ἀγαθοῦ)."[120] Acquisition of virtue was depicted as ascending toward the good. As sons, through love, the monks were encouraged to practice and habituate virtue. Pauli remarked that Dorotheos described "love as the perfection of all the virtues."[121] Indeed, Dorotheos recalled the words of Psalm 34:11: "Come, you children, listen to me: I will teach you the fear of the Lord." He carefully explained that the psalmist said, "'Come' unto me, inviting us to virtue."[122] The beckoning call of God involved the imperative to acquire virtue. Additionally, "the saints call those who have been transfigured (μεταμορφουμένους) by their word, from evil to virtue: 'children.'"[123] This interpretation of scripture gave virtue a profound role in establishing the relational status between the monk and God. Virtue acquisition was a mark of sonship that began with fear of God and progressed to transformation. Dorotheos elsewhere described this transformational aspect of virtue as spiritual health for the monk.

Dorotheos keenly observed that habituated action affected the spiritual health of his monks. Continuing to act in an evil manner habituates that evil, while renouncing evil habituates good action. As part of his monastic teaching, monks were called upon to examine themselves regularly. Dorotheos taught that "if one searches himself (ἐρευνᾷ τις ἑαυτὸν) thus every day and tries to repent for his sins and correct himself, he will begin to diminish the evil (ἄρχεται μειοῦν τὴν κακίαν) and if he used to commit nine faults, now he makes eight."[124] Through continual self-examination and "with the help of God, he gradually progresses and he does not allow the passions to become rooted in himself."[125] As an example, Dorotheos pointed to a certain monk who kept stealing food and giving it to the donkeys. When confronted, the monk could give no reply, only that he habitually stole because of his previous negligence.[126] The monk had allowed the passion to take root in his life through lack of vigilance. In such a way, "both virtue and evil, if practiced continuously, become a habit for the soul (ἕξιν τινὰ ἐμποιεῖ τῇ ψυχῇ) and this habit either damns or comforts it."[127] Habituated action could serve to promote health or destruction for the monk depending on whether he habituated virtue or habituated evil.

The effects of habituated action were intrinsically tied to Dorotheos's understanding of the role of virtue in spiritual health. He taught that "Virtue is a natural innate condition for us (ἡ μὲν ἀρετὴ φυσική ἐστι καὶ ἐν ἡμῖν ἐστιν) since, the seeds of virtue are indelible (ἀνεξάλειπτα γὰρ τὰ σπέρματα τῆς ἀρετῆς). I said therefore, that as far as we do good we become accustomed to virtue."[128] Habituated virtue was part of the healthy way of life in humanity's natural, created state. As virtue was acquired through habituation, "we rediscover our natural state and our own health (εἰς τὴν ἰδίαν ὑηείαν ἐπανερχόμεθα)."[129] Dorotheos proposed an analogy to physical health. Reestablishing the habit of virtue "is like the person that had a problem with his eyes (ἀπὸ ὀφθαλμίας) and recovers his normal sight or the person that suffered from any other sickness (ἀπὸ ἄλλης οἴας δήποτε ἀρρωστίας) and regains his natural health (κατὰ φύσιν ὑγείαν)."[130] Establishing habits of evil, on the other hand, was "unnatural (ξένην τινὰ)," a "foreign habit (παρὰ φύσιν λαμβάνομεν ἕξιν)."[131] Acquiring virtue signified a return to health through rooting out the habits of evil and constant vigilance.

On another occasion, Dorotheos recalled an encounter with Zosimas the Sophist who was unable to answer queries about how he could simultaneously display virtue and claim to be a sinner. When Zosimas offered no reply, Dorotheos interjected,

> I wonder, is this not like sophistry and medicine (ἡ σοφιστικὴ καὶ ἰατρική)? When, for example, the doctor or Sophist learns the art of medicine or sophistry well and practices it (πράττει αὐτήν), it gradually becomes a habit (γίνεταί τις ἕξις) for him, and, as I said, little by little the soul imperceptibly assumes (ἀνεπαισθήτως προσελάβετο) this art (τὴν τέκνην) by the practicing of it. This is more or less the same with humility when, where by keeping the commandments, humility becomes a habit and it is not possible to give an explanation of this in words.[132]

The slow habituation of virtue like developing a skill or a trade gradually transformed the monk. Acquiring humility was somewhat beyond explanation. Dorotheos claimed to illumine the way to humility, but "humility itself is divine and cannot be comprehended."[133] However, Dorotheos admitted that a bodily labor was necessary to acquire humility.

> Since the soul has fallen from the keeping of God's commandment, into transgression (παρεδόθη ἡ ἀθλία), the wretched thing was given up, as St. Gregory says, to the seeking of pleasure, to independence that leads to error and to the love of things of the body. In a certain sense, it was found to be at one with the body and it became 'flesh (σάρξ),' as it says, 'My spirit shall not strive with man for ever, for he is indeed flesh.'

(Gen. 6:3) From then on, the wretched soul has been suffering together with the body and it is in accordance with all things done by it. This is why the elder said that, 'hard bodily labor leads to humility (ὁ σωματικὸς κόπος ὁδηγεῖ εἰς ταπείνωσιν)'.... Hard work (ὁ κόπος), therefore, humbles the body and when it is humbled, the soul is likewise."[134]

The relation between the body and soul was a distinctive position. The soul suffered with the body in fallen humanity. Consequently, the return of the soul to health was not through dissociation with the body but through the body. Bodily labor had a positive effect on the soul.

In a similar vein, Dorotheos compared the acquisition of virtue to other skilled occupations: "Likewise, if someone wants to obtain virtue he must be neither indifferent (οὐκ ὀφείλει ἀδιαφορεῖν), nor lofty (μετεωρίζεσθαι), since, as someone who wants to learn to be a carpenter pays attention to no other art (τέκνη)."[135] The acquisition of virtue was the singular aim for the monk. It required focus of mind and labor of body. Monks

should not pay attention to anything else, but should study how to acquire it, night and day. Those who do not come to it in this way, not only will they not progress (οὐ προκόπτουσιν), but are destroyed (συντρίβονται), wandering about without any purpose. If someone is not vigilant and does not struggle, he will easily be inclined to digress (τὰς παρεκβάσεις) from the virtues.[136]

The intense devotion to virtue acquisition was a subject with which Dorotheos was readily familiar.

From his own childhood, Dorotheos recalled his study of classical education. "I was so accustomed to it that I did not know what I ate or drank or how I slept because I was aflame with enthusiasm for reading (ἐκ τῆς καύσεως τῶν ἀναγνωσμάτων). I never wanted to go and eat with any of my friends. I did not meet them at all during the time I was studying, despite the fact that I was a sociable person and loved my friends."[137] He would read late into the night by lamp light relating that, "I lived this way because I felt nothing to be sweeter than my reading."[138] Dorotheos took his zeal for learning with him to the monastic life but directed his energy toward the virtues. He confessed, "when I came to the monastery, I said to myself, 'If you had such great desire and zeal for secular learning and were so occupied with reading that it became a habit, how much more so should this be for the virtues?'"[139] Dorotheos conceived of the virtues as a middle (μέσαι) or royal way (βασιλικὴ ὁδος), as Basil stated, "The person who does not allow his thought to incline towards excess or deprivation (πρὸς ὑπερβολὴν μήτε ἔλλειψιν) but directs it to the midpoint, that of virtue, is upright in his heart."[140] Virtue, as humanity's created state, signified a return to health. Evil, on the other hand, "has neither essence nor substance (οὔτε οὐσία τίς ἐστιν, οὔτε ὑπόστασίν τινα ἔχει)."[141] Evil comes about through practice of the passions: "If the soul digresses (κλίνουσα) from the virtues it becomes a subject (γίνεται ἐμπαθὴς) of passions and in this way evil is given existence (ἀποτελεῖ τὴν κακίαν)."[142] Dorotheos compared evil in the soul to sickness arising in the body. Through excess or lack of care for the body, either excess or deficiency was produced and sickness incurred. When the body was restored to balance, the sickness disappeared. Likewise in the soul, "Evil is the sickness of the soul by which the soul is deprived of its own natural health, which is virtue (ἡ κακία ἀρρωστία ἐστὶ τῆς ψυχῆς στερουμένης τῆς ἰδίας αὐτῆς καὶ κατὰ φύσιν ὑγείας, ἥτις ἐστὶν ἡ ἀρετή)."[143] Only through acquisition of virtue could the monk return to the healthy spiritual state.

Conclusion

Virtue acquisition and bodily labor were intricately intertwined in Dorotheos's monastic vision. The metaphor of healing was heavily influential for the conception of virtue championed by Dorotheos. His emphasis on virtue recaptured the importance given it by Isaiah and countered the significant absence of virtue instruction in the Letters of Barsanuphius and John. Dorotheos also initiated a resurgence of the role of the body in the monastic life. His positive portrayal of the body was closely bound to his depiction of virtue and also resonated in other areas.

CHAPTER SIX

The Ascetic Body

This final chapter addresses the conflicting accounts of the body in the monastic school of Gaza. Dorotheos emphasized the healing and health available to his monks in this life stemming from his conception of virtue as a unified and comprehensive natural state. He stressed the interrelatedness of body and soul in the health of the human person rather than the denigration of the body for the sake of the soul. For Dorotheos, the body was an integral part of humanity and was not to be dismissed, but trained. He eschewed harsh treatment and the neglect of care for the body. This attention to the body included attention to its physical needs, especially on occasions that necessitated interpretation of illnesses. His practical knowledge of health care as well as the spiritual discernment that distinguished his monastic instruction from that of Isaiah, Barsanuphius, and John facilitated his care for the body and the soul of his monks.

The cultivation of virtue was the hallmark of Dorotheos of Gaza's monastic vision. This pursuit was not centered upon a spirituality that denigrated the body for the sake of the soul, but one that trained both body and soul to habituate virtue and return to health. Asceticism was this discipline and training.[1] In Patrik Hagman's words, "Asceticism is concerned with the body, with how body and soul are related, and with how the body can function as a symbol for different ways of living."[2] In the monastic milieu, the body was infused with different sorts of meaning. A famous epigram attributed to another ancient Christian monk named

Dorotheos witnessed the variety of ascetic approaches to the body. When collecting stones in the desert to build cells for others, he was asked why he killed his body in the heat. Dorotheos replied, "It kills me, I will kill it."[3] For this Dorotheos, the body symbolized an opponent that must be subjugated and defeated. Such an approach may not have been typical, but was not totally foreign to early Christian monastics. Hagman considered the various ways monastics related to the body and urged caution towards interpretive methods that seek a uniform approach, stating,

> While there is a great number of ways to relate to the body (or to be more specific, to be embodied), they are not unlimited. However, when it comes to the body we have another difficulty to keep in mind: the body tends to act as a symbol for so many things. Therefore it is necessary to distinguish in some way between the experience of being embodied and other experiences that use the body as a symbol.[4]

The multifarious meanings attributed to the body were products of the ascetic tradition with which one was associated. Ascetical traditions had a strong impact on early Christianity and testified to a wide range of practices.[5]

Attempts to provide a theory of asceticism have met various degrees of success, and no complete theory has been proposed.[6] Richard Valantasis has proposed a theory of asceticism that revolves around the ascetic's practice as a performance that leads to a transformation. According to Valantasis, "Asceticism may be defined as performances within a dominant social environment intended to inaugurate a new subjectivity, different social relations, and an alternative symbolic universe."[7] Ascetic activity centered upon "a self who, through behavioral changes, seeks to become a different person, a new self…. As this new self emerges, it masters the behaviors that enable it at once to deconstruct the old self and to construct the new."[8] Asceticism instantiated a new subjectivity through the habituation of certain activities. These activities were a performance that related this new subjectivity to an audience.[9] Hagman explained how "in the ascetic life, the experience of the created self is somehow connected to becoming that created self. According to ascetic logic, to step out of that performance is described as a temptation or failure, not a return to the normal way of life."[10] The ascetic slowly re-created the self through asceticism. The created self became the true self, accompanied by new relations to others through the assumed symbolic universe.

In *The Ascetic Self*, Gavin Flood provided a notable supplement to Valantasis's work. Flood proposed an ascetical theory that takes into account two important aspects that appeared in this study: tradition and cosmology. According to Flood, ascetics "performed the memory of tradition, and it is this memory of tradition that marks asceticism off from mere abstinence or abstinence for a secular pursuit, such as health."[11] Tradition played an important role in Dorotheos's development from monastic novice to spiritual leader. Flood asserted that asceticism was always set within a religious tradition, "within a shared memory that both looks back to an origin and looks forward to a future goal. But asceticism only flourishes in certain kinds of tradition that might be called 'cosmological'; in traditions where cosmology is lost, asceticism as performance becomes eroded or becomes a purely internalized performance."[12] The aim in Christian asceticism was the replacement of the self's will with the divine will. For Flood, this meant that "The self becomes passive and God active."[13] The ambiguity of the ascetic self was that only through an assertion of the will could the will become passive.

Ascetic behavior was the willful practice that unseated the individual's will. The new self, or new subjectivity, created amid this ambiguity, was "expressed as praxis in the body and as discourse in language."[14] The body was the place where the ascetic performance was most evident and relevant to communal ascetic life. Flood contended, "Paying attention to the details of everyday living—the monastic rules, the control of the body, the restriction of food—is to enact the memory of tradition. Enacting the memory of tradition reveals a particularity of existence that is subjective yet not individualistic."[15] Through ascetic performance within the Christian tradition, Flood asserted, "The ultimate goal of Christian asceticism has been the reconstitution of the pre-fall state through withdrawal (*anachoresis*) and self-mastery (*enkrateia*)."[16] Amid his matrix of influences, Dorotheos of Gaza attested an ascetic performance "through tradition-specific bodily regimes or habits and in obedience to ascetic discipline."[17] This study has shown how Dorotheos used many of the traditional themes and metaphors in his spiritual direction, but the meaning with which he infused his teaching was distinct. Dorotheos's narrative of salvation, account of virtue and the passions, and interpretation of the ascetic body distinguished his teaching from his contemporaries. For Gazan monasticism, the ascetic tradition retained a focus on the body of Christ as exemplar. Each author developed the incarnational emphasis to inscribe meaning to the suffering of illness in the body. For Isaiah, Barsanuphius, and John the monastic body was one that should be despised and conquered. Dorotheos viewed the body positively, arguing that health of the soul and health of the body were aspects of the transformation incurred though asceticism and the monastic tradition.

Significant for the role of health and illness in this study, Crislip has recently examined the role of illness in late ancient Christian asceticism. With regard to bodily illness in monastic settings, Crislip reported, "Even among those who saw illness among monks as especially meaningful, monastic authors disagree sharply over how to make meaning out of it."[18] Crislip explored a variety of monastic literature from the late ancient Christian context and found that these Christians "presented asceticism as the cure of humanity's endemic illness and illness as asceticism's apogee, the most effective mode self-mortification.... Illness points to ambiguities of embodiment: it threatens the ascetic's practice, yet could serve as the model and mode of ascetic transcendence and self-fashioning."[19] Monastics were faced with the task of understanding illness of the body as part of their ascetic effort. The meaning derived from illness differed.

For monastics, the experience of illness was problematic. However, Crislip showed how the "sustained debate over the practical, ascetical, and theological meaning of the illness experience opened up new ways for Christians to understand the self, the body, and ascetic practice."[20] Illness could be construed as a high form of asceticism: "illness, like fasting, prayer, vigils, and even intentional self-hurt, functions as a primary means of spiritual development."[21] According to Crislip, illness and asceticism were dialectical. Illness accomplished many of the goals of asceticism, but it also undermined asceticism because it rendered the ascetic unable to perform the ascetic practice.[22] Thus, Crislip claimed, "The meaning of illness [in late ancient Christianity] is polysemic and ambiguous, and thus frequently contested."[23] This ambiguity was evident in the distinct approaches of the Gazan monastics.

The distinction arose from the narratives attached to illness. Crislip explained how narrative enabled monastics to attach meaning to illness. He claimed, "The dominant 'master narratives' or cultural models that were available to early Christians—primarily biblical, but also traditional Hellenistic models—offered no consistent or reliable means for explaining illness."[24] Articulating the narrative from which illness arose was part of the interpretive process. Arthur Kleinman argued that one could shape the ambiguity of illness and the experience of illness into personal narrative; the experience became a story. For Kleinman, "Illness takes on meaning as suffering because of the way this relationship between body and self is mediated by cultural symbols of a religious, moral, or spiritual kind."[25] The ascetic teachers of Gazan monasticism provided the cultural and traditional narrative through which the monks were to elucidate and understand illness. Kleinman asserted that in order to understand the meaning of illness one "must first understand normative conceptions of the body in relation to the self and world. These integral aspects of local social systems inform how we feel, how we perceive mundane bodily processes, and how we interpret those feelings and processes."[26] The narrative provided the lens through which illness was conceived and approached. In Crislip's portrayal, "the models or master narratives are not a straitjacket; they merely provide the symbolic morphemes out of which the cultural observer creates a narrative or creates meaning."[27] The distinct narratives of salvation within the monastic school of Gaza would provide different ranges of meaning to illness.

These meanings led to divergent approaches to the bodies of ascetics with regard to illness and health.

Dorotheos's narrative distinguished his position on the role of the body's health and illness from those his contemporaries. His discourse of healing sought to return to the health of humanity at creation and set his monastic teaching on a different trajectory from other Gazan monastics. Bodily illness impaired a monk's pursuit of health. This study bolsters Brown's account, in which Dorotheos moved beyond "the sharp opposition between the pure spirit and the sensual body" to stress how the "body was allowed to become the discreet mentor of the proud soul."[28] The body was the locus of the soul's exercise, and the body's health was inextricably linked to the soul's health. Through the body, the soul was able to seek freedom from the passions. The pursuit of healing for body and soul entailed the cultivation of habits so that monks steadily moved toward a state of health. Hadot characterized the spiritual exercises of Dorotheos as monks "training themselves in little things, so as to create a habit, before moving on to greater things."[29] As a monastic teacher, Dorotheos had absolute control over his monks' way of life.[30] This way of life combined acute attention to the cultivation of healing in soul and body, seeking, in Brown's words, "the long return of the human person, body and soul together, to an original, natural and uncorrupted state."[31]

Isaiah and the Body

Isaiah understood asceticism as a gift of suffering offered to God. In a letter written to his monks, Isaiah stated, "First, I greet you in godly fear, and entreat you to be perfect in a manner pleasing to him, in order that your suffering (ὁ κόπος) may not be futile, but, rather, that it may be joyfully received from you by God."[32] Isaiah wished his monks to continue in their asceticism and also to guard their thoughts and pursue virtue. The ascetic effort of his monks was only a part of the monastic life. Ascetic effort without protection from one's thoughts left one open to disturbances. Honor and vainglory could corrupt a monk. Therefore, Isaiah warned, "A person who performs his ascetic effort (ὁ ποιῶν τὸν κόπον αὐτοῦ) but does not protect [himself] is like a house without doors or windows, into which any reptile that wants can enter."[33] For Isaiah, silence and ascetic discipline were the beginning of a way of life that led to weeping, fear of God, humility, foresight, and, finally, love. Love rendered the soul free from disease and dispassionate.[34] These monastic virtues began with the training of the body and progressed to the health of the soul.

Isaiah's concentration on the body grew out of his understanding of Adam's body and Jesus's body. In Discourse 2, Isaiah described the change in Adam's nature as a twisting of healthy senses toward that which is contrary to nature.[35] The healing of Adam was through Jesus's "holy body (διὰ τοῦ ἁγίου αὐτοῦ σώματος)."[36] Isaiah emphasized Jesus' becoming "completely human (τέλιος ἄνθρωπος)" and "in every way like us except without sin (ἐν πᾶσι τοῖς καθ᾽ ἡμᾶς ἐγένετο κατὰ πάντα χωρὶς ἁμαρτίας)."[37] Through Jesus's body, that which was contrary to nature in humanity was transformed back to a state that was according to nature. For Adam, "God returned him to Paradise (τὸν παράδεισον)."[38] The rest of humanity was resurrected by following Christ's commandments. These commandments were "indicating to us holy worship (λατρείαν ἁγίαν) and pure law (νόμον καθαρόν), that we may stay in the natural state (ἐν τῷ φυσικῷ) in which God created us."[39] Isaiah enjoined his monks to achieve

> what our Lord Jesus Christ has shown us in his holy body (ἐν τῷ ἁγίῳ αὐτοῦ σώματι)... [and] take care of ourselves (φροντίσωμεν... ἑαυτῶν), in order to please God by leading our practical life (τὸ πρακτικὸν ἡμῶν) in the best way we can, and by setting in order (σταθμίζοντες) of all our members until they are established in the state that is according to nature, so that we may find mercy in the hour of temptation which will come over the whole universe."[40]

The monastic life was an instantiation of Christ's own life in each person through ascetic discipline.

The establishment of a new person through asceticism was the supercession of the old person according to the example of Jesus. Isaiah affirmed, "Our Lord Jesus Christ revealed the New Person (φανερῶν τὸν νέον ἄνθρωπον) in his own body."[41] He argued that "the fire of his divinity (τὸ πῦρ τῆς θεότητος αὐτοῦ) came upon those who followed his sacred teachings."[42] This fire allowed Jesus's followers to hunt down the desires of the flesh and attain joy. The love of one's soul and the willingness to lose one's life for Jesus's sake (Matthew 10:39) signified the new person revealed in Jesus's body.[43]

Jesus's human body signified the natural state of humanity. Monastics were urged to follow Christ in crucifixion, death, burial, and resurrection. Only then could one "arise in newness, when he sees himself in the natural condition of Jesus, following his holy footprints which were made when he became human for us (ὅστις ἐγένετο ἄνθρωπος ὑπὲρ ἡμῶν)."[44] The renewed monk, the one who had eliminated all aspects of the state contrary to nature, "shows that he is truly from Christ, and is the son of God and brother of Jesus (υἱὸς Θεοῦ καὶ ἀδελφὸς Ἰησοῦ)."[45] Identification with Jesus's divine sonship was interpreted through the ascetic effort of the monk. Isaiah also taught that transformation through ascetic preparation enabled one to become Christ's "bride (νύμφη), and his Holy Spirit has inherited you (ἐκληρονόμησέ σε), even while you are still in the body."[46] In another discourse, Isaiah pointed to Christ as the paragon of health, saying,

> Look, brother, how [Christ] wishes a person to resemble him, healthy from everything that is contrary to nature (εἶναι ὑγιῆ ἀπὸ πάσης τῆς παραφύσεως), to be worthy of becoming a bride for him. The soul recognizes his thoughts about conduct (ἡ ψυχὴ οὖν γινώσκει τοὺς λογισμοὺς αὐτῆς ἐκ τῆς ἰδίας πράξεως), for if it practices works, the Holy Spirit lives in it, because the works cause the soul to be reborn (ἀναγεννᾷ)."[47]

Elsewhere, he encouraged his audience, "Blessed are those who acquire the New Person (τὸν καινὸν ἄνθρωπον) before meeting Christ."[48] Ascetic discipline within the monastic life opened up not only new subjective possibilities, a new person, but also new relational possibilities, becoming a brother or bride of Christ.

Isaiah described the ascetic struggle using wine as a metaphor. Wine symbolized a person's nature that desired to encounter god in purity.[49] Isaiah spoke of the cask and the wine as two aspects of the same goal, transforming grapes into wine that could be enjoyed in the end. Like "the cask that has been pitched reasonably (τὸ ἀγγεῖον πεπισσωμένον ἐστὶ μετὰ ἐπιεικείας)," so too the body was purified and healed of every passion.[50] However, if there was a crack that had not been pitched, then it could not serve or please God.[51] Without the preparation of the cask, grapes could never be vinified. Isaiah taught how young wine must receive the leaven from spiritual fathers to mature and ferment: "Without silence, perseverance, and much struggle toward God (ἄνευ ἡσυχίας, καὶ κακοπαθείας, καὶ παντὸς κόπου κατὰ Θεόν), it is not possible to settle (τὴν κατάστασιν)."[52] If wine is left with its seed and fruit, relatives and other undisciplined people, it becomes vinegar.[53] Isaiah continued to describe the monastic life as maturing wine, which vice spoiled but virtue preserved. All the purification and preparation was "done to the wine until it satisfies the farmer and he is pleased with the result."[54] The young wine was carefully prepared, matured, and preserved. "Likewise," stated Isaiah, "one has to advance in all these things until his work (τὸ ἔργον αὐτοῦ) is pleasing (ἀρέση) to God."[55] The cask and wine, body and soul, of a person were to be carefully crafted and conserved. Asceticism was the disciplined cultivation of the body and soul.

Ascetic performance was not to be interrupted by bodily weakness. Isaiah stated, "One who fears bodily weakness (ὁ φοβούμεονς ἀσθένειαν σώματος) cannot attain the way that is according to nature."[56] Asceticism could result in a weakened body, but this should not hinder one's advancing toward the natural state. Isaiah contrasted the body with the clay jars that Gideon used to hide torches at night in Judges 7. By breaking the jars and surprising the Midianites, Gideon was able to rout his enemy.

The destruction of the jars was instrumental in Gideon's victory. According to Isaiah, "If, however, he falls down before God in all his suffering (ἐν παντὶ κόπῳ αὐτοῦ), God is able to give him rest, for had Gideon not broken the water jars, he would not have seen the light of the torches (Judg. 7:19)."[57] The breaking of the body was key to experiencing the transformation into a new person. Isaiah continued, "unless a person despises the body (εἰ μὴ ὁ ἄνθρωπος καταφρονήσει τοῦ σώματος), he cannot see the light of divinity, for unless Jael, too, the wife of Heber the Kennite, had broken the post of the tent, she would not have overturned the pride of Sisara (Judg. 4:21)."[58] These varied metaphors illustrated Isaiah's approach toward the body. The body was to be prepared and sealed, broken and despised. This ascetic treatment was essential to the transformation of the self into a new person.

Isaiah regarded the body as an important aspect of asceticism, but he vacillated on its connection to the soul.[59] In one discourse he mentioned that "All these things occupy the soul when it leaves the body (ὅταν ἐξέλθῃ ἀπὸ τοῦ σώματος), and the virtues assist the soul (αἱ ἀρεταὶ δὲ βοηθοῦσιν αὐτῇ)."[60] Earlier in the same discourse, Isaiah mentioned that when a person died,

> Upon his going out from this world, he will present his work (τὸ ἔργον αὐτοῦ), and the angels will rejoice with him when they see him rid of the powers of darkness. When the soul leaves the body (ἐξέλθῃ ἡ ψυχὴ ἀπὸ τοῦ σώματος), the angels journey with it. At that moment, all the forces of darkness come out to meet the soul, wanting to possess it and examining whether it has anything that belongs to them. Then it is not the angels who war against these forces, but the good works that have been achieved which fortify and protect the soul from them, so that it may not be touched by them. If the works are victorious (νικήσῃ), then the angels lead the soul, chanting in procession, until it meets God in gladness, and at that time it forgets every worldly labor (παντὸς ἔργου) and toil (παντὸς τοῦ κόπου αὐτῆς).[61]

One's asceticism prepared the soul for its journey to God. The ascetic struggle and transformation in this life was preparation for the life to come. It aided one's ascent to the divine by protecting the soul from dark forces. All the while, angels chant and cheer.

Separation of body and soul appeared in another discourse. Isaiah wrote, "One who trusts in his own righteousness (ὁ δὲ πεποιθὼς ἐπὶ τὴν δικαιοσύνην αὐτοῦ) and holds onto his own will is unable to avoid the enemy, or to find any rest … and when this person leaves the body (ἐὰν ἐξέλθῃ ἀπὸ τοῦ σώματος), it will be difficult to find mercy."[62] One's own righteousness was insufficient for protection from the enemy. Asceticism may begin in the individual will, but its power lay elsewhere. Isaiah here emphasized that whatever was essential of the human person would leave the body. However, this separation may not have been permanent in Isaiah's thought. He also mentioned the resurrection of the body on two occasions. Quoting 1 Cor. 6:19, Isaiah instructed, "Take care of your body as a temple of God."[63] His emphasis on caring for the body arose from his conception of the body's resurrection. Isaiah wrote

> Take care [of the body] (φρόντισον), knowing that you will be resurrected (ἀναστῆναι) and give account before God… Just as when your body is wounded (ἐὰν πληγῇ σου τὸ σῶμα), you care for it so that it may be healed (φροντίζεις τοῦ θεραπεῦσαι αὐτό), make sure that it is dispassionate (ἀπαθὲς) on the day of the resurrection of all (ἐν τῇ ἀναστάσει)."[64]

The training of the body was to ensure that it was prepared for the resurrection. Preparation of the body was not for the sake of the body, but from concern for the soul. Isaiah began this discourse by establishing that "one cannot care for one's soul, so long as one is caring for the body (οὐ δύναταί τις φροντίσαι τῆς ἑαυτοῦ ψυχῆς, ὅσον φροντίζει τοῦ σώματος)."[65] Ascetic effort aimed at removing all passionate threats from the body so that the soul remained undisturbed.

The belief that the Lord would resurrect the body promulgated the need to seek cleansing of the body. Isaiah testified that "The one who believes that his body will, by nature, arise (ἐγείρεσθαι) on the day of resurrection (ἐν τῇ ἡμέρᾳ τῆς ἀναστάσεως) is obliged to care for and cleanse it from every impurity (ὀφείλει φροντίσαι καὶ καθαρίσαι αὐτὸ ἀπὸ παντὸς μολυσμοῦ)."[66] Again, Isaiah suggested that hope in the resurrection of the body should encourage asceticism. The cleansing of the body through ascetic struggle readied for resurrection at the last day. A major focus of Isaiah's ascetic teaching emphasized despising the body for the sake of the soul. This emphasis was enforced in Barsanuphius and John's approach to asceticism and the body.

Barsanuphius and John's Approach to the Body

For Barsanuphius and John, asceticism was training and discipline of the body for the sake of the soul's health.[67] Crislip described Barsanuphius and John as healers, stating, "it was primarily as spiritual healers—guides in making sense out of illness and of ridding the sufferer of anxieties and evil thoughts—that the Great Old Men corresponded."[68] It was in this mode of caring for the soul "through the language of healing that late ancients described the process of spiritual direction."[69] The Old Men understood the body as the training ground for the soul. Their spiritual direction depicted the body as important primarily as the locus of struggle for the soul. As the body was disciplined through asceticism, the soul, too, was directed toward proper attentiveness to the body and the passions.

Barsanuphius's and John's instructions revealed the ambiguity of the body in ascetic teaching by emphasizing the weakening of the body through asceticism on the one hand, and the need for bodily health to engage in asceticism on the other. In one letter, Barsanuphius told a young brother to give the body only what it requires and to not relax the body.[70] On another occasion, Barsanuphius and John did seek health of soul and body for their associates. Barsanuphius promised an elder of the monastery who lived in stillness that he would pray for him. The request was not recorded, but Barsanuphius replied, "I am praying in short for the health and salvation of your soul and body (εὔχομαι ἐν συντόμῳ περὶ τῆς ὑγιείας καὶ σωτηρίας ψυχῆς καὶ σώματος ὑμῶν)."[71] Health of body and soul could be coextensive. It remained that healing of the body was not the primary concern of Barsanuphius and John and focus on the body's health could be counterproductive to the spiritual health they intended.

Sleeping and eating were both necessary bodily activities. They could also become the sources of spiritual disruption when not undertaken with discernment. One correspondent wrote to John about his father's strict recommendations concerning food and sleep. John understood that overeating could cause one to become sleepy and tempted to fornicate. Sleep also came upon one whose body was weak because of illness. In both cases, weakness or overeating, a monk would be unable to "perform one's service (τινα λειτουργῆσαι)."[72] The regulation of diet and sleep was the responsibility of the discerning monastic father, and the disciple should be obedient in these matters. John encouraged this monk, saying, "We are required, however, to do our best and not more. The protection and mercy of God are there in order to strengthen our weakness."[73] John not only recognized the limits of embodied life, but also advised his reader to trust in divine aid as he was obedient to his monastic father.

Another monk asked John about the teaching of the fathers concerning the body. He inquired, "The fathers say that we should despise the body (καταφρονεῖν τοῦ σώματος), and then they say that we should control the body with discernment (τῇ διακρίσει κυβερνᾶν τὸ σῶμα). I entreat you to teach me the difference between the two."[74] John responded by noting Paul's distinction between caring for the body and indulging the body. He stated, "The Apostle explains the difference between the two when he says: 'Make no provision for the flesh, to gratify its desires (τῆς σαρκὸς πρόνοιαν μὴ ποιεῖσθε εἰς ἐπιθυμίαν) (Rom. 13:14)."[75] John combined this statement with another quote from "the same Apostle:" "For no one ever hates his own flesh, but nourishes and tenderly cares for it (οὐδεὶς γάρ ποτε τὴν ἑαυτοῦ σάρκα ἐμίσησε, ἀλλ᾽ ἐκτρέφει καὶ θάλπει αὐτήν) (Eph. 5:29)."[76] John explained that one must care for the body so that the body can aid one's spiritual ministry. However, when one sought to care for body out of a desire for pleasure, then one should instead despise the body. John's reply admitted the ambiguity of the body for monastics. The body should be maintained with discernment so that it did not gain prominence in the monk's thought.

Sexual thoughts were a perpetual problem for many monks. John consoled a monk who experienced dreams of fantasy at night and further temptations during the day. John understood that these thoughts were connected and could be caused by arrogance or gluttony. He proposed bodily activity to help conquer them: forty-nine prostrations while uttering a prayer.[77] Training the body to respond to evil thoughts would affect one's reaction to and rejection of evil thoughts. Natural movements of the body at night were not easily overcome, even while praying, naming the holy and consubstantial Trinity, and performing the sign of the cross.[78] John confided that through ascetic effort, "The perfect (οἱ τέλειοι) do not even experience this. For they have quenched every natural movement (ἔσβεσαν... τὸ φυσικόν), having rendered themselves spiritual eunuchs (εὐνούχισαν ἑαυτοὺς πνευματικῶς) for the heavenly kingdom. That is to say, they have mortified their own earthly members (ἐνέκρωσαν ἑαυτῶν τὰ μέλη)."[79] The ascetic elites were able to cut away the movements of the body and rest in this peace.

Elsewhere, John referred to the body as a tool of the soul that should be sharpened and honed.[80] The body was being trained because of its necessary relation to the soul. The correspondent in this letter was concerned about maintaining his ascetic routine even while ill. John responded that the body assisted the person in the monastic vocation. Caring for the body, even while ill, must not arise out of passionate desire. This same monk was healed of his bodily illness but sought Barsanuphius's counsel when a small illness remained with him. Barsanuphius's reply was that this monk should "Despise the body, which is destined to be eaten by worms (καταφρόνησον τοῦ σκωληκοβρώτου σώματος). In any case, you are not bringing any benefit to it, since it will be given over to decay."[81] The remaining illness had become a stumbling block for the monk. Barsanuphius told him to meditate on these words and not be overcome by the remaining illness.

Correctly training the body would decrease the impact of evil thoughts and the devil. When Dorotheos was battling fornication, abstinence, and a bodily illness, Barsanuphius responded, "Brother, it is out of envy that the devil has aroused within you this warfare. So guard your eyes, and do not eat to the point of satiation. Drink only a little wine, for the sake of the illness that you describe."[82] Dorotheos combined the use of wine and limitation of nourishment with prayer and humility to confront his symptoms. During Dorotheos's continual struggle with thoughts, Barsanuphius wrote, "remember that you will not be in the body long (μνήσθητι ὅτι οὐ χρονίζεις ἐν τῷ σώματι)."[83] The hope of escaping the body was an important aspect of Barsanuphius's ascetic instruction. While in the body, struggles would come to the monks in various forms. One could escape this life of suffering through preparation and healing of the soul.

John described the training of the soul through the analogous training of the body. Thoughts of vainglory and dishonor troubled Dorotheos. John's advice challenged Dorotheos to treat his soul as though it were in pain. He wrote to Dorotheos, saying,

> Listen, child, perceive what is unseen by means of what is seen (ἐκ τῶν φαινομένων νόησον τὰ μὴ φαινόμενα). When something in your body is in pain, then you should abstain from whatever harms you. So when your soul hurts (πονῶν), should you not battle to abstain likewise? There is need of great effort and toil (κόπου καὶ πόνου χρεία πολλή), as the Apostle says: 'I punish my body and enslave it (ὑπωπιάζω μου τὸ σῶμα καὶ δουλαγωγῶ)' (1 Cor. 9:27).[84]

Just as one abstained from bodily practices that caused pain, so too should one struggle in one's soul to alleviate the pain of evil thoughts through training. Alleviating the pain of evil thoughts required labor and discipline, just as the body was punished and enslaved in ascetic effort.

Analyzing a series of letters between the Old Men and a sick monk named Andrew, Crislip attested, "Asceticism or discipline (*paideia*) has the same effect on the healthy body as disease: it renders it *asthenēs*, weak or sick. This weakness/sickness has a positive effect: it limits the influence of the passions, thoughts, or demons. Illness, therefore, *is* asceticism."[85] In Crislip's analysis, illness was a substitute for asceticism, but it was also more valuable in some cases. For Andrew, Barsanuphius advised, "God does not require asceticism (ἄσκησιν) from those who are physically ill (ἀσθενούντων τῷ σώματι), but only from those who are able and healthy in body. So condescending (συγκατάβηθι) a little to your body is not a sin. For God does not require this of you."[86] John too understood that, in Andrew's case, eating and drinking were allowed as long as he did so "neither with waste nor with self-indulgence (οὔτε κατὰ ἀσωτίαν οὔτε κατὰ ἡδονὴν)."[87] John, however, construed Andrew's bodily illness as a form of asceticism, writing, "But you have the affliction of illness in the place of distress through ascetic struggle (εἰς πολιτείαν)."[88] This illness was a test for Andrew and required thankful endurance.[89] Crislip called the Old Men's correspondence with Andrew "a singular process: a dialogue between historically known people about the meaning of illness and ascetic practice."[90]

Andrew's reticent acceptance of his illness indicated his inability to follow Barsanuphius's previous consolation, "Since you have God, do not be afraid, but 'cast all your anxiety on him,' (1 Peter 5:7) and he will take care of you. Do you not know that 'if the earthly tent we live in is dissolved (ἡ ἐπίγειος ἡμῶν τοῦ σκήνους οἰκία καταλυθῇ), then we have a building (οἰκοδομὴν) from God, a house not made with [human] hands (ἀχειροποίητον), one which is eternal in the heavens'?"[91] The dissolution of the earthly body and promise of a heavenly body was not a consolation. Crislip argued that this collection of correspondence offered "a rare glimpse at the traditions of ancient psychological healing, 'the care of the soul,' hē therapeia tēs psykhēs."[92]

Barsanuphius had earlier written to Andrew with a warning: "How shall we call the holy martyrs blessed on account of the sufferings they endured for the sake of Christ, if we are unable to bear a simple fever? Say to the afflicted soul: 'Is not the fever better for you than [the fire of] hell?' Let us not despair in illness; for the Apostle said: 'Whenever I am weak, then I am strong (2 Cor. 12:10)."[93] According to Crislip, "Barsanuphius uses a number of techniques to guide Andrew to make sense of his illness. One technique is to guide Andrew in interpreting his illness within their shared symbolic system."[94] Barsanuphius compared Andrew's sickness to the suffering of Job, recalling "Job's words: 'If we have received the good from the hand of the Lord, shall we not also endure the bad?' (Job 2:10)"[95] This illness was a test brought by God, "And if in testing he brings upon us illness, we nevertheless have the Apostle softening it for us by saying: 'God is faithful, and will not allow you to be tested beyond your strength, but together with the testing will also provide for you the way out, so that you may be able to endure it.' (1 Cor. 10:13)"[96] Barsanuphius encouraged Andrew to endure his illness and trust that God would strengthen him.

Crislip attested to Barsanuphius's role as "a symbolic healer [who] draws on shared symbols from the world of meaning of healer and patient, and he manipulates or applies the symbols."[97] Barsanuphius utilized the story of Job's sufferings to help Andrew understand his own sickness from an ascetic perspective. Barsanuphius even testified to his own bouts with sickness, writing, "Never have I in sickness laid down to rest or put down my handiwork; and yet great illnesses have come to me."[98] Barsanuphius witnessed the power of God to enable monks to endure illness and maintain their ascetic labor.[99]

When the monk Theodore was confronted with thoughts, he sought Barsanuphius's advice on the source of those thoughts. Theodore asked about thoughts that come from God and cause him joy when they are accomplished. Barsanuphius explained that even in these thoughts one should recall the words of Paul, "I punish my body and enslave it (Δουλαγωγῶ μου τὸ σῶμα καὶ ὑπωπιάζω). (1 Cor. 9:27)"[100] For those who desired to be spiritual, Barsanuphius recalled Paul's advice to reject the flesh.[101] Barsanuphius justified his interpretation by claiming that living according to the spirit entailed dying to the flesh, for "just as natural desires no longer remain within a person who has died physically, so also they do not remain within a person who has died according to the flesh spiritually. Now, if you have died according to the flesh, how is it that natural desires still live inside you?"[102] The natural, fleshly desires indicated that Theodore had not yet reached the spiritual level and required more instruction. Barsanuphius instructed Theodore: "humble your intellect (τῷ νοΐ ταπεινώθητι) and submit to your teacher, so that he might instruct you with compassion."[103]

Barsanuphius and John understood asceticism to be the process of putting away the old self and putting on a new self. In a series of letters, Barsanuphius clarified the central message of his instruction to a monk living in stillness:

> All you have written to me, asking God through my nothingness, my lethargic brother, converges into one thing, namely, your liberation from the old self (τὸ ἐλευθερωθῆναι ἀπὸ τοῦ παλαιοῦ ἀνθρώπου) and your salvation in the kingdom of God and in the ineffable joy of the saints. This is precisely the place of which I spoke to you, namely, the measure of being released and cleansed from the old self (τὸ μέτρον τοῦ ἀπαλλαγῆναι καὶ καθαρισθῆναι ἀπὸ τοῦ παλαιοῦ ἀνθρώπου) and being found in sanctification of soul and body (εὑρεθῆναι ἐν τῷ ἁγιασμῷ τῆς ψυχῆς καὶ τοῦ σώματος).[104]

Barsanuphius contrasted the new self and old self in a letter to John. The old self was driven by earthly desires while the new self was created according to God and was "estranged from the sensory world (τοῦ γενέσθαι τῆς γῆς ἀλλότριον τῆς αἰσθητῆς)."[105] Barsanuphius insisted that the monks become a temple for God, warning them that "the divine does not dwell in a temple stained by passions (ἐν ναῷ μεμιασμένῳ πάθεσιν, οὐ κατοικεῖ τὸ θεῖον)."[106] When John joined the monastic community of Seridos, Barsanuphius encouraged Abba John to "bear 'the death of Jesus in your body' (2 Cor. 4:10) through everything (τοῦ βαστάξαι τὴν νέκρωσιν τοῦ Ἰησοῦ ἐν τῷ σώματί σου διὰ παντός)."[107] The monastic life was an instantiation of Christ's death, dying to the world. Barsanuphius had begun to call his cell a cemetery, the tomb that holds death as well as the womb that gives life. He called his cell a cemetery because

> he has found rest from all passions there (ἀνεπαύσατο ἀπὸ τῶν παθῶν ὅλων). For he has died completely to sin (ἀπέθανε … τελείως τῇ ἁμαρτίᾳ), and his cell, wherein he is enclosed as if in a tomb (ὡς ἐν τῷ τάφῳ) for the sake of Jesus' name, is the place of rest, where neither demon nor the devil, the chief of demons, treads. Indeed, it has become a sanctuary inasmuch as it contains the dwelling-place of God.[108]

Barsanuphius himself had experienced the birth of a new self through his asceticism. The new life he led was one of rest and peace from the passions. Though few would attain the peace Barsanuphius experienced, asceticism still was preparation for a new life, a resurrected life.

In his correspondence with Abba Euthymius, Barsanuphius described the relation of the soul to the body, writing, "If we believe the Savior, who says: 'Let it be done to you according to your faith,' (Matt. 9:29) let him now say to the soul that dwells in our body (εἰπάτω καὶ νῦν πρὸς τὴν ἐνοικοῦσαν ἐν τῷ σώματι ἡμῶν ψυχὴν): 'take heart, daughter, your faith has saved you' (Matt. 9:22)."[109] Abba Euthymius also asked about the resurrection of the body. He was confused about the bodies of the saints and the bodies of the sinners that were buried in the same tomb.[110] Barsanuphius assured Euthymius that when the resurrection took place, the separation of tares and wheat would take place. Barsanuphius explained that "this age is a threshing-ground." At the resurrection, God would separate people from one another "as the shepherd separates the sheep from the goats."[111]

In Letter 607, Barsanuphius responded to a question from a monk concerning the resurrection of saint's bodies.[112] The monk questioned the nature of the resurrected body, whether it would have bones and nerves or whether it would be aerial and spherical. His question concerned the nature of Christ's resurrected body and "the body of glory (τῷ σώματι τῆς δόξης αὐτοῦ)" mentioned in Paul's letter to the Philippians (Phil. 3:21).[113] Barsanuphius began his response by referring to the reconstituted dry bones of Ezekiel's vision (Ezek. 37). In the passage from Ezekiel, the bodies were restored bone upon bone, joint upon joint, with veins and flesh and nerves. Barsanuphius continued, "The Apostle also knew that we would rise in our bodies (ἐγειρόμεθα τοῖς σώμασιν), and so he taught: 'For this perishable body must put on imperishability (Δεῖ γὰρ τὸ φθαρτὸν τοῦτο ἐνδύσασθαι ἀφθαρσίαν), and this mortal body must put on immortality.' (1 Cor. 15:53) Do not be deceived; the bodies will rise with their bones, nerves, and hair (σὺν τοῖς ὀστέοις καὶ νεύροις καὶ θριξὶ τὰ σώματα ἐγείρονται)."[114] Though Barsanuphius could not report on the glory of the resurrected body, he did note that in the age to come they "shall be brighter and more glorious (ὅμως φωτεινότερα καὶ ἐνδοξότερα), according to the voice of the Lord: 'Then the righteous will shine like the sun in the kingdom of heaven' (Matt. 13:43)."[115] These new bodies would be like the "God-bearers (θεοφόροι)."[116] The resurrected bodies of Abraham, James, and Stephen would be the same bodies but "incorruptible, immortal, and more glorious (ἄφθαρτα δὲ καὶ ἀθάνατα καὶ ἐνδοξότερα)."[117] The bodies of humans were sown in dishonor but raised in honor; sown as unspiritual bodies, but raised as spiritual bodies.[118] These spiritual bodies would receive glory. These glorified bodies would be rendered light-like according to Christ's own body, they will be "the sons of light (υἱοὶ φωτός)" (Eph. 5:8).[119] God would resurrect the body prepared through asceticism in this life to a new glory commensurate with Christ's body.

The body in Barsanuphius and John's ascetic teaching carried a variety of meanings. For the troubled monk, the body could be cast as in need of further discipline. For the sick monk, the body might need nourishment and convalescence to return to health, or the illness could be a period of testing by God. Strict discernment was needed to correctly evaluate how one should attend to the body. The varied meanings carried by the body were always interpreted through the desire to promote health for the soul. The aim of asceticism was the destruction of the old self and the institution of the new self. Only through this transformation of subjectivity could the monk truly be prepared for the eventual departure of the soul from the body and the body's consequent resurrection. Asceticism prepared the soul and body for the glory of the resurrection even at the expense of the body's health in this life.

Dorotheos and the Body

Irénée Hausherr analyzed Dorotheos's mentorship of Dositheos as a mark of Dorotheos's monastic instruction. Referring to Dorotheos's instruction for Dositheos to pray constantly as long as he was able, Hausherr indicated, "the entire biography of Dosithee illustrates both the firmness of the guidance he received and the director's desire not to impose anything that would have been beyond the physical and moral strength of this exceptional novice."[120] Dorotheos released Dositheos from his prayers when he was too ill to continue. Dorotheos's spiritual direction of Dositheos was indicative of the instruction he offered in his own monastery. He recognized that Dositheos had a habit of overindulging in food and taught him to gradually decrease the amount of food he ate until "he went down from eating six pounds to eating eight ounces."[121] Dositheos trained his body to function on the minimal amount of food necessary without being hungry or malnourished. When Dorotheos asked him if he was hungry, Dositheos replied, "I am well, father (καλῶς εἰμί, κῦρι)."[122]

The culmination of Dorotheos's guidance was manifest when, after Dositheos died, "a saintly man, an elder" was given a vision of the saints from the community who had passed away.[123] Among the saints was a young monk the elder did not recognize. When he described to the brothers of the monastery the facial features they realized that it was Dositheos. The author of the *Life* emphasized the bodily features of Dositheos after death in contrast to his frailty during his sickness. Dositheos was so sick that he had to be carried in a sheet. After the report of the vision, everyone

> glorified God, marveling at the fact that Dositheos had become worthy of reaching such a great height (ποῖα μέτρα κατηξιώθη φθάσαι) in such a short time, despite his

earlier life and discipline (ἀπὸ ποίου βίου καὶ οἵας πρώτης ἀγωγῆς), simply through obedience and denying his own will."[124]

Dositheos's short monastic life was fruitful under Dorotheos's care. His bodily demise illustrated his desire to be obedient and cut out his will even when he knew that certain foods could comfort his condition.[125]

Sickness was a common theme in Dorotheos's spiritual direction. In cases such as Dositheos's, the hope for bodily health was in vain. Dorotheos recognized that the health of the body had limits. To a brother with a prolonged sickness, Dorotheos wrote, "I beg you, my child, be patient and thankful for the symptoms of your sickness, according to the person who says, 'Accept everything that happens to you as good,' so that the aim of the providence be fulfilled in you, my child, according to the will of God, 'be brave, be strong,' (1 Cor. 16:13) by the grace of the Lord and His economy for you."[126] This illness was not described, but the call for patience and thankfulness was characteristic of enduring sickness as seen in Isaiah, Barsanuphius, and John. However, the broader context of Dorotheos's emphasis on bodily health revealed a different perspective.

Explaining the sickness of the soul, Dorotheos illustrated his understanding of bodily sickness. He wrote, "The same thing happens with sickly bodies. When someone lives to excess and takes no care of his health either an excess of something or a deficiency will be produced and thus he will lose his health. Before that sickness did not exist and there was no other problem. When the body is healed again, the sickness disappears completely."[127] Dorotheos was working within an understanding of the body whereby harmony of the body symbolized health. Disruption of the body resulted in sickness. Dale Martin developed two contrasting models of disease etiology for understanding ancient medical theory in *The Corinthian Body*: imbalance and invasion. The imbalance etiology viewed "the body [as] normally a balanced ecosystem whose elements or forces are all necessary: good health results when none of these elements or forces oversteps its natural bounds."[128] On this view, the causation of disease is not invasion by a hostile, foreign element but the influence of outside forces on the internal harmony and balance of the body. Alternately, the invasion etiology views the body as "a closed but penetrable entity that remains healthy by fending off hostile forces and protecting its boundaries."[129] This etiological theory analyzed the sickly body's reaction to outside stimuli rather than internal disharmony. Dorotheos's approach to bodily sickness was most akin to the imbalance etiology in which outside stimuli could exacerbate the situation but were not the primary causes of the illness.[130]

Dorotheos displayed his experience with sickly bodies and their reaction to nourishment. He wrote,

Since, as there are feeble and sickly bodies (σώματα μελαγχολικά, κακόχυμα) where all the food consumed is changed (τρέπουσι) according to their sickness, even if the food is good, and evidently the cause (ἡ αἰτία) of their sickness is not the food but the body itself which, as I have said, has bad health (δύσκρατόν) and necessarily owing to its bad condition, works and changes the food."[131]

The internal disruption of sick bodies reacted badly to proper nourishment. Even appropriate foods were incorrectly digested. Bodies that were healthy reacted differently. They were able to absorb the nourishment from good food and even transform bad food into nourishing food. Dorotheos claimed that the healthy person, "Even if he eats something harmful (βλαβερόν), he transforms it into nourishing food (τρέπει αὐτὸ εἰς εὐχυμίαν) according to his own condition and even this bad food does not harm him because, as I have said, his body is vigorous (εὐχυμίαν) and transforms the food according to its condition (πρὸς τὴν κρᾶσιν αὐτοῦ)."[132] A healthy body was unperturbed by food that could be harmful, because the inner disposition was able to transform it. Asceticism was, for Dorotheos, the means whereby a person maintained the balance within the body; it required constant vigilance.

Ignoring small imbalances within the body could lead to longer and more disruptive illnesses. Concerning a brother with a fever, Dorotheos explained, "I once visited a brother and found him recovering from an illness. After some discussion, I was informed that he had been alone with a fever (ἐπύρεξε) for seven days. In spite of the fact that a further forty days had passed since the fever left, he had still not recovered."[133] This brother had neglected to find the source of the fever and suffered because of this negligence. By disregarding his small disorder, he required "much time and effort before recovering (πολλοῦ πάνυ χρεία κόπου καὶ χρόνου πρὶν ἢ γένηται αὐτοῦ ἡ κατόρθωσις)."[134] In another discourse, Dorotheos discussed the role of one's way of life in the suffering of a fever. He asked,

When a person has a fever (πυρέσσῃ) what is it that burns him, what kind of fire? What wood produces this fire? If someone happens to have a weak body, a body of bad temperament (σῶμα μελαγχολικὸν δύσκρατον), is it not the bad temperament (δυσκρασία αὐτοῦ) that burns him up (καίει αὐτὸν) and always disturbs (ταράσσει) and troubles (θλίβει) his life?"[135]

Fever itself was the illness and resulted from a life that was not properly comported. Through the imbalance of one's body, weakness and fever resulted. Avoiding fever required interpreting the temperament of the body. Consistent discernment of the body's condition was necessary to remain in a healthy state.

Dorotheos retained a similar discourse with regard to the body to that evident in Isaiah, Barsanuphius, and John. One of Dorotheos's sayings connected the cutting off of one's will with despising certain elements of communal life. Doro-theos said, "The person who does not despise all material things, glory and bodily comfort, even his own rights, cannot cut off his own will, nor can he be delivered from wrath and sadness or comfort his neighbor."[136] Despising bodily comfort, however, was not the same emphasis as despising the body. Here the context was the communal life of the monastery.

The body also functioned as a metaphor for the monastic community. Dor-otheos stated, "Let us help (βοηθήσωμεν) one another since we are members of the same body (ἰδίοις μέλεσι)" and all are "one body (πάντες ἓν σῶμά ἐσμεν)."[137] As members of one body, each should seek the health of all the other members. A wound in one's hand or foot would not induce one to simply cut off the injured member, so, too, with one's brothers. Dorotheos referred to Zosimas on the value of an ill member, saying, "Would we not rather bath it, clean it, put a plaster on it, make the sign of the cross over it, bless it with holy water, pray and ask the saints to pray for us—as Abba Zosimas used to say—and to put it simply, not abandon, or dislike our own member or even the bad smell of it, but instead do everything to try to heal it?"[138] Though figurative, Dorotheos displayed his approach to the physical body as therapeutic and restorative. The monastic life offered a communal therapy for physical and spiritual sicknesses.

In a letter to the superiors of other monks, Dorotheos encouraged them to set forth a good example in their deeds. For the healthy, this meant bodily works. For the sick elder, Dorotheos specified, "model for them through your good spir-itual state (τῇ τῆς ψυχῆς καλῇ καταστάσει) and through the fruits of the spirit (enumerated by the Apostle): love, joy, peace, long suffering, gentleness, goodness, faith, and temperance which is the contrary of all the passions (Gal. 5:22–23)."[139] TIllness may have inhibited the elder from performing bodily deeds, but he should still exhibit spiritual fruits that display spiritual health. In a response to the cel-lar-keeper, Dorotheos emphasized the importance of spiritual progress and the fruits reaped from it. When one served the sick, God would send someone to serve him in his sickness. When bodily or spiritual afflictions came, the judgment of one's faults would prepare him to endure these afflictions with patience. By culti-vating the virtues of sympathy and humility, one was prepared for the disruptions of life and could endure them appropriately.[140]

Dorotheos's view of the ascetic body encouraged his monks to seek health for the body. The body, in turn, enabled the soul to attain virtue. Brown noted Dorotheos's distinct position on this issue as opposed to his mentor Barsanu-phius.[141] Whereas Barsanuphius taught Dorotheos to despise the body, Doro-theos taught his monks that the body was interconnected with the soul and that they should work for the health of both. Brown called the ascetic transformation in Dorotheos's teaching "the inextricable interdependence of body and soul."[142] Through asceticism of the body one could bring humility to the soul. In Discourse 2, Dorotheos discussed the connection between bodily labor and humility, claiming, "Hard work, therefore, humbles the body and when it is humbled, the soul is likewise (ὁ κόπος οὖν ταπεινοῖ τὸ σῶμα· τοῦ δὲ σώματος ταπεινουμένου, συνταπεινοῦται αὐτῷ καὶ ἡ ψυχή)."[143] The body was a means of healing the soul through habituation of the virtues. Brown called this interdependence "a sense of the shared momentum of body and soul."[144] Dorotheos retained a dual emphasis on body and soul in his monastic guidance in which the soul depended upon the body for its health.

For Dorotheos, it was through the body that the soul escaped the passions. When discussing some monks who viewed death as an escape from troubles, Dorotheos insisted that affliction in this life prepared one for comfort in the next life. Quoting Evagrius, Dorotheos stated, "The person that prays to God to leave this world sooner whilst he is still full of passions (ἐμπαθής τις ὢν) seems like the person who asked the carpenter to immediately destroy the bed of a sick person."[145] These monks, who desired death, were unprepared for it. They viewed their struggles as a burden to bear and death as the only escape.

Dorotheos understood the promise of health in this life as opposed to the mystery of death, saying, "It is a great philanthropy of God (μεγάλη φιλανθρωπία τοῦ Θεοῦ), brethren, to be in this world) but we, not knowing how things are there, consider the things which we suffer here as a burden (βαρέα), but this is not so."[146] Dorotheos contended, "Through the body the soul escapes from her passions and is comforted (διὰ γὰρ τοῦ σώματος τούτου περισπᾶται ἡ ψυχὴ ἀπὸ τῶν παθῶν αὐτῆς καὶ παρακαλεῖται·). It eats, drinks, sleeps, lives with others and it is with friends."[147] The communal life provided an environment where the monk engaged in an embodied struggle against the passions fought in solidarity with others. However, when the soul

gets away from the body (ἐπὰν δὲ ἐξέλθῃ ἀπὸ τοῦ σώματος) it becomes alone with its passions (μονοῦται αὕτη καὶ τὰ πάθη αὐτῆς) and therefore it is always held by them (λοιπὸν κολάζεται πάντοτε ὑπ᾽ αὐτῶν), remaining always with them and burning from the annoyance of them so that it cannot even remember God, for the remembrance of God comforts the soul, as it says in the psalms, 'I was mindful of God and I was made glad.' (Ps. 77:3) However, the passions do not allow even this to happen.[148]

The body, though a possible source for disruption, was a safe haven for the soul, a place where the soul could be nurtured. Dorotheos continued to describe these despondent monks who "are so upset by their troubles that they do not even want to carry on living and they consider death as something pleasant that will deliver them."[149] Death, as a separation of the soul from the body, contravened the body and soul's interdependence.

Even depriving a monk of companionship and physical stimuli was tortuous. Dorotheos gave an example of a monk locked in a dark cell. Under these conditions,

> He will not eat, drink, sleep or be in contact with anyone for three days. He will not sing, not pray and not remember God at all and he will learn what his passions are doing to him. This is what it is like whilst we are still here. How much worse will it be when the soul escapes from the body? It will be delivered to the passions and will be alone with them (ποσῷ γε μᾶλλον μετὰ τὸ ἐξελθεῖν τὴν ψυχὴν ἀπὸ τοῦ σώματος καὶ προδοθῆναι αὐτοῖς καὶ μονωθῆναι μετ᾽ αὐτῶν)."[150]

Death for the unprepared would indeed be hell for the monks. Without the body, the soul would be left on its own and would be forced to battle its thoughts and memories without aid. Dorotheos explained, "What the soul has done with regard to the virtues and the passions it always remembers and none of that is lost…The soul, as I have said, forgets nothing concerning the actions done in this world but keeps them all after it leaves the body and remembers them all more clearly and precisely when it is freed from the earthly body."[151] Dorotheos was unclear about what exactly the soul remembered after death, but he was clear that one should train one's thoughts in preparation for the soul's separation from the body.

The ascetic body, for Dorotheos, was a body being recreated in the likeness of Christ. Dorotheos connected his monastic teaching to the narrative of salvation. The monastic life was a life of return to the natural state through the work of Christ. He observed that Christ

> has assumed our essence (τὴν οὐσίαν ἡμῶν), the first fruit of our nature and He became a new Adam (γίνεται νέος Ἀδὰμ) 'according to the image of Him who created him (κατ᾽ εἰκόνα τοῦ κτίσαντος αὐτόν).' (Col. 3:10) He renews human nature and makes our senses perfect again (ἀνανεοῖ γὰρ τὸ κατὰ φύσιν καὶ σώας πάλιν ποιεῖ τὰς αἰσθήσεις), as they were at the beginning. He renewed fallen Man by becoming Man (ἀνενέωσεν τὸν πεσόντα ἄνθρωπον γενόμενος ἄνθρωπος). He liberated him from the dominion of sin, which had compelled him by force."[152]

The immortality, free-will, and virtue granted at creation belonged to humanity's natural state.[153] Through sin, humanity assumed a state contrary to nature, was dominated by the passions, and death reigned.[154] Acetic labor enabled the transformation envisioned, one in which the soul and body were both regenerated and restored to the natural state. Through monastic obedience to Christ's commandments, one could rediscover and renew the divine light.[155]

Conclusion

The body attained significance in Dorotheos's teaching because of its connection to virtue acquisition and habituation. For Dorotheos, the monastic pursuit was living the virtuous life in the present; ascetic activity and virtue were interrelated. Practicing a virtue entailed the belief that one was not virtuous as well as the rejection of praise as an ascetic.[156] Dorotheos affirmed that virtue was practiced when one acted with self-control (ἐγκρατευόμενος) and abstained from believing that the action was virtuous and from the desire to be praised as an ascetic (θέλει ἐπαινεῖσθαι ὡς ἀσκητής). Virtuous monks had cultivated humility (ἡ ταπείνωσις) through self-control (ἡ ἐγκράτεια) and discretion (ἡ σωφροσύνη).[157] Dorotheos clarified some of the ambiguity illustrated in Barsanuphius's and John's instruction by closely linking the health of the body and the health of the soul into one harmonious vision through his emphasis on virtue. The habituation of virtue, for Dorotheos, was not accomplished at the expense of the body. In his linkage of virtue acquisition with the body, he also avoided the harsh regard for the body as seen in Isaiah. For Dorotheos, asceticism conditioned the body and soul to respond appropriately to any circumstance and dissolve potential disruption. This positive role of the body emphasized a distinct vision of the ascetic body in the monastic school of Gaza.

CHAPTER SEVEN

Conclusion

This work has sought to revive Dorotheos's importance among his monastic contemporaries by providing a fresh perspective from which to demonstrate his contribution to his tradition. Our goal was to compare the Gazan monastics' use of the discourse of healing in their monastic guidance with a focus upon Dorotheos's distinctive approach. His contribution lay in his stressing the centrality of Christ as physician and teacher in the drama of salvation, the role of virtue in living the healthy life, and the positive role of the body for his monastics. Dorotheos articulated his distinctive contribution within a common discourse. The discourse of healing was a shared discourse in which Dorotheos and his contemporaries expounded their visions of the monastic life and established a connection between the conceptual frameworks of the members of the monastic school of Gaza. Important differences in spiritual direction arose from within the discourse of healing and reflected the particular emphases of each monastic. On Dorotheos's part, the discourse of healing was a traditional means to elaborate upon his view of the healthy life of humanity as inclusive of soul and body. The subtle distinctions highlighted in this study indicate that Dorotheos of Gaza was a decisive figure in the monastic school of Gaza who transformed his tradition and inaugurated a renewed emphasis on the interrelatedness of the health of soul and body for the healing of humanity through the discourse of healing.

While his contemporaries—Isaiah, Barsanuphius, and John—engaged the discourse of healing to communicate their understanding of the monastic life, Dorotheos, remaining faithful to his tradition, expanded upon his inherited tradition and incorporated a view of healing that clarified the place of monasticism in the drama of salvation, more fully addressed the role of virtue in the monastic life, and ensured the importance of the body's health as conducive to the healing of the whole person. Dorotheos employed the discourse of healing in a way that engaged the contemporary discourse of his monastic heritage and a broader Christian discourse that took into account medical approaches to healing.

Three distinct developments marked Dorotheos's contribution to his monastic tradition. First, Dorotheos's vision of the healing that the Christian life entailed began with an analysis of the drama of salvation. He espoused a view of humanity's salvation that reflected his conception of Christ enabling a return to humanity's created condition. For Dorotheos, the monastic life was firmly situated within his understanding of the healing offered by Christ. Dorotheos expressed his conception of the narrative of salvation and the monastic life through the language of health and healing. Dorotheos depicted "Christus ... als dem Arzt der Seelen."[1] Christ the Physician brought spiritual healing to humanity, and Christ's teaching provided the means to continue to live the healthy life. Dorotheos emphasized that Christ "knows everything and gives the proper prescription for every passion."[2] In Pauli's words, "Für jedes Leiden der Seele hält Christus ein entsprechendes 'Medikament' bereit."[3] Christ was the physician able to renew humanity and affect the possibility of a return to humanity's created state: "Durch Christus, den neuen Adam, wird die Natur des Menschen erneuert, und seine Sinne erhalten ihre ursprüngliche Gesundheit zurück."[4] The metaphor of healing provides the key to understanding how Dorotheos envisioned the efficacy of Christ's activity. As a physician, Christ brought healing to humanity that was otherwise unavailable. In addition, Christ provided the prescription for healthy living through his teachings. Dorotheos explained that "In this way, [Christ] has given us the cure for the cause [of sin], so that we shall be able to obey and be saved.... Here briefly, in one word, he has shown us the root and cause of every evil and the treatment for it and also the cause of every good."[5] Christ's role as Physician and Teacher functioned as a primary theme that textured and elucidated Dorotheos's use of the discourse of healing and his own monastic instruction on the life of health.

Second, Dorotheos conceived the habituation of virtue as essential for the healthy life. In contrast to his contemporaries in the Gazan monastic tradition, he stated, "virtue is a natural innate condition for us since the seeds of virtue are indelible. I said therefore that as far as we do good we become accustomed to virtue. That is to say, we rediscover our natural state and our own health."[6] The correlation between virtue and the healthy life arose in Dorotheos's teaching at several points. For example, the importance of cultivating virtue in the monastic life led Dorotheos to rehabilitate the motif of a dwelling for the soul as a house built of the virtues. He concluded, "Briefly, we must practice each virtue in such a way that we reach it and it becomes a habit for us. Thus, as we have said, we are a good and skilled builder, able to build our house securely."[7] It was precisely in the construction of the house of virtue that Dorotheos returned again to service of the sick. He reflected, "I myself knew a brother who was battling with an evil desire and, because he served a sick person suffering from dysentery with knowledge, he was freed from the struggle."[8] In this case, he likened the "good and skilled builder" to one who serves the sick with compassion. Through the security of the construction of the soul with compassion, Dorotheos's monastic brother was able to maintain his healthy state amid an infection of evil desires. Virtue became the primary vehicle for the restoration of a person's health. The habituation and acquisition of virtue reinforced the importance of the body in the monastic life.

Third, Dorotheos rejuvenated the positive role of the body in the monastic life. He did not advise denigrating the body for the sake of the soul but taught that a proper understanding of the body and attending to bodily needs was essential for physical and spiritual health. When discussing fasting, Dorotheos explained that the goal was to feed the body according to its need and to eliminate gluttonous desire. In a proper fast, a monk "rightly searches out his need and receives exactly what is necessary, not for pleasure, but for the strengthening of his body."[9] The body's health and the soul's health were inseparable. Dorotheos also posited that through bodily action the soul could attain improved health. Specifically, one obtained the virtue of humility through bodily labor. Dorotheos taught that, "Hard work, therefore, humbles the body and when it is humbled, the soul is likewise."[10] Pauli explained that the body was not inimical to the soul's health but an essential component: "Positiv gewendet wird nun der Leib zum Instrument, durch das die Seele sich von den Leidenschaften reinigen kann. Dies verdeutlicht Dorotheos am Zusammenhang von körperlichen Mühen und Demut."[11] Health of the soul and health of the body were interconnected. The body was so important for the health of the soul that Dorotheos stated, "Through the body the soul escapes from her passions and is comforted."[12] In his distinct use of the discourse of healing, Dorotheos overcame the dichotomy of body and soul in a unitive way that brought the two together as important for the whole person. For Dorotheos, the monastic life was characterized by the pursuit of health for the soul and the body.

In conclusion, Dorotheos brought his distinct perspective to bear upon the monastic school of Gaza to enrich and invigorate it. Adapting the discourse of healing to highlight his own concerns was an important aspect of his monastic tradition. Bitton-Ashkelony and Kofsky aptly described the monastic school of Gaza as "firmly rooted in earlier ascetic traditions, reshaping them through its interpretation and selective adoption, demonstrating that we are dealing here with a dynamic monastic culture in an ongoing process of shaping and reevaluating its own tradition."[13] The dynamism of his tradition allowed Dorotheos to express his spiritual teaching in a form that was traditional but with particularities that were distinct. Dorotheos made use of the established discourse of healing to articulate the monastic life while adding his own emphasis on the type of healing one should pursue. This new lens illumines new facets of his thought and signals his importance in the use of healing as a mode of discourse. Dorotheos employed a tradition of perspectives and techniques that attempted to define and cultivate healing. This comparative study of the Gazan monastics' use of the discourse of healing distinguishes Dorotheos from his colleagues, establishes the importance of virtue in the monastic life, deepens a spiritual trajectory that incorporates the body, complicates the role of the body in asceticism, and reevaluates the notions of health and illness in early Christianity.

Notes

Chapter 1: Introduction

1. Peter Brown, *The Body and Society: Men, Women, and Sexual Renunciation in Early Christianity*, 2nd ed. (New York: Columbia University Press, 2008), 236.
2. Lucien Regnault, "Théologie de la vie monastique selon Barsanuphe et Dorothée," in *Théologie De La Vie Monastique; Études Sur La Tradition Patristique* (Paris: Aubier, 1961), 322. "Rather than dwell on points of detail where Dorotheos is only the echo of the tradition, we chose to emphasize what seems most important and most characteristic."
3. Ibid. "Dorotheos is faithful to the tradition, to the whole tradition, and leaves nothing to be lost."
4. The observations of Jonathan Zecher on John Climacus' significance within his monastic tradition were helpful. See, Jonathan L. Zecher, "The Symbolics of Death and the Construction of Christian Asceticism: Greek Patristic Voices from the Fourth through the Seventh Centuries" (PhD diss., Durham University, 2011), 35.
5. Lampe defined πάθος as "emotion, passion" of the soul. G. W. H. Lampe, *A Patristic Greek Lexicon.* (Oxford: The Clarendon Press, 1961), 992. Additionally, Liddell and Scott offered the examples of "love and hate." Liddell and Scott, *A Greek-English Lexicon.* (Oxford: The Clarendon Press, 1999), 1285. The specific use of πάθος in Gazan monasticism is explored below, pages 127–148. For Dorotheos, πάθος always referred to a disease of the soul. For further development on the role of passions in Greek thought, see William V. Harris, *Restraining Rage: The Ideology of Anger Control in Classical Antiquity* (Harvard: Harvard

University Press, 2004); David Constans, *The Emotions of the Greeks: Studies in Aristotle and Greek Literature* (Toronto: University of Toronto Press, 2006).

6. Averil Cameron, *Christianity and the Rhetoric of Empire: The Development of Christian Discourse* (Berkeley: University of California Press, 1991), 58.

7. Ibid., 170.

8. Michael Dörnemann, *Krankheit und Heilung in der Theologie der frühen Kirchenväter*, Studien und Texte zu Antike und Christentum (Tübingen: Mohr Siebeck, 2003), 10. "In dieser Arbeit meint der Begriff Metapher...nicht nur eine sprachliche Ausdrucksform, sondern bereits eine Form des Denkens." Metaphor is "not only a linguistic expression, but is already a form of thinking."

9. For instance, Dörnemann explained Basil of Caesarea's use of medical metaphors to explain certain theological ideas. "In weiteren theologischen Fragen greift Basilius auf medizinale Metaphern zurück: Das Böse ist eine Krankheit..." "In other theological matters, Basil relies on medical metaphors: Evil is an illness." Ibid., 206.

10. Ibid., 6–7.

11. George Lakoff and Mark Johnson, *Metaphors We Live By* (Chicago: University of Chicago Press, 1980), 5.

12. Ibid., 6.

13. Ibid., 19.

14. Ibid., 5.

15. Christa Baldauf, "Sprachliche Evidenz metaphorischer Konzeptualisierung: Probleme und Perspektive der kognitivistischen Metapherntheorie," in *Bildersprache verstehen: Zur Hermeneutik der Metapher und anderer bildlicher Sprachformen* (München: W. Fink, 2000), 132. "Eine Beschäftigung mit der Metapher zielt weniger auf Sprachverständnis als vielmehr auf das Verständnis kognitiver Routinen. Auch ist die Metaphern nicht mehr Reflex individueller Sichtweisen, sondern Ausdruck eines überindividuellen Verständnisses der Welt. Metaphorische Konzeptualisierungsweisen bilden in ihrer Konventionalisiertheit ein Raster der Erfahrungsbewältigung, welches kognitive Anstrengung reduziert und Nicht-Greifbares begreifbar werden lässt."
"An approach to metaphor aims less at dealing with language comprehension and more on the understanding of cognitive routines. Nor is the metaphor reflective of individual perspectives, but represents a supra-individual understanding of the world. Metaphorical methods of conceptualization constitute, in a conventional manner, a pattern of managed experience that reduces cognitive effort and one in which non-tangibles can be understandable."

16. Amanda Porterfield, *Healing in the History of Christianity* (New York: Oxford University Press, 2005), 44.

17. Ibid.

18. Anne Elizabeth Meredith, "Illness and Healing in the Early Christian East" (PhD diss., Princeton University, 1999), 157. Meredith commented, "The use of metaphor and analogy enabled Christian writers and orators to express the inexpressible and to describe a God they felt to be indescribable." Ibid., 154.

19. Dorotheos of Gaza, *Abba Dorotheos: Practical Teaching on the Christian Life*, translation, introduction, and glossary by Constantine Scouteris (Athens: Constantine Scouteris, 2000),

157; Dorotheos of Gaza, Œuvres spirituelles, trans. Lucien Regnault and J. de Préville, vol. 92, Sources chrétiennes (Paris: Éditions du Cerf, 1963), 316, Discourse 8.

20. Dorotheos of Gaza, *Abba Dorotheos*, 157, Discourse 8.

21. Ibid.

22. Brown, *The Body and Society*, 233.

23. Ibid.

24. Barsanuphius and John, *Letters*, trans. John Chryssavgis, Fathers of the Church (Washington, D.C.: Catholic University of America Press, 2006), 260, Letter 256. Brown's translation, 236.

25. Dorotheos of Gaza, Œuvres spirituelles, 204–206, Discourse 2.

26. Brown, *The Body and Society*, 236.

27. Ibid., 425.

28. Pierre Hadot, *What Is Ancient Philosophy?*, trans. Michael Chase (Cambridge, MA: Belknap Press of Harvard University Press, 2004), 134–136.

29. Ibid., 136–138.

30. Pierre Hadot, *Philosophy as a Way of Life: Spiritual Exercises from Socrates to Foucault*, trans. Michael Chase (Malden, MA: Wiley-Blackwell, 1995), 136.

31. Ibid., 135.

32. Ibid., 139.

33. Hadot, *What Is Ancient Philosophy?*, 240–241. Hadot argued, "The Christians adopted the Greek word *philosophia* to designate monasticism as the perfection of the Christian life, and were able to do so because the work *philosophia* designated a way of life." Ibid., 247.

34. Judith Pauli, *Menschsein und Menschwerden nach der geistlichen Lehre des Dorotheus von Gaza* (St. Ottilien: EOS Verlag, 1998).

35. Judith Pauli, *Doctrinae Diversae: Die geistliche Lehre*, 2 vols., vol. 37 (Freiburg: Herder, 2000).

36. Jennifer Lee Hevelone-Harper, *Disciples of the Desert: Monks, Laity, and Spiritual Authority in Sixth-Century Gaza* (Baltimore: Johns Hopkins University Press, 2005).

37. Brouria Bitton-Ashkelony and Aryeh Kofsky, *The Monastic School of Gaza* (Leiden: Brill, 2006), 3.

38. Ibid., 223.

39. Ibid., 44.

40. Ibid.

41. Ibid., 142.

42. Rosa Marie Parrinello, *Comunità monastiche a Gaza: Da Isaia a Doroteo (secoli IV–VI)*, Temi e Testi (Roma: Edizioni di Storia e Letteratura, 2010), 6.

43. Ibid., 39.

44. Ibid., 215–216.

45. Pierre Canivet, "Dorothée de Gaza: est-il un disciple d'Évagre?," *Revue des Études Greques* 78 (1965): 337.

46. Lorenzo Perrone, "Scripture for a Life of Perfection. The Bible in Late Antique Monasticism: The Case of Palestine," in *The Reception and Interpretation of the Bible in Late Antiquity: Proceedings of the Montréeal Colloquium in Honour of Charles Kannengiesser, 11–13 October 2006*, ed. Lorenzo DiTommaso and Lucian Turcescu (Boston: Brill, 2008), 414.

47. For ease of reference, I use the term '*Spiritual Discourses*' to indicate the full collection of Dorotheos's works—discourses, letters, and sayings—and often refer to a specific work within this collection, i.e. *Discourse* 1, *Letter* 2.

48. Lucien Regnault and Jacques de Préville, Œuvres spirituelles, Sources chrétiennes (Paris: Éditions du Cerf, 1963).

49. Pauli, *Doctrinae Diversae: Die geistliche Lehre.*

50. Lucien Regnault and Jean de Préville's critical edition made use of two unpublished dissertations: Brun, P. M. *Dorotheos archimandrita seu Gazaeus* (Rome 1932) and Wijnen, J. *Dorotheos van Gaza: Prolegomena tot een tekstuitgave* (Louvain 1954) as compared to the Minge text of Dorotheos of Gaza, *S. Dorotheus, Archimandrita* ed. J. -P Migne, vol. 88, Patrologiae Cursus Completus, Series Graeca (Paris: J.-P. Migne, 1860), cols. 1611–1844. Regnault and Préville noted that the first fourteen discourses were preserved in almost all of the manuscripts in the same order, while other discourses vary greatly in number and order. They observed that the first fourteen discourses constituted a block or unit of text around which other literature was added. "Il est à remarquer que ce groupe de quatorze se retrouve dans presque tous les manuscrits et, à part une exception accidentelle, dans le meme ordre, alors que pour les autres *Doctrines*, le nombre et l'ordre varient beaucoup. Certains manuscrits ne contiennent que ces quatorze instructions, qui ont pu constituer une 'bloc' fondamental et primitif, auquel auraient été ajoutées postérieurement d'autres pieces." Regnault and Préville, Œuvres spirituelles, 30–31. Of the twenty-four discourses and eight letters available in Migne's *Patrologiae Graeca vol. 88*, *Discourse* 24 was recognized by Irénée Hausherr as the work of John of Dalyatha, also known as John of Saba. See, Irénée Hausherr, "La "Doctrine XXIV" de saint Dorothée," *Orientalia christiana periodica* 6 (1940): 220–221. Also, *Discourse* 21 was found to be from the correspondence of Barsanuphius and John (*Letters* 285, 277, 278, 288, 307, 322, 345, 523, and 545). In addition, *Discourses* 16, 17, 18, and 20 were found to be letters from Dorotheos to his monks rather than discourses and *Discourse* 19 was determined to be a collection of Dorotheos's sayings. The text of *Letter* 6, *Letter* 12, portions from the *Introductory Letter*, and the *Life of Dositheos* were absent in Migne's edition. Regnault and Préville, Œuvres spirituelles, 30–34. Judith Pauli re-examined the importance of Brun and Wijnen's work for the critical edition published by Regnault and Préville. She charted the contents from Wijnen's study of 150 manuscripts and rescension into five families by focusing on forty-one important manuscripts from the ninth century to the sixteenth century. She concluded that only *Paris Coislin* 260 (eleventh century) and *Sinai gr.* 412 (twelfth century) contain the entire corpus of texts that now comprise the critical edtion of Dorotheos's works. *Paris Coislin* 260 also served as the model from which Regnault and Préville ordered the textual elements of their critical edition. For charts and further analysis, see Pauli, *Menschsein und Menschwerden*, 25–36.

51. Siméon Vailhé, "Saint Dorothée et Saint Zosime," Échos d'*Orient* 4 (1905): 361–362.

52. There are two English translations of Dorotheos's *Spiritual Discourses*. The widely available translation published by Eric Wheeler did not address the entirety of works concerning Dorotheos and was based upon the inferior Migne text. See Dorotheos of Gaza, *Dorotheos of Gaza: Discourses and Sayings*, trans. Eric P. Wheeler (Kalamazoo: Cistercian Publications, 1977), 20. Alternatively, the translation of Constantine Scouteris was based upon the

critical edition of Regnault and Préville and, in addition to the *Discourses*, contained the *Prologue, Introductory Letter*, and *Life of Dositheos*. See *Abba Dorotheos*, 13.

53. Dorotheos of Gaza, *Abba Dorotheos*, 55–56, Life of Dositheos.

54. Ibid., 169–170, Discourse 10.

55. Parrinello argued that the work of Abba Zosimas provided another resource for Dorotheos and provided a connection to Basil of Caesarea's ascetical works. She claimed that Dorotheos compiled and edited this collection of monastic discourses. Parrinello proposed that "Probabilmente egli raccolse e redasse le conversazioni spirituali (*Adloquia*) del monaco fenicio Zosima, vissuto per un po' di tempo nella laura di San Gerasimo e il cui arco cronologico dovette compiersi tra la seconda metà del V secolo e la prima metà del VI: Zosima fondò una propria comunità monastica a Cesarea e potrebbe dunque essere il tramite attraverso il quale Doroteo entra in contatto con Basilio, uno degli autori più presenti nell' opera zosimiana proprio con le Regole." Parrinello, *Communità monastiche a Gaza*, 215–216. "He probably collected and wrote the spiritual conversations (*Alloquia*) of the Phoenician monk Zosimas, who lived for a time in the laura of St. Gerasimos and whose span had ended in the second half of the fifth century and the first half of the sixth: Zosimas formed his own monastic community at Caesarea and thus may be the means by which Dorotheos comes into contact with Basil, whose *Rules* are one of the most prominent authors in the Zosimian works." Zosimas's *Alloquia* is available in Zosimas, *ΤΟΥ ΟΣΙΟΥ ΠΑΤΡΟΣ ΗΜΩΝ ΑΒΒΑ ΖΩΣΙΜΑ ΚΕΦΑΛΑΙΑ ΠΑΝΥ ΩΦΕΛΙΜΑ* (Jerusalem: Augustinos Monachos Iordanitos, 1913); Zosimas, "Alloquia," in *Νέα Σιών*, ed. Augoustinos Iordanites (1912), 93–100, 697–701, 854–865. An English translation appeared in John Chryssavgis, *In the Heart of the Desert: The Spirituality of the Desert Fathers and Mothers: With a Translation of Abba Zosimas' Reflections* (Bloomington: World Wisdom, Inc., 2008), 123–150.

56. Derwas J. Chitty, "Abba Isaiah," *Journal of Theological Studies* 22, no. 1 (April 1971): 59–60.

57. Barsanuphius and John, *Letters*, 293, Letter 311; ibid., vol. 1, 192, Letter 185; 245–247, Letter 240; 256–257, Letter 252; vol. 2, 120–121, Letter 528

58. Derwas Chitty, surveying the most relevant manuscripts and translations of Isaiah's work, illustrated the need for a critical edition of Isaiah's *Asceticon* (p. 52). See Chitty, "Abba Isaiah," 47–72. For an English translation and Greek and Syriac texts, see Isaiah of Scetis, *Abba Isaiah of Scetis: Ascetic Discourses*, trans. John Chryssavgis and Pachomios Penkett (Kalamazoo: Cistercian Publications, 2002); Isaiah of Scetis, *ΤΟΥ ΟΣΙΟΥ ΠΑΤΡΟΣ ΗΜΩΝ ΑΒΒΑ ΗΣΑΙΟΥ ΛΟΓΟΙ ΚΘ* (Jerusalem: Augoustinos Hilarion Monachoi, 1911); Isaiah of Scetis, *Tou hosiou patros hēmōn abba Esaiou logoi XXIX*, 2nd ed. (Volos: Typographeion tēs Hagioreitikēs Bibliothēkēs, 1962); Isaiah of Scetis, *Les cinq recensions de l'Ascéticon syriaque d'abba Isaïe*, vol. 289–290, 293–294, Corpus scriptorium christianorum orientalium (Louvain: Secrétariat du Corpus scriptorum Christianorum Orientalium, 1968).

59. Barsanuphius and John, *Letters*, 256–309, Letters 252–338.

60. Derwas J. Chitty, *The Desert a City: An Introduction to the Study of Egyptian and Palestinian Monasticism Under the Christian Empire* (Oxford: Blackwell, 1999), 140.

61. Hevelone-Harper mentioned, "The letters, which number more than 850, were compiled by a sixth-century monk who belonged to the monastic community at Tawatha. This compiler selected and grouped letters by recipient, adding summaries of each petitioner's ques-

tion. Through this contextualizing, the compiler certainly exercised some editorial shaping of the collection we have inherited." Hevelone-Harper, *Disciples of the Desert*, 7.

62. For the critical editions, see Barsanuphius and John, *Correspondance*, trans. François Neyt, eds. Paula de Angelis-Noah, and Lucien Regnault, vol. 426 (Paris: Éditions du Cerf, 1997); ———, *Correspondance*, trans. François Neyt, eds. Paula de Angelis-Noah, and Lucien Regnault, vol. 427 (Paris: Éditions du Cerf, 1998); ———, *Correspondance*, trans. François Neyt, eds. Paula de Angelis-Noah, and Lucien Regnault, vol. 450 (Paris: Éditions du Cerf, 2000); ———, *Correspondance*, trans. François Neyt, eds. Paula de Angelis-Noah, and Lucien Regnault, vol. 451 (Paris: Éditions du Cerf, 2001); ———, *Correspondance*, trans. François Neyt, eds. Paula de Angelis-Noah, and Lucien Regnault, vol. 468 (Paris: Éditions du Cerf, 2002). For the English translation, see Barsanuphius and John, *Letters*, trans. John Chryssavgis, 2 vols., Fathers of the Church (Washington, D.C.: Catholic University of America Press, 2006–2007).

63. The most important work on the use of scripture by the Egyptian monastics is Douglas Burton-Christie, *The Word in the Desert: Scripture and the Quest for Holiness in Early Christian Monasticism* (New York: Oxford University Press, 1993).

64. Perrone, "Scripture for a Life of Perfection," 401.

65. Ibid., 416. Interestingly, Dorotheos's own disciple Dositheos claimed to have never heard the Word of God before entering the monastery. Perrone interprets his interaction with scripture in the monastery. Ibid., 400–413.

66. Ibid., 413.

67. John Chryssavgis, "From Egypt to Palestine: Discerning a Thread of Spiritual Direction," in *Abba: The Tradition of Orthodoxy in the West. Festschrift for Bishop Kallistos (Ware) of Diokleia*, ed. John Behr, Andrew Louth, and Dimitri Conomos (Crestwood, NY: St. Vladimir's Seminary Press, 2003), 300.

68. Ibid.

69. Ibid., 300–301.

70. Jean-Claude Guy, "Educational Innovation in the Desert Fathers," *Eastern Churches Review* 6 (1974): 44.

71. Perrone, "Scripture for a Life of Perfection," 415.

Chapter 2: Monasticism in Gaza

1. François Neyt, "La formation au monastère de l'abbé Séridos à Gaza," in *Christian Gaza in Late Antiquity*, ed. Bruria Bitton-Ashkelony and Aryeh Kofsky (Boston: Brill, 2004), 153. "The region of Gaza, from Tawatha to Maiumas along the sea, became a cultural and spiritual crossroads where seekers of God came from the North and South, often attracted by the holy sites in Jerusalem."

2. The spiritual traditions of these two monastic centers has most recently been studied in Lorenzo Perrone, "Byzantine Monasticism in Gaza and in the Judaean Desert: A Comparion of their Spiritual Traditions," *Proche-Orient Chrétien* 62 (2012). As late as 2006, Lorenzo Perrone argued that "Holy Land monasticism, despite the noteworthy amount of relevant available sources—both literary and archaeological—has not yet attracted the

attention it deserves, at least not as far as the topic of this presentation [scripture in the monastic life] is concerned." Perrone, "Scripture for a Life of Perfection," 394.

3. Recent studies of Judean monasticism include: Joseph Patrich, ed., *The Sabaite Heritage in the Orthodox Church from the Fifth Century to the Present* (Leuven: Peeters, 2001); Kathleen Hay, "Impact of St. Sabas: The Legacy of Palestinian Monasticism," in *The Sixth Century, End or Beginning?*, ed. Pauline Allen and Elizabeth Jeffreys (Brisbane: Australian Association for Byzantine Studies, 1996); Joseph Patrich, *Sabas, Leader of Palestinian Monasticism: A Comparative Study in Eastern Monasticism, Fourth to Seventh Centuries* (Washington: Dumbarton Oaks Research Library and Collection, 1995); John Binns, *Ascetics and Ambassadors of Christ: The Monasteries of Palestine, 314–631* (Oxford: Clarendon Press, 1994); Bernard Flusin, *Miracle et histoire dans l'œuvre de Cyrille de Scythopolis* (Paris: Études Augustiniennes, 1983).

4. Derwas Chitty's research illuminated the historical circumstances surrounding Palestinian monasticism. He also provided early edited and translated portions of Barsanuphius and John's *Correspondence*. See Chitty, *The Desert a City*; Derwas J. Chitty, *Barsanuphius and John: Questions and Answers*, trans. Derwas J. Chitty, vol. 31/3, Patrologia Orientalis (Paris: Firmin-Didot et C Éditeurs, 1966). For the impact of Peter the Iberian see Cornelia B Horn, *Asceticism and Christological Controversy in Fifth-century Palestine: The Career of Peter the Iberian* (Oxford: Oxford University Press, 2006). On later monastic communities in Gaza, including Barsanuphius and John, see Parrinello, *Comunità monastiche a Gaza*; Jennifer Hevelone-Harper, "Ecclesiastics and Ascetics: Finding Spiritual Authority in Fifth- and Sixth-Century Palestine," *Hugoye: Journal of Syriac Studies* 9, no. 1 (January 2006); Bitton-Ashkelony and Kofsky, *The Monastic School of Gaza*; Jennifer Hevelone-Harper, "Anchorite and Abbot: Cooperative Spiritual Authority in Late Antique Gaza," *Studia Patristica* 39 (2006); John Chryssavgis, "Barsanuphius and John: The Identity and Integrity of the Old Men of Gaza," ibid.; Hevelone-Harper, *Disciples of the Desert*; Daniël Hombergen, "Barsanuphius and John of Gaza and the Origenist Controversy," in *Christian Gaza in Late Antiquity*, ed. Bruria Bitton-Ashkelony and Aryeh Kofsky (Boston: Brill, 2004); Aryeh Kofsky, "The Byzantine Holy Person: The Case of Barsanuphius and John of Gaza," in *Saints and Role Models in Judaism and Christianity*, ed. Marcel Poorthuis and Joshua Schwartz (Boston: Brill, 2004); Lorenzo Perrone, "The Necessity of Advice: Spiritual Direction as a School of Christianity in the Correspondence of Barsanuphius and John of Gaza," in *Christian Gaza in Late Antiquity*, ed. Bruria Bitton-Ashkelony and Aryeh Kofsky (Boston: Brill, 2004); Leah Di Segni, "Monk and Society: The Case of Palestine," in *The Sabaite Heritage in the Orthodox Church from the Fifth Century to the Present*, ed. Joseph Patrich, Orientalia Lovaniensia Anelecta (Leuven: Uitgeverij Peeters in Departement Oosterse Studies, 2001); Jennifer Hevelone-Harper, "Letters to the Great Old Man: Monks, Laity, and Spiritual Authority in Sixth Century Gaza" (phD diss., Princeton University, 2000).

5. Lorenzo Perrone, "Monasticism in Gaza: A Chapter in the History of Byzantine Palestine," in *Zwischen Polis, Provinz und Peripherie: Beiträge zu byzantinischen Geschichte und Kultur*, ed. Lars M. Hoffmann and Anuscha Monchizadeh (Wiesbaden: Harrassowitz Verlag, 2005), 59. For a critical overview of monasticism in Gaza, see Bitton-Ashkelony and Kofsky, *The Monastic School of Gaza*, 6–48.

6. Chitty, *The Desert a City*, 179.

7. John Chryssavgis, *Soul Mending: The Art of Spiritual Direction* (Brookline, Mass.: Holy Cross Orthodox Press, 2000), 91.

8. Samuel Rubenson, "The Egyptian Relations of Early Palestinian Monasticism," in *The Christian Heritage in the Holy Land*, ed. Anthony O'Mahony, Göran Gunner, and Kevork Hintlian (London: Scorpion Cavendish Ltd., 1995), 41.

9. Ibid.

10. Chryssavgis, "From Egypt to Palestine," 307.

11. Bitton-Ashkelony and Kofsky, *The Monastic School of Gaza*, 3.

12. Rubenson, "The Egyptian Relations of Early Palestinian Monasticism," 43. The argument for compilation and editing of the Apophthegmata Patrum appeared in Lucien Regnault, "Les apophtegemes des pères en Palestine aux Ve–VIe siécles," *Irénikon* 54 (1981): 320–330. Regnault noted several distinguishing features from Gazan monastic literature that indicate Gaza as the locus of compilation.

13. Rubenson, "The Egyptian Relations of Early Palestinian Monasticism," 41.

14. Perrone, "Monasticism in Gaza: A Chapter in the History of Byzantine Palestine," 68.

15. Ibid.

16. Columba Stewart, "Evagrius Ponticus on Monastic Pedagogy," in *Abba: The Tradition of Orthodoxy in the West. Festschrift for Bishop Kallistos (Ware) of Diokleia*, ed. John Behr, Andrew Louth, and Dimitri Conomos (Crestwood, NY: St. Vladimir's Seminary Press, 2003), 269.

17. John Chryssavgis, "From Egypt to Palestine: Discerning a Thread of Spiritual Direction," ibid., 310–311.

18. Ibid., 315.

19. Ibid.

20. Burton-Christie, *The Word in the Desert*, 299.

21. Chryssavgis, "From Egypt to Palestine," 300–301.

22. Quoted in Brown, *The Body and Society*, 233. See, Lucien Regnault, *Barsanuphe et Jean de Gaza, Correspondance* (Sable-sur-Sarthe: Abbaye Saint-Pierre de Solesmes, 1972), 6. "Ce que les Apophtegmes des Pères nous laissaient seulement entrevoir en quelques leurs fugitives, en de rares instantanés, se déroule ici sous nos yeux comme un film…"

23. Michael Avi-Yonah, *The Madaba Mosaic Map: With Introduction and Commentary* (Jerusalem: Israel Exploration Society, 1954).

24. Ibid., Plate 9.

25. Yizhar Hirschfeld, "The Monasteries of Gaza: An Archaeological Review," in *Christian Gaza in Late Antiquity*, ed. Bruria Bitton-Ashkelony and Aryeh Kofsky (Boston: Brill, 2004), 66.

26. Hirschfeld's archaeological and geographic survey includes illustrations and numerous photographs of Gazan monastic locations. Ibid., 61. See also, Yizhar Hirschfeld, "The Monasteries of Palestine in the Byzantine Period," in *Christians and Christianity in the Holy Land: From the Origins to the Latin Kingdoms*, ed. Ora Limor and Guy G. Stroumsa (Turnhout: Brepols, 2006), 401–419. Hirschfeld provided a summary of the monastic remains at Deir e-Nuserat: "The excavation [at Deir e-Nuserat] uncovered remains of a large and splendid coenobium. Within the walls of the monastery was a courtyard surrounded by

halls and numerous rooms. Among them may be identified a church with a crypt below, a bathhouse, and a hospice. The church had a polychrome mosaic pavement, and the original limestone facing was preserved on its walls." Hirschfeld, "The Monasteries of Gaza: An Archaeological Review," 76–77.

27. Hirschfeld, "The Monasteries of Gaza," 61. See also, Yizhar Hirschfeld, *The Judean Desert Monasteries in the Byzantine Period* (New Haven: Yale University Press, 1992).

28. Hirschfeld, "The Monasteries of Gaza," 77.

29. Ibid. Hirschfeld listed the following villages: Bethelea, Thabatha, Beth Dallatha, and Kefar Shearta.

30. Ibid.

31. Hevelone-Harper, *Disciples of the Desert*, 6.

32. John Chryssavgis and Pachomios Penkett, *Abba Isaiah of Scetis: Ascetic Discourses*, trans. John Chryssavgis and Pachomios Penkett (Kalamazoo: Cistercian Publications, 2002), 15.

33. Perrone, "Monasticism in Gaza: A Chapter in the History of Byzantine Palestine," 67–68.

34. Hirschfeld, "The Monasteries of Gaza," 75.

35. Chryssavgis, "Barsanuphius and John," 307.

36. Chryssavgis and Penkett, *Ascetic Discourses*, 19. See John Rufus, *John Rufus: The Lives of Peter the Iberian, Theodosius of Jerusalem, and the Monk Romanus*, trans. Cornelia B. Horn and Robert R. Phenix (Atlanta: Society of Biblical Literature, 2008), xci, 243–245.

37. Zachariah the Rhetor, "Vita Isaiae monachi," in *Vitae virorum apud Monphysitas celeberrimorum*, Corpus scriptorum Christianorum Orientalium (Louvain: L. Durbecq, 1955), 2–16.

38. John Rufus, *The Lives*, 243–247.

39. John Chryssavgis, "Abba Isaiah of Scetis: Aspects of Spiritual Direction," *Studia Patristica* 35 (2001): 30.

40. Horn, *Asceticism and Christological Controversy*, 155.

41. Ibid.

42. Chryssavgis and Penkett, *Ascetic Discourses*, 24.

43. Chryssavgis, "Abba Isaiah of Scetis," 32.

44. Ibid.

45. Rubenson, "The Egyptian Relations of Early Palestinian Monasticism," 44.

46. Ibid.

47. Chryssavgis and Penkett, *Ascetic Discourses*, 23.

48. Ibid., 24.

49. Chryssavgis, "From Egypt to Palestine," 307.

50. Eric P. Wheeler, *Discourses and Sayings*, trans. Eric P. Wheeler (Kalamazoo: Cistercian Publications, 1977), 30.

51. Hirschfeld, "The Monasteries of Gaza," 76. See also, Chitty, *The Desert a City*, 132–140.

52. Hirschfeld, "The Monasteries of Gaza," 76.

53. Ibid.

54. Hirschfeld, *The Judean Desert Monasteries*, 24–26, 36–38.

55. Hevelone-Harper, *Disciples of the Desert*, 36.

56. Ibid., 35. Chryssavgis also noted that "the monastery in Thavatha assumed the form of a loose community with many cells, where monks enjoyed varying degrees of enclosure. It

rapidly became known for its far-reaching activities, including workshops (*Letters* 553–554), two guest-houses (*Letters* 570, 595–596), a hospital (*Letters* 327, 548), and a large church (*Letter* 55)." Chryssavgis, "Barsanuphius and John," 308.

57. Bitton-Ashkelony and Kofsky, *The Monastic School of Gaza*, 183. Bitton-Ashkelony and Kofsky indicated that "The 'library' of the monastic communities of Gaza was likely to include a major portion of the classics as well as the 'best-sellers' of the monastic literature of the age, such as the Pachomian writings, Basil's ascetic works, certain works of Evagrius, and the *apophthegmata*. Yet the general picture of these communities that emerges does not conform to any specific and coherent monastic tradition."

58. Evagrius Scholasticus remarked that Barsanuphius was an Egyptian who then resided near Gaza in contemplation. Evagrius Scholasticus, *The Ecclesiastical History of Evagrius Scholasticus*, trans. Michael Whitby (Liverpool: Liverpool University Press, 2000), 333, Book 4.33.

59. Chryssavgis, "Barsanuphius and John," 308.

60. François Neyt, "A Form of Charismatic Authority," *Eastern Churches Review* 6 (1974): 61.

61. Ibid., 62.

62. Hevelone-Harper, "Anchorite and Abbot," 383.

63. Hirschfeld, *The Judean Desert Monasteries*, 24–26, 36–38.

64. Hevelone-Harper, *Disciples of the Desert*, 17.

65. Ibid.

66. Ibid.

67. François Neyt and Paula de Angelis-Noah, "Introduction," in *Correspondance* (Paris: Éditions du Cerf, 1997), 20.

68. Parrinello, *Comunità monastiche a Gaza*, 72. "[I]t seems to me that there are a considerable number of points of contact between Basil and the *Letters* of John and Barsanuphius, while much smaller are the points of convergence with the Pachomian regulations: Basilian directives, moreover, seem to fit much more to a type of monasticism embodied by Barsanuphius and John, who could hardly express themselves in a far more rigid Pachomian community."

69. Di Segni clarified the following, "Many of the lay correspondents appear by the context to have been city dwellers, and in only two cases are the questions related to country life…. Several epistles were sent collectively to the citizens of Gaza, and some to the city bishop, advising them how to act vis-à-vis the authorities—the emperor, the *dux Palaestinae*, imperial officers, the metropolitan—so that the city should not suffer." Di Segni, "The Monk and Society," 33.

70. Hevelone-Harper, *Disciples of the Desert*, 4.

71. Di Segni, "The Monk and Society," 31. Di Segni's essay is in response to the influential article Peter Brown, "The Rise and Function of the Holy Man in Late Antiquity," *Journal of Roman Studies* 61 (1971).

72. Di Segni, "The Monk and Society," 32–33.

73. Barsanuphius and John, *Letters*, 227, Letter 224. John told Dorotheos, "If all of us are one–both the [Great] Old Man in God and I with the Old Man–then I dare to say that, if he gave you his word [to pray for you], I, too, give mine through him." Ibid., 290, Letter 305.

74. Barsanuphius and John, *Letters*, trans. John Chryssavgis, Fathers of the Church (Washington, D.C.: Catholic University of America Press, 2007), 152–154, Letters 571–572.

75. Barsanuphius and John, *Letters*, 32, Letter 13.

76. Hevelone-Harper, *Disciples of the Desert*, 19.
77. Ibid., 21.
78. Perrone, "The Necessity of Advice," 133–134.
79. Hevelone-Harper, *Disciples of the Desert*, 19.
80. Perrone, "Monasticism in Gaza: A Chapter in the History of Byzantine Palestine," 71.
81. Chryssavgis, "From Egypt to Palestine," 307.
82. Ibid., 302.
83. Perrone, "The Necessity of Advice," 148.
84. Ibid., 131–132. Perrone continued to explain, "There is enough evidence to support the claim that we have here a 'school-situation,' one in which Barsanuphius and (to a lesser extent) John the Prophet are dealing with pupils or disciples and engaging them in a lengthy and demanding program. Within this 'educational' framework, the message the letters are intended to convey to their addressees can be summarized as follows: their essential goal is to ensure salvation, which usually means to walk properly on the path leading to perfection. Such a path has to be learned from those who have already gone along it and have, to a greater or lesser extent, achieved the sought-after condition" (ibid., 133).
85. Ibid., 135.
86. John Moschos, *The Spiritual Meadow*, trans. John Wortley (Kalamazoo, Mich: Cistercian Publications, 1992), 136, Chapter 166.
87. Dorotheos of Gaza, *Abba Dorotheos*, 65, Discourse 1; Dorotheos of Gaza, Œuvres spirituelles, 146, Discourse 1.
88. Hirschfeld, "The Monasteries of Gaza," 77.
89. Dorotheos of Gaza, *Abba Dorotheos*, 55, Life of Dositheos.
90. Hevelone-Harper, *Disciples of the Desert*, 62. Antioch was mentioned in the anonymous Vita S. Barsanorii (Life of Barsanuphius). "At ille, ordinatis quae agenda instabant, quendam Antiochensam virum, nomine Dorotheum, prudentem atque providum..." "Incipit vita sancti Barsanorii abbatis," in *Catalogus codicum hagiographicorum latinorum antiquiorum saeculo XVI qui asservantur in Bibiotheca nationali parisiensi, ediderunt hagiographi Bollandiani* (Bruxellis: Apud Editores, 1889), 530. Dorotheos was also described in Godefrido Henschennio and Daniele Papebrochio, ed., *Acta Sanctorum*, vol. April, Tome 2 (Paris: Victorem Palmé, 1866), 22–27.
91. Hevelone-Harper, *Disciples of the Desert*, 64, n.12.
92. Dorotheos of Gaza, *Abba Dorotheos*, 55, Life of Dositheos 1. For comparative charts of manuscript contents see Pauli, *Menschsein und Menschwerden*, 26–36.
93. Pauli, *Menschsein und Menschwerden*, 8.
94. On Dorotheus' relationship with Barsanuphius and John, see Neyt, "A Form of Charismatic Authority," 52–65.
95. Dorotheos of Gaza, *Abba Dorotheos*, 55, Life of Dositheos; Dorotheos of Gaza, Œuvres spirituelles, 122, Life of Dositheos. For early Christian approaches to healing, see Giovanni Battista Bazzana, "Early Christian Missionaries as Physicians: Healing and its Cultural Value in the Greco-Roman Context," *Novum Testamentum* 51 (2009): 232–251. For two recent studies of hospitals in Byzantine monastic contexts, see Timothy S. Miller, *The Birth of the Hospital in the Byzantine Empire* (Baltimore: Johns Hopkins University Press, 1997), 118–140; Andrew T. Crislip, *From Monastery to Hospital: Christian Monasticism & the*

Transformation of Health Care in Late Antiquity (Ann Arbor: University of Michigan Press, 2005), 100–142.

96. Hevelone-Harper, *Disciples of the Desert*, 65.

97. Dorotheos of Gaza, *Abba Dorotheos*, 184, Discourse 11.

98. Hevelone-Harper, *Disciples of the Desert*, 68.

99. Ibid., 61.

100. Perrone, "Monasticism in Gaza: A Chapter in the History of Byzantine Palestine," 72.

101. Parrinello, *Comunità monastiche a Gaza*, 215–216. Zosimas "could therefore be the means through which Dorotheos came into contact with Basil, one of the most widely present authors in the Zosimas's own work with the Rule."

102. Pauli, *Menschsein und Menschwerden*, 53. Dorotheos "reflects a greater theological of the ascetical conception of the Cappadocians."

103. Ibid., 54. "The analogy between medicine and soul healing, i.e. between physical illness to the understanding of the passions as a mental illness, is found both in the Stoic and Hellenistic moral philosophy and also in Basil."

104. Ibid., 56. "Dorotheos often resorts back to the knowledge of ancient medicine to illustrate spiritual relationships. He follows the concept of medicine of Hippocrates (humoral), that health and disease are understood as harmony or disturbance of the equilibrium of the four humors. The idea of the passions as a disease of the soul puts this approach in close proximity in any case, but Dorotheos's comparisons demonstrate that it is not an effectively used stylistic device: From them the author speaks of his own knowledge and practical experience."

105. Bitton-Ashkelony and Kofsky, *The Monastic School of Gaza*, 223.

106. See, Hevelone-Harper, *Disciples of the Desert*, 61–78. Hevelone-Harper provided a thorough analysis of Dorotheos's position and work in Seridos's coenobium. Her study of Letters 262–338 is invaluable for establishing the context and interpretation of Dorotheos's work in the infirmary.

107. Ibid., 62.

108. Ibid., 64, n.12.

109. Dorotheos of Gaza, *Abba Dorotheos*, 49, Introductory Letter.

110. Ibid., 50, Introductory Letter 6; Dorotheos of Gaza, Œuvres spirituelles, 118, Introductory Letter 6.

111. Pauli, *Menschsein und Menschwerden*, 8.

112. Barsanuphius and John, *Letters*, 287, Letter 295; see also 286, Letters 293–394.

113. Dorotheos of Gaza, *Abba Dorotheos*, 55, Life of Dositheos; Dorotheos of Gaza, Œuvres spirituelles, 122, Life of Dositheos.

114. Dorotheos of Gaza, *Abba Dorotheos*, 56, Life of Dositheos. Seridos was wary of admitting Dositheos because he feared he might be in the service of an official or had stolen something and wanted to escape. Plus, "Neither his stance nor his appearance are that of someone who wants to become a monk." Ibid., 55–56, Life of Dositheos.

115. Ibid., 55, Life of Dositheos (§2); 60, Life of Dositheos (§9).

116. Ibid., 117, Discourse 4.

117. Neyt, "A Form of Charismatic Authority," 60.

118. Barsanuphius and John, *Letters*, 308, Letter 336; Barsanuphius and John, *Correspondance*, trans. Lucien Regnault, vol. 450 (Paris: Éditions du Cerf, 2000), 342, Letter 336.

119. Barsanuphius and John, *Letters*, 294–295, Letter 313.

120. Ibid., 302, Letter 328; Barsanuphius and John, *Correspondance*, 328, Letter 328.

121. Dorotheos of Gaza, *Abba Dorotheos*, 60, Life of Dositheos.

122. Ibid., 61, Life of Dositheos.

123. Barsanuphius and John, *Letters*, 302, Letter 327; Barsanuphius and John, *Correspondance*, 326, Letter 327.

124. Miller, *The Birth of the Hospital*, 63.

125. Barsanuphius and John, *Letters*, 302, Letter 327; Barsanuphius and John, *Correspondance*, 326, Letter 327.

126. Barsanuphius and John, *Letters*, 302, Letter 327; Barsanuphius and John, *Correspondance*, 326, Letter 327.

127. Dorotheos certainly accessed and utilized "medical books" as noted in the Old Men's correspondence. However, no indication was given as the exact texts he used. This work is narrowly focused on the comparison of Dorotheos with his contemporaries within the context of his discourse of healing. It is enough to establish that Dorotheos was familiar with ancient medical texts even if one cannot determine which texts those were. According to Miller, "many Byzantine medical texts are either unpublished or available in uncritical editions. Moreover, the manuscript traditions of these texts are so complicated and contain so many different rescensions that historians and philologists have been unable to date most of them or to determine their authors." Miller, *The Birth of the Hospital*, 167. Of the surviving medical treatises available, Oribasius of Pergamon and Aetios of Amida may provide parallels to the medical treatments mentioned by Dorotheos and prove a fruitful avenue of research for further study into a strictly medicinal analysis of Dorotheos's spiritual teaching.

128. Barsanuphius and John, *Letters*, 307, Letter 334.

129. Ibid., 295–296, Letter 315.

130. Ibid., 296, Letter 315.

131. Ibid., 304–305, Letter 330.

132. Perrone, "Monasticism in Gaza: A Chapter in the History of Byzantine Palestine," 72.

133. Ibid.

134. Regnault, "Théologie de la vie monastique selon Barsanuphe et Dorothée," 316. Dorotheos was "remaining very close to reality, concrete and practical as Barsanuphius, Dorotheos seems to have had some concerns to identify details of tradition and experience, essential elements that sketch the main lines of Christian and monastic spirituality."

135. Bitton-Ashkelony and Kofsky, *The Monastic School of Gaza*, 45.

136. Ibid.

137. Samuel Rubenson, "'As Already Translated to the Kingdom While Still in the Body' The Transformation of the Ascetic in Early Egyptian Monasticism," in *Metamorphoses: Resurrection, Body, and Transformative Practices in early Christianity*, ed. Turid Karlsen Seim and Jorunn Økland (New York: W. de Gruyter, 2009), 271.

138. Ibid., 272.

Chapter 3: The Discourse of Healing and Gazan Monasticism

1. Gary B. Ferngren and Darrel W. Amundsen, "Virtue and Health/Medicine in Pre-Christian Antiquity," in *Virtue and Medicine: Explorations in the Character of Medicine*, ed. Earl E. Shelp (Boston: D. Reidel Publishing Company, 1985), 6.

2. Galen, *Selected Works*, trans. P. N. Singer (New York: Oxford University Press, 1997), 347, The Art of Medicine 2.

3. Ibid., 349, The Art of Medicine 4.

4. Guenter B. Risse, *Mending Bodies, Saving Souls: A History of Hospitals* (New York: Oxford University Press, 1999), 77.

5. "Physicians in the classical world emphasized individual treatment. The treatment of disease usually took the form of a holistic approach that involved the use of regimen, pharmacology, and surgery. Preventative medicine was regarded as the best way to maintain health. This was accomplished by means of a detailed classification of food and drink based on the properties of each, whether strong, weak, dry, moist, cool, hot, constricting, or laxative. Sleep, sexual activity, and exertion were also regulated. Treatment was adjusted to the individual, and a physician was expected to know his patients well so that he would be able to adjust their treatment in order to maintain a balance of the constituent elements of the human body." Gary B. Ferngren, *Medicine and Health Care in Early Christianity* (Baltimore: Johns Hopkins University Press, 2009), 20.

6. Ibid., 15.

7. Hippocrates, *Hippocrates*, trans. W. H. S. Jones, vol. 2, The Loeb Classical Library (Cambridge, MA: Harvard University Press, 1959), 139, The Sacred Disease 1.1.

8. Ibid., 141, The Sacred Disease 1.2.

9. Galen, *Selected Works*, 33, The best Doctor is also a Philosopher 3.

10. Ibid.

11. Ibid., 374, The Art of Medicine 23.

12. Ibid., 33, The best Doctor is also a Philosopher 3.

13. Ibid., 34, The best Doctor is also a Philosopher 4.

14. Ferngren, *Medicine and Health Care in Early Christianity*, 29. See, Plato, *The Republic of Plato*, trans. Allan Bloom (United States of America: Basic Books, 1991), 123, 443 D–E.

15. Ludwig Edelstein, "The Relation of Ancient Philosophy to Medicine," in *Ancient Medicine: Selected Papers of Ludwig Edelstein*, ed. Owsei Temkin and Lilian C. Temkin (Baltimore: The Johns Hopkins Press, 1967), 366.

16. Ferngren, *Medicine and Health Care in Early Christianity*, 29.

17. Ferngren and Amundsen, "Virtue and Health/Medicine in Pre-Christian Antiquity," 3.

18. Ibid., 5.

19. Plato, *The Republic of Plato*, 105, 427e. Ferngren and Amundsen summarize Plato's approach to virtue and the tripartite soul: "In the Platonic scheme the soul is composed of three parts. The first is the intellect, which gives to man the power to think and deliberate. The second is the will or the spirited part of the personality. The third is the appetite, which has a natural desire for physical satisfaction. Corresponding to these elements of the tri-partite soul are the appropriate virtues: wisdom, which is appropriate to the intellect;

courage, which is appropriate to the will; and temperance, which is appropriate to the appetite. The fourth of the virtues, justice, is not related to one of the parts of the soul. Rather it is conceived as the virtue that regulates the others. Justice in the soul results from each part of the soul fulfilling its proper function. Virtue arises from a harmony of the constituent parts of the soul, which are organized for the best performance of living. Since for Plato virtue is one, all four of the virtues overlap and it is impossible to have one virtue without having them all. An individual whose soul is well ordered will be wise, since his reason will be in command; brave, as his will enables him to carry out what reason prescribes; and temperate, as his appetites are kept under control by his reason." Ferngren and Amundsen, "Virtue and Health/Medicine in Pre-Christian Antiquity," 10. Also, they noted, "Plato's concept of virtue includes both the virtues of the body and the soul, and hence he makes the virtues of the body (Health, beauty, and strength) parallel to the virtues of the soul." Ibid., 11.

20. Later in Republic, the character Socrates stated, "To produce health is to establish the parts of the body in a relation of mastering, and being mastered by, one another that is according to nature, while to produce sickness is to establish a relation of ruling and being ruled by, one another that is contrary to nature... Virtue, then, as it seems, would be a certain health, beauty and good condition of a soul, and vice a sickness, ugliness and weakness." Plato, *The Republic of Plato*, 124, 444d–e.

21. Galen, *Galen: Method of Medicine*, trans. Ian Johnston and G. H. R. Horsley, vol. 1, Loeb Classical Library (Cambridge, M.A.: Harvard University Press, 2011), 65–67, 1.5. The notion of health and the able-bodied in ancient Greece raises some interpretive questions as seen in the collection of essays in Helen King, ed., *Health in Antiquity* (New York: Routledge, 2005). Foremost is the role of blindness in the poet: does blindness contribute to the *ars poetica*? This question is pursued in Nicholas Vlahogiannis, "'Curing' disability," in *Health in Antiquity*, ed. Helen King (New York: Routledge, 2005), 180–191.

22. Galen, *Galen: Method of Medicine*, 67, 1.5.

23. Ferngren and Amundsen, "Virtue and Health/Medicine in Pre-Christian Antiquity," 10.

24. Ibid.

25. Ibid., 15.

26. Ibid.

27. Ibid., 16–17.

28. Ibid., 17.

29. Ibid.

30. Ibid.

31. Darrel W. Amundsen and Gary B. Ferngren, "Virtue and Medicine from Early Christianity Through the Sixteenth Century," ibid., 19.

32. Stephen D'Irsay, "Patristic Medicine," *Annals of Medical History* 9 (1928): 364.

33. Ferngren and Amundsen, "Virtue and Health/Medicine in Pre-Christian Antiquity," 12.

34. Ibid., 20.

35. Ibid., 34.

36. Darrel W. Amundsen and Gary B. Ferngren, "Virtue and Medicine from Early Christianity Through the Sixteenth Century," ibid., 23–62.

37. Adolf Harnack, *The Mission and Expansion of Christianity in the First Three Centuries*, trans. James Moffatt, vol. 1 (New York: G. P. Putnam's Sons, 1908), 120.

38. Adolf Harnack, *Medicinisches aus der ältesten Kirchengeschichte* (Leipzig: J. C. Hinrichs'sche Buchhandlung, 1892), 89. "The Gospel itself has come as the message of the Savior and the healing of the world. It is aimed at sick humanity and promises its health."

39. Meredith, "Illness and Healing in the Early Christian East," 33.

40. Ibid., 153.

41. Ibid.

42. Ferngren and Amundsen, "Virtue and Health/Medicine in Pre-Christian Antiquity," 7.

43. Porterfield, *Healing in the History of Christianity*, 4. Meredith, too, signaled the power inherent in the ability of religion to provide an etiology for disease. "The process of providing an etiological explanation for disease is not neutral. This claim to be able to interpret the afflicted bodies of the ill was an enormously powerful form of social control." Meredith, "Illness and Healing in the Early Christian East," 60.

44. "By making available a wide variety of medical analogues, Hippocratic medicine became a vital part of Christian theological exegesis and pastoral practice....At the head of spiritual medicine stood Christ, the physician of the soul. As a physician, Christ added luster to the medical profession, without however entering into the substance of the science and the art of Hippocratic medicine." Owsei Temkin, *Hippocrates in a World of Pagans and Christians* (Baltimore: The Johns Hopkins University Press, 1991), 177.

45. Meredith, "Illness and Healing in the Early Christian East," 44–45.

46. Ibid., 153.

47. Ferngren, *Medicine and Health Care in Early Christianity*, 13.

48. Miller, *The Birth of the Hospital*, 29.

49. Teresa M Shaw, *The Burden of the Flesh: Fasting and Sexuality in Early Christianity* (Minneapolis, MN: Fortress Press, 1998), 27.

50. Darrel W. Amundsen, "Medicine and Faith in Early Christianity," in *Medicine, Society, and Faith in the Ancient and Medieval Worlds* (Baltimore: The Johns Hopkins University Press, 1996), 127.

51. Hippocrates, *Hippocrates*, 227.

52. Eusebius of Caesarea, *The History of the Church from Christ to Constantine*, trans. G. A. Williamson (New York: New York University Press, 1966), 386, 10.4.11–12; Origen of Alexandria, *Contra Celsum*, trans. Henry Chadwick (New York: Cambridge University Press, 1980), 193, 4.15.

53. Origen of Alexandria, *Contra Celsum*, 498, 8.60.

54. Gregory of Nyssa, *Saint Gregory of Nyssa: Ascetical Works*, trans. Virginia Woods Callahan, The Fathers of the Church (Washington D.C.: The Catholic Universtiy Press, 1967), 199, On the Soul and the Resurrection 1.1.

55. Ibid., 185, Life of Macrina.

56. Gregory Nazianzen, *Funeral Orations*, trans. Leo P. McCauleyibid. (New York: Fathers of the Church, Inc., 1953), 47, On St. Basil the Great 23. Vivian Nutton depicted Basil's position, "It is not that Christianity is necessarily opposed to secular healing; but it presupposes an alternative medicine on which true Christians may be expected to rely...But even those who, like St. Basil, knew and approved of secular medicine, were always careful

to leave room for this peculiarly Christian type of healing." Vivian Nutton, "From Galen to Alexander: Aspects of Medicine and Medical Practice in Late Antiquity," in *Symposium on Byzantine Medicine*, ed. John Scarborough, Dumbarton Oaks Papers (Washington, District of Columbia: Dumbarton Oaks Research Library and Collection, 1984), 5.

57. On Basil's monastic and medical endeavors, see Philip Rousseau, *Basil of Caesarea* (Berkeley: University of California Press, 1994), 139–178, 190–232. Basil's influence in Gaza was discussed above. See also Parrinello, *Communità monastiche a Gaza*.

58. Crislip, *From Monastery to Hospital*, 27.

59. Risse, *Mending Bodies, Saving Souls: A History of Hospitals*, 77.

60. Vivian Nutton, *Ancient Medicine* (New York: Routledge, 2004), 41.

61. Basil of Caesarea, *Saint Basil: Letters (186–368)*, trans. Agnes Clare Way, vol. 2, The Fathers of the Church (New York: Fathers of the Church, Inc., 1955), 25, Letter 189 To Eusthathius the Physician.

62. Meredith, "Illness and Healing in the Early Christian East," 33.

63. Basil of Caesarea, "Homily Explaining that God is not the Cause of Evil," in *On the Human Condition*, Popular Patristics Series (Crestwood, N.Y.: St. Vladimir's Seminary Press, 2005), 73.

64. Ibid.

65. Ibid., 67.

66. Ibid., 68.

67. Ibid., 69.

68. Basil of Caesarea, "Homily 9: On the Hexaemeron," in *Saint Basil: Exegetical Homilies*, The Fathers of the Church (Washington, D.C.: The Catholic University of America Press, 1963), 141.

69. Basil of Caesarea, "Homily 10: A Psalm on the Lot of the Just Man (Psalm 1)," in *Saint Basil: Exegetical Homilies*, The Fathers of the Church (Washington, D.C.: The Catholic University of America Press, 1963), 160.

70. Ibid., 157.

71. Ibid., 152.

72. Basil of Caesarea, *The Asketikon of St. Basil the Great*, trans. Anna M. Silvas (New York: Oxford University Press, 2005), 264. Silvas also noted, "*LR* 55 is Basil's final revision and restatement of his position." Ibid., 264, n.459.

73. Ibid., 265, Longer Response 55.

74. Ibid.

75. Meredith, "Illness and Healing in the Early Christian East," 106.

76. Basil of Caesarea, *The Asketikon of St. Basil the Great*, 265.

77. Ibid., 266, Longer Response 55.

78. Ibid. Italics included in the published text.

79. Ibid., 266, Longer Response 55.

80. Ibid.

81. Ibid., 267–268, Longer Response 55.

82. Ibid., 268, Longer Response 55.

83. Ibid., 268–269, Longer Response 55.

84. Ibid.

85. Temkin, *Hippocrates in a World of Pagans and Christians*, 175.

86. Gillian Clark, "The Health of the Spiritual Athlete," in *Health in Antiquity*, ed. Helen King (New York: Routledge, 2005), 228. Clark connected Christian asceticism with earlier Greek examples, namely Plato: "Plato's comment (Rep. 403e–404a) on the training of guardians, the elite class of warriors and philosophers who rule his ideal state, helped to inspire philosophical and Christian tradition with the metaphor of the spiritual athlete. This athlete's 'greatest contest' is for the integrity of the soul, and he or she must be always in training, *askêsis*, for the fight against the onslaughts of desire. The training is both for soul and body, but it is the training of the body that has pre-empted the name of asceticism." Ibid., 216.

87. Ibid., 229.

88. Susan Ashbrook Harvey, "Physicians and Ascetics in John of Ephesus: An Expedient Alliance," in *Symposium on Byzantine Medicine*, ed. John Scarborough, Dumbarton Oaks Papers (Washington, D.C.: Dumbarton Oaks Research Library and Collection, 1984), 89.

89. Meredith, "Illness and Healing in the Early Christian East," 50.

90. Ferngren, *Medicine and Health Care in Early Christianity*, 151.

91. Miller, *The Birth of the Hospital*, 119. See Basil of Caesarea, *The Asketikon of St. Basil the Great*, 184–185, Longer Response 7.

92. Judith Perkins, *The Suffering Self: Pain and Narrative Representation Inearly Christianity* (London ; New York: Routledge, 1995), 207–208.

93. Crislip, *From Monastery to Hospital*, 8.

94. Ibid.

95. Ibid. For the spread of the hospital in the Byzantine empire, see Miller, *The Birth of the Hospital*.

96. Crislip, *From Monastery to Hospital*, 9.

97. Ibid., 14.

98. Ibid.

99. Ibid., 9.

100. Ibid., 19.

101. Ibid.

102. Ibid., 21.

103. "We should begin by recognizing that nonmedical healing was central to the monastic life, at least in the eyes of many in the ancient world. By *nonmedical* I designate healing techniques that do not attempt to treat perceived internal humoral imbalances, visible wounds, or external environmental conditions through the therapy of a human healer. Rather, nonmedical healing draws exclusively on the perceived aid of a divine or quasi-divine agent; this divine aid could, of course, be invoked through a variety of techniques, none of which held any specific sympathetic or oppositional relationship to perceived humoral imbalance, external wound, or external environmental cause." Ibid.

104. "Dietary therapy was in monasteries, just as outside of monasteries, the first line of defense in the treatment of illness. To a large extent, food was given to the sick simply to comfort and strengthen them, rather than out of a well-formulated medical theory. This treatment is typical of the lay care provided in lavras. In addition to the universally prescribed foods such as gruel, a standard component of Greco-Roman therapy, sick monastics were

often treated to comfort foods, foods to lift the spirits of the infirm. These comfort foods included fresh bread, wine, honey, stewed plums, eggs, and pastries." Ibid., 28. "Next to dietary therapy, hygiene and comfort care were the most common forms of treatment for sick monastics. Much of this care was of a mundane nature: the provisions of various kinds of clothing, pillows and cushions, good blankets, or beds to comfort the sick and infirm. It also involved hygienic care of the sick." Ibid., 30.

105. "Beyond dietary and hygienic therapy, monastic infirmaries treated monastics with *material medica*, or pharmaceuticals." Ibid., 31.

106. Ibid.

107. Ibid., 28.

108. Peregrine Horden, "The Death of Ascetics: Sickness and Monasticism in the early Byzantine Middle East," in *Monks, Hermits and the Ascetic Tradition: Papers Read at the 1984 Summer Meeting and the 1985 Winter Meeting of the Ecclesiastical History Society*, ed. W. J. Sheils (Oxford: Blackwell, 1985), 48–49.

109. Isaiah of Scetis, *Ascetic Discourses*, 88, Discourse 8; Isaiah of Scetis, *ΤΟΥ ΟΣΙΟΥ ΠΑΤΡΟΣ ΗΜΩΝ ΑΒΒΑ ΗΣΑΙΟΥ ΛΟΓΟΙ ΚΘ*, 54, Discourse 8. "[Ε]ἰ μὴ ὁ Κύριος ἡμῶν Ἰησοῦς Χριστὸς ἐθεράπευσε πάντα τὰ πάθη τοῦ ανθρώπου, δι᾽ ὅν ἐπεδήμησεν, οὐκ ἀνῆλθεν ἐπὶ τὸν σταυρόν·"

110. Isaiah of Scetis, *Ascetic Discourses*, 88, Discourse 8; Isaiah of Scetis, *ΤΟΥ ΟΣΙΟΥ ΠΑΤΡΟΣ ΗΜΩΝ ΑΒΒΑ ΗΣΑΙΟΥ ΛΟΓΟΙ ΚΘ*, 54, Discourse 8.

111. Isaiah of Scetis, *Ascetic Discourses*, 88, Discourse 8; Isaiah of Scetis, *ΤΟΥ ΟΣΙΟΥ ΠΑΤΡΟΣ ΗΜΩΝ ΑΒΒΑ ΗΣΑΙΟΥ ΛΟΓΟΙ ΚΘ*, 55, Discourse 8.

112. Chryssavgis and Penkett, *Ascetic Discourses*, 25; Isaiah of Scetis, *ΤΟΥ ΟΣΙΟΥ ΠΑΤΡΟΣ ΗΜΩΝ ΑΒΒΑ ΗΣΑΙΟΥ ΛΟΓΟΙ ΚΘ*, 62, Discourse 8.

113. Isaiah of Scetis, *Ascetic Discourses*, 84, Discourse 7.

114. Ibid., 101–102, Discourse 11.

115. Ibid., 158, Discourse 21; Isaiah of Scetis, *ΤΟΥ ΟΣΙΟΥ ΠΑΤΡΟΣ ΗΜΩΝ ΑΒΒΑ ΗΣΑΙΟΥ ΛΟΓΟΙ ΚΘ*, 129, Discourse 21.

116. Isaiah of Scetis, *Ascetic Discourses*, 45, Discourse 2; Isaiah of Scetis, *ΤΟΥ ΟΣΙΟΥ ΠΑΤΡΟΣ ΗΜΩΝ ΑΒΒΑ ΗΣΑΙΟΥ ΛΟΓΟΙ ΚΘ*, 6, Discourse 2.

117. Isaiah of Scetis, *Ascetic Discourses*, 45, Discourse 2; Isaiah of Scetis, *ΤΟΥ ΟΣΙΟΥ ΠΑΤΡΟΣ ΗΜΩΝ ΑΒΒΑ ΗΣΑΙΟΥ ΛΟΓΟΙ ΚΘ*, 6, Discourse 2.

118. Num. 21:7–9.

119. Isaiah of Scetis, *Ascetic Discourses*, 197, Discourse 25; Isaiah of Scetis, *ΤΟΥ ΟΣΙΟΥ ΠΑΤΡΟΣ ΗΜΩΝ ΑΒΒΑ ΗΣΑΙΟΥ ΛΟΓΟΙ ΚΘ*, 167, Discourse 25.

120. Isaiah of Scetis, *Ascetic Discourses*, 220, Discourse 27.

121. Ibid., 113, Discourse 14; Isaiah of Scetis, *ΤΟΥ ΟΣΙΟΥ ΠΑΤΡΟΣ ΗΜΩΝ ΑΒΒΑ ΗΣΑΙΟΥ ΛΟΓΟΙ ΚΘ*, 81, Discourse 14.

122. Isaiah of Scetis, *Ascetic Discourses*, 113, Discourse 14.

123. Ibid., 206, Discourse 25; Isaiah of Scetis, *ΤΟΥ ΟΣΙΟΥ ΠΑΤΡΟΣ ΗΜΩΝ ΑΒΒΑ ΗΣΑΙΟΥ ΛΟΓΟΙ ΚΘ*, 177, Discourse 25.

124. Isaiah of Scetis, *ΤΟΥ ΟΣΙΟΥ ΠΑΤΡΟΣ ΗΜΩΝ ΑΒΒΑ ΗΣΑΙΟΥ ΛΟΓΟΙ ΚΘ*, 4, Discourse 2.

125. Ibid., 48, Discourse 7.

126. Isaiah of Scetis, *Ascetic Discourses*, 94, Discourse 8; Isaiah of Scetis, *ΤΟΥ ΟΣΙΟΥ ΠΑΤΡΟΣ ΗΜΩΝ ΑΒΒΑ ΗΣΑΙΟΥ ΛΟΓΟΙ ΚΘ*, 62, Discourse 8.

127. Isaiah of Scetis, *Ascetic Discourses*, 94, Discourse 8.

128. Ibid., 92, Discourse 8; Isaiah of Scetis, *ΤΟΥ ΟΣΙΟΥ ΠΑΤΡΟΣ ΗΜΩΝ ΑΒΒΑ ΗΣΑΙΟΥ ΛΟΓΟΙ ΚΘ*, 60, Discourse 8.

129. Isaiah of Scetis, *Ascetic Discourses*, 92, Discourse 8; Isaiah of Scetis, *ΤΟΥ ΟΣΙΟΥ ΠΑΤΡΟΣ ΗΜΩΝ ΑΒΒΑ ΗΣΑΙΟΥ ΛΟΓΟΙ ΚΘ*, 60, Discourse 8.

130. Isaiah of Scetis, *Ascetic Discourses*, 93, Discourse 8.

131. Ibid., 142, Discourse 18; Isaiah of Scetis, *ΤΟΥ ΟΣΙΟΥ ΠΑΤΡΟΣ ΗΜΩΝ ΑΒΒΑ ΗΣΑΙΟΥ ΛΟΓΟΙ ΚΘ*, 113, Discourse 18.

132. Isaiah of Scetis, *Ascetic Discourses*, 163, Discourse 22; Isaiah of Scetis, *ΤΟΥ ΟΣΙΟΥ ΠΑΤΡΟΣ ΗΜΩΝ ΑΒΒΑ ΗΣΑΙΟΥ ΛΟΓΟΙ ΚΘ*, 133, Discourse 22.

133. Isaiah of Scetis, *Ascetic Discourses*, 82–83, Discourse 7; Isaiah of Scetis, *ΤΟΥ ΟΣΙΟΥ ΠΑΤΡΟΣ ΗΜΩΝ ΑΒΒΑ ΗΣΑΙΟΥ ΛΟΓΟΙ ΚΘ*, 48, Discourse 7.

134. Isaiah of Scetis, *Ascetic Discourses*, 213, Discourse 26.

135. Ibid., 204, Discourse 25; Isaiah of Scetis, *ΤΟΥ ΟΣΙΟΥ ΠΑΤΡΟΣ ΗΜΩΝ ΑΒΒΑ ΗΣΑΙΟΥ ΛΟΓΟΙ ΚΘ*, 174, Discourse 25.

136. Isaiah of Scetis, *Ascetic Discourses*, 141, Discourse 18; Isaiah of Scetis, *ΤΟΥ ΟΣΙΟΥ ΠΑΤΡΟΣ ΗΜΩΝ ΑΒΒΑ ΗΣΑΙΟΥ ΛΟΓΟΙ ΚΘ*, 112, Discourse 18.

137. Isaiah of Scetis, *Ascetic Discourses*, 141, Discourse 18; Isaiah of Scetis, *ΤΟΥ ΟΣΙΟΥ ΠΑΤΡΟΣ ΗΜΩΝ ΑΒΒΑ ΗΣΑΙΟΥ ΛΟΓΟΙ ΚΘ*, 113, Discourse 18, n. 1 (following the Latin variant).

138. Isaiah of Scetis, *Ascetic Discourses*, 57, Discourse 4; Isaiah of Scetis, *ΤΟΥ ΟΣΙΟΥ ΠΑΤΡΟΣ ΗΜΩΝ ΑΒΒΑ ΗΣΑΙΟΥ ΛΟΓΟΙ ΚΘ*, 19, Discourse 4.

139. Barsanuphius and John, *Letters*, 207, Letter 199; Barsanuphius and John, *Correspondance*, trans. Lucien Regnault, vol. 427 (Paris: Éditions du Cerf, 1998), 628, Letter 199.

140. Barsanuphius and John, *Letters*, 130, Letter 109.

141. See also ibid., 221, Letter 212; ibid., 123–124, Letter 532; 138, Letter 553.

142. Ibid., 219, Letter 211; Barsanuphius and John, *Correspondance*, 658, Letter 211.

143. Barsanuphius and John, *Letters*, 78–79, Letter 61; Barsanuphius and John, *Correspondance*, trans. Lucien Regnault, vol. 426 (Paris: Éditions du Cerf, 1997), 298, Letter 61.

144. Barsanuphius and John, *Letters*, 79, Letter 61; Barsanuphius and John, *Correspondance*, 300, Letter 61.

145. Barsanuphius and John, *Letters*, 80, Letter 61; Barsanuphius and John, *Correspondance*, 302, Letter 61.

146. Barsanuphius and John, *Letters*, 80, Letter 61.

147. Ibid.

148. Ibid., 81, Letter 61.

149. Barsanuphius and John, *Letters*, 278, Letter 770; Barsanuphius and John, *Correspondance*, trans. Lucien Regnault, vol. 468 (Paris: Éditions du Cerf, 2002), 216, Letter 770.

150. Barsanuphius and John, *Letters*, 121, Letter 529; Barsanuphius and John, *Correspondance*, trans. Lucien Regnault, vol. 451 (Paris: Éditions du Cerf, 2001), 668, Letter 529.

151. Barsanuphius and John, *Letters*, 108, Letter 508.

152. Ibid., 122–123, Letter 532.

153. Ibid., 123–124, Letter 532; Barsanuphius and John, *Correspondance*, 672, Letter 532.

154. Barsanuphius and John, *Letters*, 228, Letter 226.

155. Barsanuphius and John, *Letters*, 125, Letter 534.

156. Barsanuphius and John, *Letters*, 148–149, Letter 126; Barsanuphius and John, *Correspondance*, 480, Letter 126.

157. Barsanuphius and John, *Letters*, 170, Letter 148.

158. Barsanuphius and John, *Letters*, 117, Letter 520.

159. Barsanuphius and John, *Correspondance*, 656, Letter 520.

160. Barsanuphius and John, *Letters*, 117, Letter 520.

161. Barsanuphius and John, *Letters*, 110, Letter 88.

162. Barsanuphius and John, *Letters*, 110, Letter 510.

163. Barsanuphius and John, *Letters*, 177–178, Letter 157; Barsanuphius and John, *Correspondance*, 552, Letter 157.

164. Barsanuphius and John, *Letters*, 179, Letter 159.

165. Barsanuphius and John, *Letters*, 109, Letter 510; Barsanuphius and John, *Correspondance*, 638, Letter 510.

166. Barsanuphius and John, *Letters*, 43, Letter 23.

167. Ibid., 176, Letter 154.

168. Barsanuphius and John, *Letters*, 116, Letter 519.

169. Ibid., 111, Letter 511.

170. Ibid., 52, Letter 424.

171. Ibid.

172. Barsanuphius and John, *Letters*, 104, Letter 78.

173. Ibid., 97, Letter 72.

174. Barsanuphius and John, *Letters*, 198, Letter 613.

175. Ibid., 199, Letter 613; Barsanuphius and John, *Correspondance*, 850, Letter 613.

176. Barsanuphius and John, *Letters*, 320, Letter 348; Barsanuphius and John, *Correspondance*, 368, Letter 348.

177. Barsanuphius and John, *Letters*, 320, Letter 348; Barsanuphius and John, *Correspondance*, 368, Letter 348.

178. Barsanuphius and John, *Letters*, 320, Letter 348; Barsanuphius and John, *Correspondance*, 368, Letter 348.

179. Barsanuphius and John, *Letters*, 175, Letter 599; Barsanuphius and John, *Correspondance*, 800, Letter 599.

180. Barsanuphius and John, *Letters*, 224, Letter 218; Barsanuphius and John, *Correspondance*, 670, Letter 218.

181. Barsanuphius and John, *Letters*, 225, Letter 220. Regnault proposed that the monk in question was Dositheos, the associate of Dorotheos. See Regnault and Préville, Œuvres spirituelles, 139, n. 2.

182. Barsanuphius and John, *Letters*, 225, Letter 221.

183. Ibid., 225, Letter 222.

184. Ibid., 226, Letter 223. Zecher considered Barsanuphius's notion of death for monastics: "The ascetic dies out of obedience to Christ and in thanksgiving for his death. However, the ascetic's 'death' becomes a means of imitating Christ—to 'die' for Christ means being 'crucified.' By such language, Barsanuphius contextualizes ascetic practices and ideals

within an incarnational framework. Thus 'death'—and particularly that obedient form of death which excises the will—underpins the Christ like virtues of obedience, humility, and love." Zecher, "The Symbolics of Death," 177.

185. Zosimas, "Reflections," in *In the Heart of the Desert: The Spirituality of the Desert Fathers and Mothers: With a Translation of Abba Zosimas' Reflections* (Bloomington: World Wisdom, Inc., 2008), 132.

186. Ibid.; Zosimas, "Alloquia," 699. "Καὶ ὀφείλεις μεμνῆσθαι αὐτοῦ ὡς ἰατροῦ πεμθέντος σοι ὑπὸ τοῦ Χριστοῦ."

187. Zosimas, "Reflections," 126; Zosimas, "Alloquia," 699.

188. Zosimas, "Reflections," 126; Zosimas, "Alloquia," 700.

189. Zosimas, "Reflections," 126; Zosimas, "Alloquia," 700.

190. Zosimas, "Reflections," 127; Zosimas, "Alloquia," 700.

191. Zosimas, "Reflections," 127; Zosimas, "Alloquia," 700. See, Evagrius of Pontus, *Euagrius Ponticus*, trans. Wilhelm Frankenberg, vol. 13.2, Abhandlungen der königlichen Gesellschaft der Wissenschaften zu Göttingen, Philologische-historische Klasse (Berlin: Weidmannsche Buchhandlung, 1912), Letter 51, 600–601.

192. Zosimas, "Reflections," 127; Zosimas, "Alloquia," 700.

193. Zosimas, "Reflections," 132.

194. Ibid.; Zosimas, "Alloquia," in *Νέα Σιών*, ed. Augoustinos Iordanites (1913), 857.

195. Zosimas, "Reflections," 132; Zosimas, "Alloquia," 857.

196. Dorotheos of Gaza, *Abba Dorotheos*, 78, Discourse 1; 92, Discourse 2; 95–96, Discourse 2; 139, Discourse 6; and 154–157, Discourse 8.

197. Ibid., 179, Discourse 11.

198. Ibid., 72, Discourse 1.

199. Dorotheos of Gaza, Œuvres spirituelles, 152, Discourse 1.

200. Ibid., 156, Discourse 1.

201. Dorotheos of Gaza, *Abba Dorotheos*, 75, Discourse 1.

202. Ibid., 73–74, Discourse 1; Dorotheos of Gaza, Œuvres spirituelles, 156, Discourse 1.

203. Dorotheos of Gaza, *Abba Dorotheos*, 71–72, Discourse 1.

204. Ibid.

205. Ibid., 186, Discourse 11; Dorotheos of Gaza, Œuvres spirituelles, 374, Discourse 1.

206. Dorotheos of Gaza, *Abba Dorotheos*, 171, Discourse 10; Dorotheos of Gaza, Œuvres spirituelles, 342, Discourse 10. Translation slightly altered.

207. Dorotheos of Gaza, *Abba Dorotheos*, 171, Discourse 10; Dorotheos of Gaza, Œuvres spirituelles, 342, Discourse 10. Translation slightly altered.

208. Dorotheos of Gaza, *Abba Dorotheos*, 171, Discourse 10; Dorotheos of Gaza, Œuvres spirituelles, 342, Discourse 10.

209. Dorotheos of Gaza, *Abba Dorotheos*, 102, Discourse 3; Dorotheos of Gaza, Œuvres spirituelles, 212, Discourse 3.

210. Dorotheos of Gaza, *Abba Dorotheos*, 185–186, Discourse 11; Dorotheos of Gaza, Œuvres spirituelles, 372, Discourse 11.

211. Dorotheos of Gaza, *Abba Dorotheos*, 184, Discourse 11.

212. Ibid., 103–104, Discourse 3.

213. Ibid., 154, Discourse 8; Dorotheos of Gaza, Œuvres spirituelles, 308–310, Discourse 8. See Basil of Caesarea, "Homily 10: Against Those Who Are Prone to Anger," in *Ascetical Works*, The Fathers of the Church (New York: Fathers of the Church, 1950), 449.

214. Dorotheos of Gaza, *Abba Dorotheos*, 179, Discourse 11; Dorotheos of Gaza, Œuvres spirituelles, 356, Discourse 11.

215. Dorotheos of Gaza, *Abba Dorotheos*, 179, Discourse 11; Dorotheos of Gaza, Œuvres spirituelles, 357–358, Discourse 10.

216. Dorotheos of Gaza, *Abba Dorotheos*, 179, Discourse 11; Dorotheos of Gaza, Œuvres spirituelles, 358, Discourse 10.

217. Dorotheos of Gaza, *Abba Dorotheos*, 186–187, Discourse 11; Dorotheos of Gaza, Œuvres spirituelles, 376, Discourse 11.

218. Dorotheos of Gaza, *Abba Dorotheos*, 186, Discourse 11; Dorotheos of Gaza, Œuvres spirituelles, 376, Discourse 10.

219. Dorotheos of Gaza, *Abba Dorotheos*, 186, Discourse 11; Dorotheos of Gaza, Œuvres spirituelles, 376, Discourse 10. "Evidently, it is not bad for the health if one eats cabbage, lentils or any of them once or twice, but if one eats them continuously, in excess, this produces fever. Hence, all those who suffer from this literally burn and suffer a myriad of adversities. It is also like this with the soul. If a person continues to sin, it becomes a somewhat evil habit in the soul and this is precisely what torments him."

220. Dorotheos of Gaza, Œuvres spirituelles, 280, Discourse 12.

221. Dorotheos of Gaza, *Abba Dorotheos*, 191, Discourse 12; Dorotheos of Gaza, Œuvres spirituelles, 380, Discourse 12.

222. Dorotheos of Gaza, *Abba Dorotheos*, 128, Discourse 5.

223. Ibid.

224. Ibid.; Dorotheos of Gaza, Œuvres spirituelles, 264, Discourse 5.

225. Dorotheos of Gaza, *Abba Dorotheos*, 96, Discourse 2.

226. Ibid., 256, Letter 1; Dorotheos of Gaza, Œuvres spirituelles, 496, Letter 1. Translation slightly altered.

227. Dorotheos of Gaza, *Abba Dorotheos*, 138, Discourse 6.

228. Benedicta Ward, *The Sayings of the Desert Fathers: The Alphabetical Collection* (London: Mowbrays, 1975), 30, Alonios 4.

229. Dorotheos of Gaza, *Abba Dorotheos*, 165, Discourse 9; Dorotheos of Gaza, Œuvres spirituelles, 330, Discourse 9.

230. Dorotheos of Gaza, *Abba Dorotheos*, 149, Discourse 7; Dorotheos of Gaza, Œuvres spirituelles, 302, Discourse 7.

231. Dorotheos of Gaza, *Abba Dorotheos*, 149, Discourse 7; Dorotheos of Gaza, Œuvres spirituelles, 302, Discourse 7.

Chapter 4: Healing in the Drama of Salvation

1. See also Basil of Caesarea, *The Asketikon of St. Basil the Great*, 162–171, Longer Response 2.

2. Bitton-Ashkelony and Kofsky, *The Monastic School of Gaza*, 143.

3. The categories used here, "creation," "fall," "healing," and "monastic life," are terms Dorotheos used in his depiction of the narrative of salvation. See each section below for references.

4. Dorotheos of Gaza, *Abba Dorotheos*, 69, Discourse 1; Dorotheos of Gaza, Œuvres spirituelles, 146, Discourse 1. "Ἐν ἀρχῇ ὅτε ἐποίησεν ὁ Θεὸς τὸν ἄνθρωπον…κεκοσμημένον πάσῃ ἀρετῇ"

5. Dorotheos of Gaza, *Abba Dorotheos*, 69, Discourse 1; Dorotheos of Gaza, Œuvres spirituelles, 146, Discourse 1. "ἔχων σώας τὰς αἰσθήσεις καὶ ὢν ἐν τῷ κατὰ φύσιν καθὼς καὶ ἐκτίσθη"

6. Dorotheos of Gaza, *Abba Dorotheos*, 69, Discourse 1; Dorotheos of Gaza, Œuvres spirituelles, 146, Discourse 1.

7. Dorotheos of Gaza, *Abba Dorotheos*, 69, Discourse 1; Dorotheos of Gaza, Œuvres spirituelles, 146, Discourse 1.

8. Dorotheos of Gaza, Œuvres spirituelles, 146, Discourse 1.

9. Isaiah of Scetis, *Ascetic Discourses*, 43, Discourse 2; Isaiah of Scetis, *ΤΟΥ ΟΣΙΟΥ ΠΑΤΡΟΣ ΗΜΩΝ ΑΒΒΑ ΗΣΑΙΟΥ ΛΟΓΟΙ ΚΘ*, 4, Discourse 2. "σώας ἔχοντα τὰς αἰσθήσεις καὶ ἑστηκυίας ἐν τῷ φυσικῷ."

10. Isaiah of Scetis, *Ascetic Discourses*, 43, Discourse 2; Isaiah of Scetis, *ΤΟΥ ΟΣΙΟΥ ΠΑΤΡΟΣ ΗΜΩΝ ΑΒΒΑ ΗΣΑΙΟΥ ΛΟΓΟΙ ΚΘ*, 4, Discourse 2. "When Adam listened to the one who deceived him, all of his senses were twisted (μετεστράφησαν) toward that which is contrary to nature (εἰς παρὰ φύσιν)." Concerning the contrasted natures in Isaiah, Perrone stated, "There are other elements in the ascetic doctrine of Isaiah of Gaza, which become a common heritage for the monks of subsequent generations, as we see both in the two Old Men of Gaza and in Dorotheos. We may briefly record the idea that the monastic way of life should take as its goal the restoration of the human condition 'according to nature' (kata physin), an indication which at first sight sounds rather philosophical. Yet such a perspective, despite its very stoic flavour, is strictly connected to the motif of the discipleship of Jesus, thus reshaping in an original way the philosophical tradition of the 'spiritual exercises.'" Perrone, "Monasticism in Gaza: A Chapter in the History of Byzantine Palestine," 69.

11. Isaiah of Scetis, *Ascetic Discourses*, 45, Discourse 2; Isaiah of Scetis, *ΤΟΥ ΟΣΙΟΥ ΠΑΤΡΟΣ ΗΜΩΝ ΑΒΒΑ ΗΣΑΙΟΥ ΛΟΓΟΙ ΚΘ*, 6, Discourse 2.

12. Isaiah of Scetis, *Ascetic Discourses*, 44–45, Discourse 2.

13. Barsanuphius and John, *Letters*, 41, Letter 404.

14. Barsanuphius and John, *Letters*, 251, Letter 246; Barsanuphius and John, *Correspondance*, 198, Letter 246. "God made both the soul and the body dispassionate (ἀπαθῆ), but through disobedience (διὰ δὲ τῆς παρακοῆς) people fell away to passions (εἰς πάθη)."

15. Barsanuphius and John, *Letters*, 251, Letter 246; Barsanuphius and John, *Correspondance*, 198, Letter 246. "Καὶ τὴν ψυχὴν καὶ τὸ σῶμα ἀπαθῆ ἔκτισεν ὁ Θεός, διὰ δὲ τῆς παρακοῆς ἐξέπεσαν εἰς πάθη."

16. Barsanuphius and John, *Letters*, 251, Letter 245; *Correspondance*, 196, Letter 245.

17. Barsanuphius and John, *Letters*, 251, Letter 245; Barsanuphius and John, *Correspondance*, 196, Letter 245.

18. Barsanuphius and John, *Letters*, 275, Letter 763; Barsanuphius and John, *Correspondance*, 206, Letter 763.

19. Barsanuphius and John, *Letters*, 31, Letter 389; Barsanuphius and John, *Correspondance*, 442, Letter 389. John explained that, "people are themselves to blame for their own evils, he allowed them their freedom so that they may be without any excuse on the day of judgment, when each would accuse the other."

20. Dorotheos of Gaza, *Abba Dorotheos*, 69, Discourse 1; Dorotheos of Gaza, Œuvres spirituelles, 148, Discourse 1.

21. Dorotheos of Gaza, *Abba Dorotheos*, 71, Discourse 1; Dorotheos of Gaza, Œuvres spirituelles, 150, Discourse 1.

22. Dorotheos of Gaza, *Abba Dorotheos*, 70–71, Discourse 1; Dorotheos of Gaza, Œuvres spirituelles, 150, Discourse 1. Dorotheos interpreted this passage to say that Babylon, "has not repented, it has not been afraid, it has not returned from its sinfulness."

23. Isaiah of Scetis, *Ascetic Discourses*, 43–44, Discourse 2; Isaiah of Scetis, *ΤΟΥ ΟΣΙΟΥ ΠΑΤΡΟΣ ΗΜΩΝ ΑΒΒΑ ΗΣΑΙΟΥ ΛΟΓΟΙ ΚΘ*, 4, Discourse 2.

24. Isaiah of Scetis, *Ascetic Discourses*, 43, Discourse 2.

25. Ibid., 45, Discourse 2.

26. Barsanuphius and John, *Letters*, 92, Letter 69.

27. Ibid.

28. Dorotheos of Gaza, *Abba Dorotheos*, 71, Discourse 1.

29. Ibid.; Dorotheos of Gaza, Œuvres spirituelles, 150, Discourse 1.

30. Dorotheos of Gaza, *Abba Dorotheos*, 71, Discourse 1.

31. Ibid.

32. Ibid., 71, Discourse 1; Dorotheos of Gaza, Œuvres spirituelles, 152, Discourse 1.

33. Isaiah of Scetis, *Ascetic Discourses*, 43, Discourse 2.

34. Ibid.

35. Ibid., 43–44, Discourse 2; Isaiah of Scetis, *ΤΟΥ ΟΣΙΟΥ ΠΑΤΡΟΣ ΗΜΩΝ ΑΒΒΑ ΗΣΑΙΟΥ ΛΟΓΟΙ ΚΘ*, 4, Discourse 2.

36. Isaiah of Scetis, *Ascetic Discourses*, 43, Discourse 2.

37. Ibid., 88–89, Discourse 8.

38. Ibid., 219, Discourse 27.

39. Ibid., 101–102, Discourse 11; Isaiah of Scetis, *ΤΟΥ ΟΣΙΟΥ ΠΑΤΡΟΣ ΗΜΩΝ ΑΒΒΑ ΗΣΑΙΟΥ ΛΟΓΟΙ ΚΘ*, 70, Discourse 11.

40. Isaiah of Scetis, *Ascetic Discourses*, 101–102, Discourse 11.

41. Ibid., 206, Discourse 25.

42. Ibid., 192–193, Discourse 25.

43. Barsanuphius and John, *Letters*, 94, Letter 70; Barsanuphius and John, *Correspondance*, 338, Letter 70.

44. Barsanuphius and John, *Letters*, 94, Letter 70; Barsanuphius and John, *Correspondance*, 338, Letter 70.

45. Barsanuphius and John, *Letters*, 94, Letter 70.

46. Ibid., 208, Letter 199; Barsanuphius and John, *Correspondance*, 630, Letter 199.

47. Barsanuphius and John, *Letters*, 208, Letter 199.

48. Zecher explained that for Barsanuphius, "the destruction of the old self—a process of dying—is not the end. It only enables a monk to put on a 'new human' self, one which is Godly. Barsanuphius considers the 'new self' to be more properly human, and certainly

more godlike, than the old one. Death, then, leads to the formation of a properly *human* being—which is a god. Ceasing to do his own will, the monk accomplishes God's; giving up his blood relations, he is adopted as a son of God." Zecher, "The Symbolics of Death," 170.

49. Dorotheos of Gaza, *Abba Dorotheos*, 72, Discourse 1; Dorotheos of Gaza, Œuvres spirituelles, 152, Discourse 1.

50. Dorotheos of Gaza, *Abba Dorotheos*, 72, Discourse 1; Dorotheos of Gaza, Œuvres spirituelles, 154, Discourse 1.

51. Dorotheos of Gaza, *Abba Dorotheos*, 73, Discourse 1.

52. Dorotheos of Gaza, Œuvres spirituelles, 356–358, Discourse 11." Ὁ Χριστὸς γάρ ἐστιν ὁ ἰατρὸς τῶν ψυχῶν ἡμῶν" The portrayal of Christ as physician was common in early Christianity. For a survey of references to Christ as physician, see Jean-Claude Larchet, *Thérapeutique des maladies spirituelles: Une introduction à la tradition ascétique de l'*Église Orthodoxe, 2 ed. (Suresnes: Éditions de l'Ancre, 1993), 342–344, n.123. In Letter 199, Barsanuphius claimed, "Jesus is the Physician of souls and bodies." (Ὁ Ἰησοῦς ἰατρός ἐστι τῶν ψυχῶν καὶ τῶν σωμάτων.) Barsanuphius and John, *Letters*, 207, Letter 199; Barsanuphius and John, *Correspondance*, 628, Letter 199. This remark would have appeared to presuppose Dorotheos's comments on Christ as physician were it not for the broader conception of salvation at work in each. For Barsanuphius, healing involved enduring suffering until death, while, for Dorotheos, the healing of Christ was present in this life.

53. Dorotheos of Gaza, *Abba Dorotheos*, 73–74, Discourse 1; Dorotheos of Gaza, Œuvres spirituelles, 154–156, Discourse 1.

54. Dorotheos of Gaza, *Abba Dorotheos*, 74, Discourse 1.

55. Ibid., 76, Discourse 1; Dorotheos of Gaza, Œuvres spirituelles, 162, Discourse 1.

56. Dorotheos of Gaza, *Abba Dorotheos*, 76–77, Discourse 1; Dorotheos of Gaza, Œuvres spirituelles, 164, Discourse 1.

57. Dorotheos of Gaza, *Abba Dorotheos*, 77, Discourse 1.

58. Ibid.

59. Ibid., 78, Discourse 1.

60. Ibid., 81–82, Discourse 1; Dorotheos of Gaza, Œuvres spirituelles, 176, Discourse 1.

61. Dorotheos of Gaza, *Abba Dorotheos*, 77, Discourse 1.

62. Isaiah of Scetis, *Ascetic Discourses*, 204, Discourse 25.

63. Ibid., 213, Discourse 26.

64. Ibid., 107, Discourse 13; Isaiah of Scetis, *ΤΟΥ ΟΣΙΟΥ ΠΑΤΡΟΣ ΗΜΩΝ ΑΒΒΑ ΗΣΑΙΟΥ ΛΟΓΟΙ ΚΘ*, 77, Discourse 13.

65. Isaiah of Scetis, *Ascetic Discourses*, 82–83, Discourse 7.

66. Barsanuphius and John, *Letters*, 208, Letter 199; Barsanuphius and John, *Correspondance*, 630, Letter 199.

67. Barsanuphius and John, *Letters*, 64, Letter 49; Barsanuphius and John, *Correspondance*, 262–264, Letter 49.

68. Barsanuphius and John, *Letters*, 143–144, Letter 124., my emphasis; Barsanuphius and John, *Correspondance*, 466, Letter 124.

69. Barsanuphius and John, *Letters*, 2, Letter 351; Barsanuphius and John, *Correspondance*, 372, Letter 351.

70. Barsanuphius and John, *Letters*, 25, Letter 2.
71. Ibid., 95–96, Letter 71.
72. Ibid., 89, Letter 67.
73. Ibid., 209, Letter 200.
74. Ibid., 102, Letter 77.
75. Ibid., 144, Letter 124.
76. Ibid., 31, Letter 389; Barsanuphius and John, *Correspondance*, 442, Letter 389.
77. Barsanuphius and John, *Letters*, 315–316, Letter 345; Barsanuphius and John, *Correspondance*, 360, Letter 345. One could not expect to arrive at "the holy rest of perfection, unless one first suffers with Christ and endures all of his sufferings, recalling the Apostle, who said: 'Let us suffer with him so that we may be glorified with him.' (Rom. 8:17) Therefore, do not be deceived; for there is no other way of salvation but this."
78. Larchet, *Thérapeutique des maladies spirituelles: Une introduction à la tradition ascétique de l'Église Orthodoxe*, 501.
79. Isaiah of Scetis, *Ascetic Discourses*, 227–228, Discourse 28; Isaiah of Scetis, *ΤΟΥ ΟΣΙΟΥ ΠΑΤΡΟΣ ΗΜΩΝ ΑΒΒΑ ΗΣΑΙΟΥ ΛΟΓΟΙ ΚΘ*, 194–197, Discourse 28.
80. Isaiah of Scetis, *Ascetic Discourses*, 229, Discourse 28.
81. Ibid., 99, Discourse 10; Isaiah of Scetis, *ΤΟΥ ΟΣΙΟΥ ΠΑΤΡΟΣ ΗΜΩΝ ΑΒΒΑ ΗΣΑΙΟΥ ΛΟΓΟΙ ΚΘ*, 67, Discourse 10.
82. Isaiah of Scetis, *Ascetic Discourses*, 99, Discourse 10; Isaiah of Scetis, *ΤΟΥ ΟΣΙΟΥ ΠΑΤΡΟΣ ΗΜΩΝ ΑΒΒΑ ΗΣΑΙΟΥ ΛΟΓΟΙ ΚΘ*, 67, Discourse 10.
83. Isaiah of Scetis, *Ascetic Discourses*, 89, Discourse 8; Isaiah of Scetis, *ΤΟΥ ΟΣΙΟΥ ΠΑΤΡΟΣ ΗΜΩΝ ΑΒΒΑ ΗΣΑΙΟΥ ΛΟΓΟΙ ΚΘ*, 56, Discourse 8.
84. Isaiah of Scetis, *Ascetic Discourses*, 99, Discourse 10.
85. Ibid., 101, Discourse 11.
86. Ibid., 96, Discourse 9; Isaiah of Scetis, *ΤΟΥ ΟΣΙΟΥ ΠΑΤΡΟΣ ΗΜΩΝ ΑΒΒΑ ΗΣΑΙΟΥ ΛΟΓΟΙ ΚΘ*, 64, Discourse 9.
87. Isaiah of Scetis, *Ascetic Discourses*, 136, Discourse 17; Isaiah of Scetis, *ΤΟΥ ΟΣΙΟΥ ΠΑΤΡΟΣ ΗΜΩΝ ΑΒΒΑ ΗΣΑΙΟΥ ΛΟΓΟΙ ΚΘ*, 108, Discourse 17.
88. Isaiah of Scetis, *Ascetic Discourses*, 183–184, Discourse 25; Isaiah of Scetis, *ΤΟΥ ΟΣΙΟΥ ΠΑΤΡΟΣ ΗΜΩΝ ΑΒΒΑ ΗΣΑΙΟΥ ΛΟΓΟΙ ΚΘ*, 152, Discourse 25.
89. Isaiah of Scetis, *Ascetic Discourses*, 124, Discourse 16; Isaiah of Scetis, *ΤΟΥ ΟΣΙΟΥ ΠΑΤΡΟΣ ΗΜΩΝ ΑΒΒΑ ΗΣΑΙΟΥ ΛΟΓΟΙ ΚΘ*, 93, Discourse 16.
90. Isaiah of Scetis, *Ascetic Discourses*, 60, Discourse 4; Isaiah of Scetis, *ΤΟΥ ΟΣΙΟΥ ΠΑΤΡΟΣ ΗΜΩΝ ΑΒΒΑ ΗΣΑΙΟΥ ΛΟΓΟΙ ΚΘ*, 23, Discourse 4.
91. Isaiah of Scetis, *Ascetic Discourses*, 89, Discourse 8; Isaiah of Scetis, *ΤΟΥ ΟΣΙΟΥ ΠΑΤΡΟΣ ΗΜΩΝ ΑΒΒΑ ΗΣΑΙΟΥ ΛΟΓΟΙ ΚΘ*, 56, Discourse 8.
92. Isaiah of Scetis, *Ascetic Discourses*, 230, Discourse 28; Isaiah of Scetis, *ΤΟΥ ΟΣΙΟΥ ΠΑΤΡΟΣ ΗΜΩΝ ΑΒΒΑ ΗΣΑΙΟΥ ΛΟΓΟΙ ΚΘ*, 195, Discourse 28.
93. Isaiah of Scetis, *Ascetic Discourses*, 177, Discourse 23; Isaiah of Scetis, *ΤΟΥ ΟΣΙΟΥ ΠΑΤΡΟΣ ΗΜΩΝ ΑΒΒΑ ΗΣΑΙΟΥ ΛΟΓΟΙ ΚΘ*, 146, Discourse 23.
94. Isaiah of Scetis, *Ascetic Discourses*, 155–156, Discourse 21.
95. Barsanuphius and John, *Letters*, 251, Letter 246. "God created both the soul and the body dispassionate, but through disobedience people fell away to passions."

96. Ibid., 251, Letter 245.

97. Ibid., 89, Letter 67; Barsanuphius and John, *Correspondance*, 326, Letter 67.

98. Barsanuphius and John, *Letters*, 137, Letter 118.

99. Ibid., 138, Letter 119.

100. Ibid., 137, Letter 118.

101. Ibid., 251, Letter 244; Barsanuphius and John, *Correspondance*, 196, Letter 244.

102. Barsanuphius and John, *Letters*, 124, Letter 102.

103. Ibid.

104. Ibid., 97, Letter 72.

105. Ibid., 258–259, Letter 256; Barsanuphius and John, *Correspondance*, 214, Letter 256.

106. Barsanuphius and John, *Letters*, 119–120, Letter 526; Barsanuphius and John, *Correspondance*, 664, Letter 526.

107. Barsanuphius and John, *Letters*, 104, Letter 78; Barsanuphius and John, *Correspondance*, 362, Letter 78.

108. Barsanuphius and John, *Letters*, 228–229, Letter 226; Barsanuphius and John, *Correspondance*, 142, Letter 226.

109. Barsanuphius and John, *Letters*, 75, Letter 59; Barsanuphius and John, *Correspondance*, 290, Letter 59.

110. Barsanuphius and John, *Letters*, 52, Letter 424; Barsanuphius and John, *Correspondance*, 498, Letter 424.

111. Barsanuphius and John, *Letters*, 52, Letter 424.

112. Barsanuphius and John, *Letters*, 165, Letter 142; Barsanuphius and John, *Correspondance*, 520, Letter 142.

113. Barsanuphius and John, *Letters*, 165, Letter 142; Barsanuphius and John, *Correspondance*, 520, Letter 142.

114. Barsanuphius and John, *Letters*, 289–290, Letter 304; Barsanuphius and John, *Correspondance*, 294, Letter 304.

115. Barsanuphius and John, *Letters*, 289–290, Letter 304; Barsanuphius and John, *Correspondance*, 294, Letter 304.

116. Barsanuphius and John, *Letters*, 290, Letter 304; Barsanuphius and John, *Correspondance*, 296, Letter 304.

117. Barsanuphius and John, *Letters*, 290, Letter 304; Barsanuphius and John, *Correspondance*, 296, Letter 304.

118. Barsanuphius and John, *Letters*, 76, Letter 462; Barsanuphius and John, *Correspondance*, 556–558, Letter 462.

119. Barsanuphius and John, *Letters*, 14, Letter 372; Barsanuphius and John, *Correspondance*, 402, Letter 372.

120. Barsanuphius and John, *Letters*, 14, Letter 372; Barsanuphius and John, *Correspondance*, 402, Letter 372.

121. Barsanuphius and John, *Letters*, 252, Letter 248; Barsanuphius and John, *Correspondance*, 200, Letter 248.

122. Barsanuphius and John, *Letters*, 25, Letter 385; Barsanuphius and John, *Correspondance*, 430, Letter 385.

123. Dorotheos of Gaza, *Abba Dorotheos*, 207, Discourse 13; Dorotheos of Gaza, Œuvres spirituelles, 412, Discourse 13.

124. Dorotheos of Gaza, *Abba Dorotheos*, 173, Discourse 10.

125. Ibid., 175, Discourse 10.

126. Ibid.; Dorotheos of Gaza, Œuvres spirituelles, 352, Discourse 10.

127. Dorotheos of Gaza, *Abba Dorotheos*, 175, Discourse 10; Dorotheos of Gaza, Œuvres spirituelles, 352, Discourse 10.

128. Dorotheos of Gaza, *Abba Dorotheos*, 176, Discourse 10.

129. Ibid., 186–187, Discourse 11.

130. Ibid., 195, Discourse 12; Dorotheos of Gaza, Œuvres spirituelles, 392, Discourse 12.

131. Dorotheos of Gaza, *Abba Dorotheos*, 155, Discourse 8.

132. Ibid., 181, Discourse 11.

133. Ibid., 184, Discourse 11; Dorotheos of Gaza, Œuvres spirituelles, 370, Discourse 11.

134. Dorotheos of Gaza, *Abba Dorotheos*, 145, Discourse 7; Dorotheos of Gaza, Œuvres spirituelles, 294, Discourse 7.

135. Dorotheos of Gaza, *Abba Dorotheos*, 145, Discourse 7.

136. Ibid., 208, Discourse 13; Dorotheos of Gaza, Œuvres spirituelles, 416, Discourse 13.

137. Dorotheos of Gaza, *Abba Dorotheos*, 196, Discourse 12.

138. Ibid.

139. Ibid., 196–197, Discourse 12.

140. Ibid.

141. Ibid. "Each passion has its opposing virtue–pride has humility, avarice has charity, wastefulness has temperance, impatience has patience, wrath has gentleness, hate has love, and in short, every passion, as I have said, has its opposing virtue."

142. Ibid., 197, Discourse 12; Dorotheos of Gaza, Œuvres spirituelles, 396, Discourse 12.

143. Dorotheos of Gaza, *Abba Dorotheos*, 197, Discourse 12; Dorotheos of Gaza, Œuvres spirituelles, 396, Discourse 12.

144. Dorotheos of Gaza, *Abba Dorotheos*, 197, Discourse 12; Dorotheos of Gaza, Œuvres spirituelles, 396, Discourse 12.

145. Dorotheos of Gaza, *Abba Dorotheos*, 81, Discourse 1; Dorotheos of Gaza, Œuvres spirituelles, 176, Discourse 1.

146. Dorotheos of Gaza, *Abba Dorotheos*, 81, Discourse 1.

147. Ibid.; Dorotheos of Gaza, Œuvres spirituelles, 176, Discourse 1.

148. Nikolas Egender, "Dorotheus of Gaza and Benedict of Nursia," *Cistercian Studies Quarterly* 44, no. 2 (2009): 151. First published as Nikolas Egender, "Dorotheus von Gaza und Benedikt von Nursia," *Regulae Benedicti Studia Annuarium Internatioale* 17 (1992).

149. Dorotheos of Gaza, *Abba Dorotheos*, 77–78, Discourse 1. Whereas the image of the suffering and crucified Christ was pronounced in Isaiah, Barsanuphius and John as an example to be emulated, it is absent in Dorotheos's first discourse. Instead, Dorotheos turned to the idea of crucifixion in Galatians 6:14 as the motivation to pursue the monastic life. Here crucifixion resembles intentionality to a way of life rather than physical suffering. The crucifixion of oneself to the world and the world to oneself in Galatians was an amplification of the healing and prescription for life that Christ offered to all his followers.

Chapter 5: Virtue in the Monastic Life

1. Pauli, *Menschsein und Menschwerden*, 64. Pauli noted the relation of humanity to the divine in the realm of virtue: "Nur an dieser Stelle bringt Dorotheos die Ausübung der Tugend mit der Gottähnlichkeit in Zusammenhang; gewöhnlich spricht er von ihr as der 'Gesundheit der Seele.'"

2. William Harmless, "Monasticism," in *The Oxford Handbook of Early Christian Studies*, ed. Susan Ashbrook Harvey and David G. Hunter (New York: Oxford University Press, 2008), 509–510.

3. Larchet, *Thérapeutique des maladies spirituelles: Une introduction à la tradition ascétique de l'Église Orthodoxe*, 502. "Cette remise en ordre s'effectue par l'acquisition de la totalité des vertus, mais en premier lieu dans les vertus dites principales ou génériques non dans le sens où elles engendreraient toutes les autres, mais où elles sont les conditions de leur acquisition et constituent en quelque sorte la base de tout l'édifice spirituel qu'elles doivent former."

4. George Lavere reported on Plato's use of justice as a virtue and the unity of virtue: "In the *Republic*, Plato resolved this dilemma by invoking a transcendent source of virtue administered by a select group (true philosophers) who qualified by temperament and education as interpreters of ultimate reality–the world of ideas. Such guardians or philosopher kings would establish the order of virtue in this world as a reflection of the eternal idea of virtue in the world of ideas. Accordingly, each virtue, properly defined, would take its place in the hierarchy of virtue under the direction of the overarching virtue, justice. Wisdom would rule, and properly so, reflecting its position above courage and temperance respectively in the transcendental scale of virtue. The outcome, in Plato's view, would be a well-ordered city-state and, applied to the citizen, a virtuous individual." George J. Lavere, "Virtue," in *Augustine Through the Ages: An Encyclopedia*, ed. Allan D. Fitzgerald (Grand Rapids: Wm. B. Eerdmans Publishing Company, 2009), 872.

5. The spiritual building of virtue is evident in many authors. See Origen of Alexandria, "Genesis Homily XIII," in *Origen: Homilies on Genesis and Exodus*, The Fathers of the Church (Washington D.C.: The Catholic University of America Press, Inc., 1982), 193; Evagrius, *Evagrius of Pontus: Talking Back: A Monastic Handbook for Combating Demons*, trans. David Brakke (Trappist, KY: Cistercian Publications, 2009), 65; Ward, *The Sayings of the Desert Fathers: The Alphabetical Collection*, 79, John the Dwarf 34.

6. 1 Peter 2:5 NRSV, Nestle-Aland.

7. Isaiah of Scetis, *Ascetic Discourses*, 97, Discourse 9. Isaiah stated, "Just as a house that is destroyed outside a city becomes a place of stench, the soul of a cowardly beginner becomes the dwelling-place of every dishonourable passion."

8. Ibid., 174, Discourse 23; Isaiah of Scetis, *ΤΟΥ ΟΣΙΟΥ ΠΑΤΡΟΣ ΗΜΩΝ ΑΒΒΑ ΗΣΑΙΟΥ ΛΟΓΟΙ ΚΘ*, 143, Discourse 23.

9. Isaiah of Scetis, *Ascetic Discourses*, 174, Discourse 23.

10. Ibid.; Isaiah of Scetis, *ΤΟΥ ΟΣΙΟΥ ΠΑΤΡΟΣ ΗΜΩΝ ΑΒΒΑ ΗΣΑΙΟΥ ΛΟΓΟΙ ΚΘ*, 143, Discourse 23.

11. Isaiah of Scetis, *Ascetic Discourses*, 175, Discourse 23; Isaiah of Scetis, *ΤΟΥ ΟΣΙΟΥ ΠΑΤΡΟΣ ΗΜΩΝ ΑΒΒΑ ΗΣΑΙΟΥ ΛΟΓΟΙ ΚΘ*, 144, Discourse 23.

12. Isaiah of Scetis, *ΤΟΥ ΟΣΙΟΥ ΠΑΤΡΟΣ ΗΜΩΝ ΑΒΒΑ ΗΣΑΙΟΥ ΛΟΓΟΙ ΚΘ*, 143, Discourse 23.
13. Isaiah of Scetis, *Ascetic Discourses*, 176, Discourse 23.
14. Ibid., 177, Discourse 23.
15. Barsanuphius and John, *Letters*, 50–51, Letter 32; Barsanuphius and John, *Correspondance*, 228, Letter 32.
16. Barsanuphius and John, *Letters*, 132, Letter 112.
17. Ibid.; Barsanuphius and John, *Correspondance*, 438, Letter 112.
18. Barsanuphius and John, *Letters*, 216, Letter 208; Barsanuphius and John, *Correspondance*, 650, Letter 208.
19. Barsanuphius and John, *Letters*, 216, Letter 208.
20. Ibid.
21. Ibid.
22. Ibid.
23. Ibid.
24. Ibid.; Barsanuphius and John, *Correspondance*, 652, Letter 208.
25. Dorotheos of Gaza, *Abba Dorotheos*, 231, Discourse 14; Dorotheos of Gaza, Œuvres spirituelles, 420, Discourse 14.
26. Dorotheos of Gaza, *Abba Dorotheos*, 213, Discourse 14.
27. Ibid., 217–218, Discourse 14; Dorotheos of Gaza, Œuvres spirituelles, 430, Discourse 14.
28. Dorotheos of Gaza, *Abba Dorotheos*, 213, Discourse 14.
29. Ibid. "The person that wants to build a house needs to protect it from all sides and to raise all sides together, not just pay attention to one side whilst neglecting the others."
30. Ibid.
31. Dorotheos of Gaza, Œuvres spirituelles, 422, Discourse 14; See, John the Dwarf, *Appendix ad Palladium*, ed. J. -P Migne, vol. 65, Patrologiae Cursus Completus, Series Graeca (Paris: J.-P. Migne, 1864), 216; Ward, *The Sayings of the Desert Fathers: The Alphabetical Collection*, 79, Saying 34.
32. Dorotheos of Gaza, *Abba Dorotheos*, 214, Discourse 14; Dorotheos of Gaza, Œuvres spirituelles, 422, Discourse 14.
33. Dorotheos of Gaza, Œuvres spirituelles, 424, Discourse 14.
34. Dorotheos of Gaza, *Abba Dorotheos*, 214–215, Discourse 14.
35. Ibid., 215, Discourse 14.
36. Ibid.; Dorotheos of Gaza, Œuvres spirituelles, 424, Discourse 14.
37. Dorotheos of Gaza, *Abba Dorotheos*, 215, Discourse 14.
38. Ibid.
39. Ibid., 216, Discourse 14.
40. Ibid., 215, Discourse 14; Dorotheos of Gaza, Œuvres spirituelles, 426, Discourse 14.
41. Dorotheos of Gaza, *Abba Dorotheos*, 216, Discourse 14.
42. Ibid., 216–217, Discourse 14.
43. Dorotheos of Gaza, Œuvres spirituelles, 428, Discourse 14.
44. Dorotheos of Gaza, *Abba Dorotheos*, 217, Discourse 14.
45. Ibid. See Evagrius of Pontus, *Evagrius of Pontus: The Greek Ascetic Corpus*, trans. Robert E. Sinkewicz (Oxford: Oxford University Press, 2003), 112, Praktikos 91.

46. Rowan Williams, *The Wound of Knowledge: Christian Spirituality from the New Testament to St. John of the Cross*, 2nd. ed. (Cambridge, MA: Cowley Pubications, 1990), 125.

47. Ward, *The Sayings of the Desert Fathers: The Alphabetical Collection*, 79, John the Dwarf 34.

48. Graham Gould, "A Note on the Apophthegmata Patrum," *Journal of Theological Studies* 37, no. 1 (1986): 136.

49. Ibid., 135. Addressing the significance of this saying in the *Apophthegmata Patrum*, Gould explained that "Theologically speaking, we might want to say that after it has been uttered by an abba to his disciple, a *logos* loses its charismatic authority and its immediate relevance, and is in danger of being absorbed by a later writer into a different kind of spiritual teaching. But in the desert, an abba was surely at liberty to re-use the saying of another and adapt it to a new situation, though perhaps a similar one to that in which it was first spoken."

50. Dorotheos of Gaza, *Abba Dorotheos*, 171, Discourse 10; Dorotheos of Gaza, Œuvres spirituelles, 342, Discourse 10. "Evil is the sickness of the soul by which the soul is deprived of its own natural health, which is virtue."

51. Isaiah of Scetis, *Ascetic Discourses*, 107, Discourse 13; Isaiah of Scetis, *ΤΟΥ ΟΣΙΟΥ ΠΑΤΡΟΣ ΗΜΩΝ ΑΒΒΑ ΗΣΑΙΟΥ ΛΟΓΟΙ ΚΘ*, 77, Discourse 13.

52. Isaiah of Scetis, *Ascetic Discourses*, 126, Discourse 16; Isaiah of Scetis, *ΤΟΥ ΟΣΙΟΥ ΠΑΤΡΟΣ ΗΜΩΝ ΑΒΒΑ ΗΣΑΙΟΥ ΛΟΓΟΙ ΚΘ*, 96, Discourse 16.

53. Isaiah of Scetis, *Ascetic Discourses*, 126, Discourse 16; Isaiah of Scetis, *ΤΟΥ ΟΣΙΟΥ ΠΑΤΡΟΣ ΗΜΩΝ ΑΒΒΑ ΗΣΑΙΟΥ ΛΟΓΟΙ ΚΘ*, 96, Discourse 16.

54. Isaiah of Scetis, *Ascetic Discourses*, 181, Discourse 24; Isaiah of Scetis, *ΤΟΥ ΟΣΙΟΥ ΠΑΤΡΟΣ ΗΜΩΝ ΑΒΒΑ ΗΣΑΙΟΥ ΛΟΓΟΙ ΚΘ*, 150, Discourse 24.

55. Isaiah of Scetis, *Ascetic Discourses*, 60, Discourse 4; Isaiah of Scetis, *ΤΟΥ ΟΣΙΟΥ ΠΑΤΡΟΣ ΗΜΩΝ ΑΒΒΑ ΗΣΑΙΟΥ ΛΟΓΟΙ ΚΘ*, 23, Discourse 4. Translation altered.

56. Isaiah of Scetis, *Ascetic Discourses*, 76, Discourse 5.

57. Ibid., 150, Discourse 21; Isaiah of Scetis, *ΤΟΥ ΟΣΙΟΥ ΠΑΤΡΟΣ ΗΜΩΝ ΑΒΒΑ ΗΣΑΙΟΥ ΛΟΓΟΙ ΚΘ*, 120, Discourse 21.

58. Isaiah of Scetis, *Ascetic Discourses*, 62, Discourse 4; Isaiah of Scetis, *ΤΟΥ ΟΣΙΟΥ ΠΑΤΡΟΣ ΗΜΩΝ ΑΒΒΑ ΗΣΑΙΟΥ ΛΟΓΟΙ ΚΘ*, 25, Discourse 4.

59. Isaiah of Scetis, *Ascetic Discourses*, 62, Discourse 4; Isaiah of Scetis, *ΤΟΥ ΟΣΙΟΥ ΠΑΤΡΟΣ ΗΜΩΝ ΑΒΒΑ ΗΣΑΙΟΥ ΛΟΓΟΙ ΚΘ*, 25, Discourse 4.

60. Isaiah of Scetis, *Ascetic Discourses*, 155–156, Discourse 21; Isaiah of Scetis, *ΤΟΥ ΟΣΙΟΥ ΠΑΤΡΟΣ ΗΜΩΝ ΑΒΒΑ ΗΣΑΙΟΥ ΛΟΓΟΙ ΚΘ*, 126, Discourse 21.

61. Isaiah of Scetis, *Ascetic Discourses*, 159, Discourse 21; Isaiah of Scetis, *ΤΟΥ ΟΣΙΟΥ ΠΑΤΡΟΣ ΗΜΩΝ ΑΒΒΑ ΗΣΑΙΟΥ ΛΟΓΟΙ ΚΘ*, 129, Discourse 21.

62. Isaiah of Scetis, *Ascetic Discourses*, 158, Discourse 21; Isaiah of Scetis, *ΤΟΥ ΟΣΙΟΥ ΠΑΤΡΟΣ ΗΜΩΝ ΑΒΒΑ ΗΣΑΙΟΥ ΛΟΓΟΙ ΚΘ*, 129, Discourse 21.

63. Isaiah of Scetis, *Ascetic Discourses*, 156, Discourse 21; Isaiah of Scetis, *ΤΟΥ ΟΣΙΟΥ ΠΑΤΡΟΣ ΗΜΩΝ ΑΒΒΑ ΗΣΑΙΟΥ ΛΟΓΟΙ ΚΘ*, 126, Discourse 21.

64. Isaiah of Scetis, *Ascetic Discourses*, 156, Discourse 21.

65. Ibid., 232, Discourse 28. See also, Isaiah of Scetis, *Abbé Isaïe: Recueil ascétique*, trans. Les moines de Solesmes, vol. 7, Spiritualité orientale (1970), 264. "[D]e peur qu'en sortant de notre corps nous soyons trouvés nus quant aux vertus et que nous ne tombions au pouvoir du dragon."

66. In Letter 126, Theodore praised Barsanuphius for his virtue. In Letter 351, the editor of the letters described a brother as progressing in godly virtue. In Letter 456, a layperson asked about virtue but John did not repeat the term. The same layperson mentioned virtue again in Letter 457 and, again, John did not repeat the term. In Letter 605, another brother asked Barsanuphius about virtue, but the term was not repeated.

67. Barsanuphius and John, *Letters*, 21–22, Prologue. "As we are about to read this book, however, we are obliged to know that some of these words were spoken to anchorites, others to cenobites, still others to those living together, and yet others to priests and Christ-loving laypersons. Moreover, some were intended for younger monastics or novices, others for those already advanced in age and disciplined in their habits, and still others for those approaching the perfection of virtue—as each was able to receive the words. For not all the same teachings are suitable for everyone. Just as in the ages of the body, different foods are appropriate for the breast-feeding child, for the adolescent, and for the elderly, the same also happens in the spiritual stages. Often, these elders responded to questions bearing in mind the weakness in the thoughts of the persons inquiring, discreetly condescending to their level in order that those asking might not fall into despair, just as we find in the *Lives of the Old Men*. So we must not receive as a general rule the words spoken in a loving way to particular people for the sake of their specific weakness; instead, we should immediately discern that the response was surely addressed by the saints to the questioner in a very personal way. For it may happen that such persons will one day come to their senses through the prayers of the saints, thereby reaching a condition appropriate for monks, and then they will again hear what is beneficial to them."

68. Ibid., 21, Prologue; Barsanuphius and John, *Correspondance*, 160, Prologue.

69. Barsanuphius and John, *Letters*, 243, Letter 689; Barsanuphius and John, *Correspondance*, 126, Letter 689.

70. Barsanuphius and John, *Letters*, 81–82, Letter 469; Barsanuphius and John, *Correspondance*, 570, Letter 469.

71. Barsanuphius and John, *Letters*, 82, Letter 469.

72. Ibid., 220, Letter 643.

73. Ibid., 221–222, Letter 644; Barsanuphius and John, *Correspondance*, 72, Letter 644.

74. Barsanuphius and John, *Letters*, 247, Letter 241; Barsanuphius and John, *Correspondance*, 186, Letter 241.

75. Barsanuphius and John, *Letters*, 248, Letter 241; Barsanuphius and John, *Correspondance*, 190, Letter 241.

76. Isaiah of Scetis, *Ascetic Discourses*, 155–156, Discourse 21; Isaiah of Scetis, *ΤΟΥ ΟΣΙΟΥ ΠΑΤΡΟΣ ΗΜΩΝ ΑΒΒΑ ΗΣΑΙΟΥ ΛΟΓΟΙ ΚΘ*, 126, Discourse 21.

77. Barsanuphius and John, *Letters*, 128, Letter 106; Barsanuphius and John, *Correspondance*, 426, Letter 106.

78. Barsanuphius and John, *Letters*, 137, Letter 118; Barsanuphius and John, *Correspondance*, 448–450, Letter 118.

79. Barsanuphius and John, *Letters*, 105, Letter 503; Barsanuphius and John, *Correspondance*, 626, Letter 503.

80. Barsanuphius and John, *Letters*, 123, Letter 532; Barsanuphius and John, *Correspondance*, 672, Letter 532.

81. Barsanuphius and John, *Letters*, 213, Letter 628; Barsanuphius and John, *Correspondance*, 54, Letter 628.

82. Barsanuphius and John, *Letters*, 213–214, Letter 628; Barsanuphius and John, *Correspondance*, 54, Letter 628.

83. Abba Poemen cited John the Dwarf on the virtues, "A brother asked Abba Poemen saying, 'Can a man put his trust in one single work?' The old man said to him that Abba John the Dwarf said, 'I would rather have a bit of all the virtues.'" Ward, *The Sayings of the Desert Fathers: The Alphabetical Collection*, 145, Poemen 46.

84. Barsanuphius and John, *Letters*, 324, Letter 847; Barsanuphius and John, *Correspondance*, 330, Letter 847.

85. Barsanuphius and John, *Letters*, 149, Letter 570c.

86. Ibid.; Barsanuphius and John, *Correspondance*, 738–740, Letter 570c.

87. Barsanuphius and John, *Letters*, 150, Letter 570c; Barsanuphius and John, *Correspondance*, 740, Letter 570c.

88. Barsanuphius and John, *Letters*, 151, Letter 570c.

89. Ibid., 161, Letter 576; Barsanuphius and John, *Correspondance*, 768, Letter 576.

90. Dorotheos of Gaza, *Abba Dorotheos*, 69, Discourse 1; Dorotheos of Gaza, Œuvres spirituelles, 146, Discourse 1.

91. Dorotheos of Gaza, *Abba Dorotheos*, 220–221, Discourse 14; Dorotheos of Gaza, Œuvres spirituelles, 438, Discourse 14.

92. Dorotheos of Gaza, *Abba Dorotheos*, 169, Discourse 10; Dorotheos of Gaza, Œuvres spirituelles, 336–338, Discourse 10. See, Ward, *The Sayings of the Desert Fathers: The Alphabetical Collection*, 104, Longinus 5.

93. Dorotheos of Gaza, *Abba Dorotheos*, 76, Discourse 1; Dorotheos of Gaza, Œuvres spirituelles, 162–164, Discourse 1. Samuel Rubenson noted that for Antony of Egypt, "Virtue is nothing foreign to human nature; on the contrary, salvation is the return of the human being to a natural state." Samuel Rubenson, "Christian Asceticism and the Emergence of the Monastic Tradition," in *Asceticism*, ed. Vincent L. Wimbush and Richard Valantasis (New York: Oxford University Press, 1995), 54.

94. Dorotheos of Gaza, *Abba Dorotheos*, 63, Life of Dositheos.

95. Ibid., 82, Discourse 1; Dorotheos of Gaza, Œuvres spirituelles, 178, Discourse 1.

96. Dorotheos of Gaza, *Abba Dorotheos*, 47, Introductory Letter; Dorotheos of Gaza, Œuvres spirituelles, 110, Introductory Letter.

97. Dorotheos of Gaza, *Abba Dorotheos*, 48, Introductory Letter; Dorotheos of Gaza, Œuvres spirituelles, 112, Introductory Letter.

98. Dorotheos of Gaza, *Abba Dorotheos*, 48, Introductory Letter; Dorotheos of Gaza, Œuvres spirituelles, 112, Introductory Letter.

99. Dorotheos of Gaza, *Abba Dorotheos*, 48, Introductory Letter; Dorotheos of Gaza, Œuvres spirituelles, 112–114, Introductory Letter.

100. Dorotheos of Gaza, *Abba Dorotheos*, 216, Discourse 14.

101. Ibid., 81, Discourse 1.

102. Ibid.; Dorotheos of Gaza, Œuvres spirituelles, 176, Discourse 1.

103. Dorotheos of Gaza, *Abba Dorotheos*, 83, Discourse 1.

104. Ibid., 263, Letter 2; Dorotheos of Gaza, Œuvres spirituelles, 502, Letter 2.

105. Dorotheos of Gaza, *Abba Dorotheos*, 263, Letter 2; Dorotheos of Gaza, Œuvres spirituelles, 502–504, Letter 2.

106. Dorotheos of Gaza, *Abba Dorotheos*, 85, Discourse 1; Dorotheos of Gaza, Œuvres spirituelles, 184, Discourse 1.

107. Dorotheos of Gaza, *Abba Dorotheos*, 89, Discourse 2.

108. Ibid.; Dorotheos of Gaza, Œuvres spirituelles, 188, Discourse 2.

109. Dorotheos of Gaza, *Abba Dorotheos*, 90–91, Discourse 2.

110. Ibid., 93, Discourse 2.

111. Ibid., 94, Discourse 2; Dorotheos of Gaza, Œuvres spirituelles, 196, Discourse 2.

112. Dorotheos of Gaza, *Abba Dorotheos*, 94–95, Discourse 2; Dorotheos of Gaza, Œuvres spirituelles, 198, Discourse 2.

113. Dorotheos of Gaza, *Abba Dorotheos*, 95, Discourse 2; Dorotheos of Gaza, Œuvres spirituelles, 200, Discourse 2.

114. Dorotheos of Gaza, *Abba Dorotheos*, 109, Discourse 4; Dorotheos of Gaza, Œuvres spirituelles, 220, Discourse 4.

115. Dorotheos of Gaza, *Abba Dorotheos*, 109, Discourse 4; Dorotheos of Gaza, Œuvres spirituelles, 220, Discourse 4.

116. Dorotheos of Gaza, *Abba Dorotheos*, 109, Discourse 4; Dorotheos of Gaza, Œuvres spirituelles, 220, Discourse 4.

117. Dorotheos of Gaza, *Abba Dorotheos*, 109, Discourse 4; Dorotheos of Gaza, Œuvres spirituelles, 220, Discourse 4.

118. Basil of Caesarea, *The Asketikon of St. Basil the Great*, 156–157, The Longer Responses (Prologue).

119. Dorotheos of Gaza, *Abba Dorotheos*, 109–110, Discourse 4; Dorotheos of Gaza, Œuvres spirituelles, 222, Discourse 4.

120. Dorotheos of Gaza, *Abba Dorotheos*, 112, Discourse 4; Dorotheos of Gaza, Œuvres spirituelles, 228, Discourse 4.

121. Pauli, *Doctrinae Diversae: Die geistliche Lehre*, 59. "[D]ie Liebe als die Vollendung aller Tugenden."

122. Dorotheos of Gaza, *Abba Dorotheos*, 111, Discourse 4.

123. Ibid.; Dorotheos of Gaza, Œuvres spirituelles, 226, Discourse 4.

124. Dorotheos of Gaza, *Abba Dorotheos*, 184, Discourse 11; Dorotheos of Gaza, Œuvres spirituelles, 370, Discourse 11.

125. Dorotheos of Gaza, *Abba Dorotheos*, 184, Discourse 11.

126. Ibid., 186, Discourse 11; Dorotheos of Gaza, Œuvres spirituelles, 372, Discourse 11.

127. Dorotheos of Gaza, *Abba Dorotheos*, 186, Discourse 11; Dorotheos of Gaza, Œuvres spirituelles, 374, Discourse 11.

128. Dorotheos of Gaza, *Abba Dorotheos*, 186, Discourse 11; Dorotheos of Gaza, Œuvres spirituelles, 374, Discourse 11.

129. Dorotheos of Gaza, *Abba Dorotheos*, 186, Discourse 11; Dorotheos of Gaza, Œuvres spirituelles, 374, Discourse 11.

130. Dorotheos of Gaza, *Abba Dorotheos*, 186, Discourse 11; Dorotheos of Gaza, Œuvres spirituelles, 374, Discourse 11.

131. Dorotheos of Gaza, *Abba Dorotheos*, 186, Discourse 11; Dorotheos of Gaza, Œuvres spirituelles, 374, Dicourse 11.

132. Dorotheos of Gaza, *Abba Dorotheos*, 96, Discourse 2; Dorotheos of Gaza, Œuvres spirituelles, 200, Discourse 2.

133. Dorotheos of Gaza, *Abba Dorotheos*, 96, Discourse 2.

134. Ibid., 97–98, Discourse 2; Dorotheos of Gaza, Œuvres spirituelles, 204–206, Discourse 2.

135. Dorotheos of Gaza, *Abba Dorotheos*, 170, Discourse 10; Dorotheos of Gaza, Œuvres spirituelles, 340, Discourse 10.

136. Dorotheos of Gaza, *Abba Dorotheos*, 170, Discourse 10; Dorotheos of Gaza, Œuvres spirituelles, 340, Discourse 10.

137. Dorotheos of Gaza, *Abba Dorotheos*, 169–170, Discourse 10; Dorotheos of Gaza, Œuvres spirituelles, 338, Discourse 10.

138. Dorotheos of Gaza, *Abba Dorotheos*, 170, Discourse 10.

139. Ibid.; Dorotheos of Gaza, Œuvres spirituelles, 338–340, Discourse 10.

140. Dorotheos of Gaza, *Abba Dorotheos*, 170, Discourse 10; Dorotheos of Gaza, Œuvres spirituelles, 340, Discourse 10. See Basil of Caesarea, "Homily 11: A Psalm of David which He Sang to the Lord, for the Words of Chusi, the Song of Jemini (On Psalm 7)," 176.

141. Dorotheos of Gaza, *Abba Dorotheos*, 171, Discourse 10; Dorotheos of Gaza, Œuvres spirituelles, 340, Discourse 10.

142. Dorotheos of Gaza, *Abba Dorotheos*, 171, Discourse 10; Dorotheos of Gaza, Œuvres spirituelles, 342, Discourse 10.

143. Dorotheos of Gaza, *Abba Dorotheos*, 171, Discourse 10; Dorotheos of Gaza, Œuvres spirituelles, 342, Discourse 10.

Chapter 6: The Ascetic Body

1. A collection of essays from a variety of perspectives presented at a 1993 meeting at Union Theological Seminary in New York City was published as *Asceticism*, ed. Vincent L. Wimbush and Richard Valantasis (New York: Oxford University Press, 1995). Their introductory essay set out the difficulties in establishing ascetical theory in late antiquity. Vincent L. Wimbush and Richard Valantasis, "Introduction," in *Asceticism*, ed. Vincent L. Wimbush and Richard Valantasis (New York: Oxford University Press), xix–xxxii. For contemporary works on asceticism in early Christianity, see Philip Rousseau, *Ascetics, Authority, and the Church in the Age of Jerome and Cassian*, 2nd ed. (Notre Dame: University of Notre Dame Press, 2010); Richard Valantasis, "A Theory of the Social Function of Asceticism," in *The Making of the Self: Ancient and Modern Asceticism* (Eugene, OR: Cascade Books, 2008); Richard Valantasis, "Construction of Power in Asceticism," in *The Making of the Self: Ancient and Modern Asceticism* (Eugene, OR: Cascade Books, 2008); Brown, *The Body and Society*; Gavin Flood, *The Ascetic Self: Subjectivity, Memory and Tradition* (Cambridge University Press, 2005); Michel Foucault, *The Hermeneutics of the Subject: Lectures at the Collège de France, 1981–1982*, trans. Graham Burchell (New York: Picador, 2004); Philip Rousseau, "Ascetics as mediators and as teachers," in *The Cult of Saints in Late Antiquity and the Middle Ages: Essays on the Contribution of Peter Brown*, ed. Paul Antony Hayward and J. D

Howard-Johnston (New York: Oxford University Press, 1999); Elizabeth A Clark, *Reading Renunciation: Asceticism and Scripture in Early Christianity* (Princeton: Princeton University Press, 1999); Hadot, *Philosophy as a Way of Life*; Vincent L Wimbush, *Ascetic Behavior in Greco-Roman Antiquity: A Sourcebook* (Minneapolis: Fortress Press, 1990); Geoffrey Galt Harpham, *The Ascetic Imperative in Culture and Criticism* (Chicago: University of Chicago Press, 1987). For a recent survey of approaches to early Christian asceticism, see Patrik Hagman, *The Asceticism of Isaac of Nineveh* (New York: Oxford University Press, 2010), 1–24.

2. Hagman, *The Asceticism of Isaac of Nineveh*, 1.

3. Palladius, *The Lausiac History*, trans. Robert T. Meyer (Westminster: Newman Press, 1965), 33, Dorotheus 2.

4. Hagman, *The Asceticism of Isaac of Nineveh*, 24.

5. James Goehring argued against the notion that the origins of Christian monasticism began in the Egyptian desert, the "Big Bang" theory, in James E. Goehring, *Ascetics, Society, and the Desert: Studies in Early Egyptian Monasticism* (Harrisburg, PA: Trinity Press International, 1999), 13. Susanna Elm has shown the Christian ascetic impulse was evident in urban and familial settings, Susanna Elm, *Virgins of God: The Making of Asceticism in Late Antiquity* (New York: Oxford University Press, 1994), viii. The impact of Greco-Roman asceticism upon Christian ascetical practice was recently explored in Richard Damian Finn, *Asceticism in the Graeco-Roman World* (New York: Cambridge University Press, 2009). Richard Sorabji explores the ancient method of ascetical and psychological rigor in dealing with emotions. His analysis explores the impact of Stoic doctrines on Christian authors and monastic writers like Origen and Evagrius. This subtle distinction in Stoic thought between emotions and first movements of the soul was traced through the Christian era and the impact on Evagrius was examined. Richard Sorabji, *Emotion and Peace of Mind: From Stoic Agitation to Christian Temptation: The Gifford Lectures* (New York: Oxford University Press, 2000). Foucault's distinction between the Christian ascetic goal and the Stoic emphasis is worthy of mention. He emphasized, "The Christian athlete is on the indefinite path of progress towards holiness in which he must surpass himself even to the point of renouncing himself. Also, the Christian athlete is especially someone who has an enemy, an adversary, who keeps him on guard… The Stoic athlete, the athlete of ancient spirituality also has to struggle. He has to be ready for a struggle in which his adversary is anything coming to him from the external world: the event. The ancient athlete is an athlete of the event. The Christian athlete is an athlete of himself." Foucault, *The Hermeneutics of the Subject: Lectures at the Collège de France, 1981–1982*, 332.

6. Hagman provided vague guidelines through which one could fruitfully explore ancient Christian asceticism: Asceticism is a positive concept, a response, rational, a performance or a form of communication that involves the ascetic and an audience, has a message, is transformative, and involves the body. Hagman, *The Asceticism of Isaac of Nineveh*, 20.

7. Valantasis, "Construction of Power in Asceticism," 38.

8. Valantasis, "A Theory of the Social Function of Asceticism," 7–8. See also, Richard Valantasis, "A Theory of the Social Function of Asceticism," in *Asceticism*, ed. Vincent L. Wimbush and Richard Valantasis (New York: Oxford University Press, 1995).

9. Valantasis, "Construction of Power in Asceticism," 39.

10. Hagman, *The Asceticism of Isaac of Nineveh*, 10.

11. Flood, *The Ascetic Self: Subjectivity, Memory and Tradition*, 1.

12. Ibid., 2. Flood continued, "Asceticism within tradition is performed by a self; not a disembodied self, but a historical, language-bearing, gendered person with their own name and story... The ascetic submits her life to a form that transforms it, to a training that changes a person's orientation from the fulfillment of desire to a narrative greater than the self. The ascetic reshapes the narrative of her life to the narrative of tradition." Ibid.

13. Ibid., 13.

14. Ibid.

15. Ibid., 15.

16. Ibid., 145.

17. Ibid., 5.

18. Andrew T. Crislip, *Thorns in the Flesh: Illness and Sanctity in Late Ancient Christianity* (Philadelphia: University of Pennsylvania Press, 2013), 5.

19. Ibid.

20. Ibid., 6.

21. Ibid., 28.

22. Ibid., 24.

23. Ibid.

24. Ibid., 32.

25. Arthur Kleinman, *The Illness Narratives: Suffering, Healing, and the Human Condition* (New York: Basic Books, 1988), 27.

26. Ibid., 13.

27. Crislip, *Thorns in the Flesh*, 32.

28. Brown, *The Body and Society*, 236–237.

29. Hadot, *Philosophy as a Way of Life*, 135.

30. Ibid., 140.

31. Brown, *The Body and Society*, 223.

32. Isaiah of Scetis, *Ascetic Discourses*, 119, Discourse 16; Isaiah of Scetis, *ΤΟΥ ΟΣΙΟΥ ΠΑΤΡΟΣ ΗΜΩΝ ΑΒΒΑ ΗΣΑΙΟΥ ΛΟΓΟΙ ΚΘ*, 85, Discourse 16. Translation slightly altered.

33. Isaiah of Scetis, *Ascetic Discourses*, 124, Discourse 16; Isaiah of Scetis, *ΤΟΥ ΟΣΙΟΥ ΠΑΤΡΟΣ ΗΜΩΝ ΑΒΒΑ ΗΣΑΙΟΥ ΛΟΓΟΙ ΚΘ*, 93, Discourse 16.

34. Isaiah of Scetis, *Ascetic Discourses*, 126, Discourse 16; Isaiah of Scetis, *ΤΟΥ ΟΣΙΟΥ ΠΑΤΡΟΣ ΗΜΩΝ ΑΒΒΑ ΗΣΑΙΟΥ ΛΟΓΟΙ ΚΘ*, 96, Discourse 16.

35. Isaiah compared the nature of Jesus, the nature of Adam, and a nature worse than Adam's: "If you give someone something that he desires and let him keep it, you have imitated the nature of Jesus. If, on the other hand, you ask for it back, you have imitated the nature of Adam. If you accept interest, however, you have contravened even Adam's nature." Isaiah of Scetis, *Ascetic Discourses*, 87, Discourse 8.

36. Ibid., 43, Discourse 2; Isaiah of Scetis, *ΤΟΥ ΟΣΙΟΥ ΠΑΤΡΟΣ ΗΜΩΝ ΑΒΒΑ ΗΣΑΙΟΥ ΛΟΓΟΙ ΚΘ*, 4, Discourse 2.

37. Isaiah of Scetis, *Ascetic Discourses*, 43, Discourse 2; Isaiah of Scetis, *ΤΟΥ ΟΣΙΟΥ ΠΑΤΡΟΣ ΗΜΩΝ ΑΒΒΑ ΗΣΑΙΟΥ ΛΟΓΟΙ ΚΘ*, 4, Discourse 2.

38. Isaiah of Scetis, *Ascetic Discourses*, 43, Discourse 2; Isaiah of Scetis, *ΤΟΥ ΟΣΙΟΥ ΠΑΤΡΟΣ ΗΜΩΝ ΑΒΒΑ ΗΣΑΙΟΥ ΛΟΓΟΙ ΚΘ*, 4, Discourse 2.

39. Isaiah of Scetis, *Ascetic Discourses*, 43, Discourse 2; Isaiah of Scetis, *ΤΟΥ ΟΣΙΟΥ ΠΑΤΡΟΣ ΗΜΩΝ ΑΒΒΑ ΗΣΑΙΟΥ ΛΟΓΟΙ ΚΘ*, 5, Discourse 2.

40. Isaiah of Scetis, *Ascetic Discourses*, 45, Discourse 2; Isaiah of Scetis, *ΤΟΥ ΟΣΙΟΥ ΠΑΤΡΟΣ ΗΜΩΝ ΑΒΒΑ ΗΣΑΙΟΥ ΛΟΓΟΙ ΚΘ*, 6, Discourse 2. Translation slightly altered.

41. Isaiah of Scetis, *Ascetic Discourses*, 82–83, Discourse 7; Isaiah of Scetis, *ΤΟΥ ΟΣΙΟΥ ΠΑΤΡΟΣ ΗΜΩΝ ΑΒΒΑ ΗΣΑΙΟΥ ΛΟΓΟΙ ΚΘ*, 48, Discourse 7.

42. Isaiah of Scetis, *Ascetic Discourses*, 82–83, Discourse 7; Isaiah of Scetis, *ΤΟΥ ΟΣΙΟΥ ΠΑΤΡΟΣ ΗΜΩΝ ΑΒΒΑ ΗΣΑΙΟΥ ΛΟΓΟΙ ΚΘ*, 48, Discourse 7.

43. Isaiah of Scetis, *Ascetic Discourses*, 83, Discourse 7.

44. Ibid., 141, Discourse 18; Isaiah of Scetis, *ΤΟΥ ΟΣΙΟΥ ΠΑΤΡΟΣ ΗΜΩΝ ΑΒΒΑ ΗΣΑΙΟΥ ΛΟΓΟΙ ΚΘ*, 113, Discourse 18. Translation slightly altered.

45. Isaiah of Scetis, *Ascetic Discourses*, 142, Discourse 18; Isaiah of Scetis, *ΤΟΥ ΟΣΙΟΥ ΠΑΤΡΟΣ ΗΜΩΝ ΑΒΒΑ ΗΣΑΙΟΥ ΛΟΓΟΙ ΚΘ*, 113, Discourse 18.

46. Isaiah of Scetis, *Ascetic Discourses*, 145, Discourse 19; Isaiah of Scetis, *ΤΟΥ ΟΣΙΟΥ ΠΑΤΡΟΣ ΗΜΩΝ ΑΒΒΑ ΗΣΑΙΟΥ ΛΟΓΟΙ ΚΘ*, 116, Discourse 19.

47. Isaiah of Scetis, *Ascetic Discourses*, 206, Discourse 25; Isaiah of Scetis, *ΤΟΥ ΟΣΙΟΥ ΠΑΤΡΟΣ ΗΜΩΝ ΑΒΒΑ ΗΣΑΙΟΥ ΛΟΓΟΙ ΚΘ*, 177, Discourse 25.

48. Isaiah of Scetis, *Ascetic Discourses*, 213, Discourse 26; Isaiah of Scetis, *ΤΟΥ ΟΣΙΟΥ ΠΑΤΡΟΣ ΗΜΩΝ ΑΒΒΑ ΗΣΑΙΟΥ ΛΟΓΟΙ ΚΘ*, 183, Discourse 26.

49. Isaiah of Scetis, *Ascetic Discourses*, 103, Discourse 12.

50. Ibid.; Isaiah of Scetis, *ΤΟΥ ΟΣΙΟΥ ΠΑΤΡΟΣ ΗΜΩΝ ΑΒΒΑ ΗΣΑΙΟΥ ΛΟΓΟΙ ΚΘ*, 71, Discourse 12. Translation slightly altered.

51. Isaiah of Scetis, *Ascetic Discourses*, 103, Discourse 12.

52. Ibid.; Isaiah of Scetis, *ΤΟΥ ΟΣΙΟΥ ΠΑΤΡΟΣ ΗΜΩΝ ΑΒΒΑ ΗΣΑΙΟΥ ΛΟΓΟΙ ΚΘ*, 71, Discourse 12. Translation slightly altered.

53. Isaiah of Scetis, *Ascetic Discourses*, 103, Discourse 12.

54. Ibid., 104, Discourse 12.

55. Ibid.; Isaiah of Scetis, *ΤΟΥ ΟΣΙΟΥ ΠΑΤΡΟΣ ΗΜΩΝ ΑΒΒΑ ΗΣΑΙΟΥ ΛΟΓΟΙ ΚΘ*, 72, Discourse 12. Translation slightly altered.

56. Isaiah of Scetis, *Ascetic Discourses*, 136, Discourse 17; Isaiah of Scetis, *ΤΟΥ ΟΣΙΟΥ ΠΑΤΡΟΣ ΗΜΩΝ ΑΒΒΑ ΗΣΑΙΟΥ ΛΟΓΟΙ ΚΘ*, 107, Discourse 17.

57. Isaiah of Scetis, *Ascetic Discourses*, 136, Discourse 17; Isaiah of Scetis, *ΤΟΥ ΟΣΙΟΥ ΠΑΤΡΟΣ ΗΜΩΝ ΑΒΒΑ ΗΣΑΙΟΥ ΛΟΓΟΙ ΚΘ*, 108, Discourse 17.

58. Isaiah of Scetis, *Ascetic Discourses*, 136, Discourse 17; Isaiah of Scetis, *ΤΟΥ ΟΣΙΟΥ ΠΑΤΡΟΣ ΗΜΩΝ ΑΒΒΑ ΗΣΑΙΟΥ ΛΟΓΟΙ ΚΘ*, 108, Discourse 17.

59. Isaiah said nothing about the origin of the soul, but did gesture toward the soul's preexistence. He wrote, "In the same way those who have been judged worthy and have obtained these gifts perceive the world as their prison and do not wish to mix there lest they die, and this soul cannot love the world, even if it desires it. It remembers where it found itself in the beginning, dwelling in God, before this world made it return barren to him." Isaiah of Scetis, *Ascetic Discourses*, 192, Discourse 25.

60. Ibid., 121, Discourse 16; Isaiah of Scetis, *ΤΟΥ ΟΣΙΟΥ ΠΑΤΡΟΣ ΗΜΩΝ ΑΒΒΑ ΗΣΑΙΟΥ ΛΟΓΟΙ ΚΘ*, 88, Discourse 16.

61. Isaiah of Scetis, *Ascetic Discourses*, 119–120, Discourse 16; Isaiah of Scetis, *ΤΟΥ ΟΣΙΟΥ ΠΑΤΡΟΣ ΗΜΩΝ ΑΒΒΑ ΗΣΑΙΟΥ ΛΟΓΟΙ ΚΘ*, 86, Discourse 16. Translation slightly altered.

62. Isaiah of Scetis, *Ascetic Discourses*, 90, Discourse 8; Isaiah of Scetis, *ΤΟΥ ΟΣΙΟΥ ΠΑΤΡΟΣ ΗΜΩΝ ΑΒΒΑ ΗΣΑΙΟΥ ΛΟΓΟΙ ΚΘ*, 57, Discourse 8.

63. Isaiah of Scetis, *Ascetic Discourses*, 115, Discourse 15; Isaiah of Scetis, *ΤΟΥ ΟΣΙΟΥ ΠΑΤΡΟΣ ΗΜΩΝ ΑΒΒΑ ΗΣΑΙΟΥ ΛΟΓΟΙ ΚΘ*, 83, Discourse 15.

64. Isaiah of Scetis, *Ascetic Discourses*, 116, Discourse 15; Isaiah of Scetis, *ΤΟΥ ΟΣΙΟΥ ΠΑΤΡΟΣ ΗΜΩΝ ΑΒΒΑ ΗΣΑΙΟΥ ΛΟΓΟΙ ΚΘ*, 83, Discourse 15.

65. Isaiah of Scetis, *Ascetic Discourses*, 115, Discourse 15; Isaiah of Scetis, *ΤΟΥ ΟΣΙΟΥ ΠΑΤΡΟΣ ΗΜΩΝ ΑΒΒΑ ΗΣΑΙΟΥ ΛΟΓΟΙ ΚΘ*, 82, Discourse 15.

66. Isaiah of Scetis, *Ascetic Discourses*, 117, Discourse 15; Isaiah of Scetis, *ΤΟΥ ΟΣΙΟΥ ΠΑΤΡΟΣ ΗΜΩΝ ΑΒΒΑ ΗΣΑΙΟΥ ΛΟΓΟΙ ΚΘ*, 84, Discourse 15.

67. On spiritual exercises in the monastic school of Gaza, see Bitton-Ashkelony and Kofsky, *The Monastic School of Gaza*, 157–182.

68. Crislip, *Thorns in the Flesh*, 139.

69. Ibid., 140. "Healing (of illness) … involves the transformation of meaning, more generally through the interaction of healer and the patient as well as a variety of tertiary parties… Healing in this sense can include training and manipulating the body but usually comprises an important symbolic component, and indeed may be entirely symbolic. Through the healing process, the healer may not necessarily change, eliminate, or neutralize any independent 'disease' lurking within the body–and indeed in many cases the healer and patient may not have any such conception of an independent reified force working within the body. But through the mediation of symbols and other interventions the sufferer makes sense of his or her affliction." Ibid., 143.

70. Barsanuphius and John, *Letters*, 244–245, Letter 239.

71. Ibid., 163, Letter 139; Barsanuphius and John, *Correspondance*, 514, Letter 139.

72. Barsanuphius and John, *Letters*, 105, Letter 503; Barsanuphius and John, *Correspondance*, 628, Letter 503.

73. Barsanuphius and John, *Letters*, 105, Letter 503.

74. Ibid., 118–119, Letter 524; Barsanuphius and John, *Correspondance*, 660, Letter 524.

75. Barsanuphius and John, *Letters*, 118–119, Letter 524; Barsanuphius and John, *Correspondance*, 660–662, Letter 524.

76. Barsanuphius and John, *Letters*, 119, Letter 524; Barsanuphius and John, *Correspondance*, 662, Letter 524.

77. Barsanuphius and John, *Letters*, 184, Letter 168.

78. Ibid., 185, Letter 169.

79. Ibid., 184–185, Letter 169; Barsanuphius and John, *Correspondance*, 572, Letter 169.

80. Barsanuphius and John, *Letters*, 116, Letter 518.

81. Ibid., 115, Letter 517; Barsanuphius and John, *Correspondance*, 652, Letter 517.

82. Barsanuphius and John, *Letters*, 258, Letter 255.

83. Ibid., 265, Letter 259; Barsanuphius and John, *Correspondance*, 232, Letter 259.

84. Barsanuphius and John, *Letters*, 267, Letter 261; Barsanuphius and John, *Correspondance*, 236, Letter 261.

85. Crislip, *Thorns in the Flesh*, 156. Author's emphasis.

86. Barsanuphius and John, *Letters*, 102, Letter 77; Barsanuphius and John, *Correspondance*, 358, Letter 77.

87. Barsanuphius and John, *Letters*, 105, Letter 79; Barsanuphius and John, *Correspondance*, 366, Letter 79.

88. Barsanuphius and John, *Letters*, 105, Letter 79; Barsanuphius and John, *Correspondance*, 366, Letter 79.

89. Barsanuphius and John, *Letters*, 105, Letter 80.

90. Crislip, *Thorns in the Flesh*, 139.

91. Barsanuphius and John, *Letters*, 100, Letter 75; Barsanuphius and John, *Correspondance*, 354, Letter 75.

92. Crislip, *Thorns in the Flesh*, 139.

93. Barsanuphius and John, *Letters*, 99, Letter 74.

94. Crislip, *Thorns in the Flesh*, 147.

95. Barsanuphius and John, *Letters*, 99, Letter 74.

96. Ibid., 99–100, Letter 74.

97. Crislip, *Thorns in the Flesh*, 147–148. "Symbolic healing functions to make meaning of, to understand, and to narrativize the sufferer's illness in accordance with the mythic narratives of the sufferer's culture. Second, the object of symbolic healing is the emotions or passions, rather than the body." Ibid., 143–144.

98. Barsanuphius and John, *Letters*, 100, Letter 74.

99. Crislip, *Thorns in the Flesh*, 140. "In their *Letters* we see the development of illness as a mode of spiritual exercise, as a type of asceticism."

100. Barsanuphius and John, *Letters*, 142, Letter 124; Barsanuphius and John, *Correspondance*, 464, Letter 124.

101. Barsanuphius and John, *Letters*, 143, Letter 124.

102. Ibid., 144, Letter 124; Barsanuphius and John, *Correspondance*, 468, Letter 124. "Καθὼς οὖν οὐ μένει μετὰ τοῦ νεκροῦ τὰ φυσικὰ αὐτοῦ παντελῶς, οὕτως οὐδὲ μετὰ τοῦ νεκρωθέντος τῇ σαρκὶ πνευματικῶς. Εἰ οὖν ἀπέθανες τῇ σαρκί πῶς ζῶσιν ἐν σοὶ τὰ φυσικά;"

103. Barsanuphius and John, *Letters*, 144, Letter 124; Barsanuphius and John, *Correspondance*, 468, Letter 124.

104. Barsanuphius and John, *Letters*, 209, Letter 200; Barsanuphius and John, *Correspondance*, 632, Letter 200.

105. Barsanuphius and John, *Letters*, 64, Letter 49; Barsanuphius and John, *Correspondance*, 264, Letter 49.

106. Barsanuphius and John, *Letters*, 95–96, Letter 71; Barsanuphius and John, *Correspondance*, 344, Letter 71.

107. Barsanuphius and John, *Letters*, 28, Letter 6; Barsanuphius and John, *Correspondance*, 172, Letter 6.

108. Barsanuphius and John, *Letters*, 165, Letter 142; Barsanuphius and John, *Correspondance*, 520, Letter 142.

109. Barsanuphius and John, *Letters*, 75, Letter 59; Barsanuphius and John, *Correspondance*, 290, Letter 59.

110. Barsanuphius and John, *Letters*, 77, Letter 60.

111. Ibid., 78, Letter 60.

112. Barsanuphius and John, *Letters*, 191–192, Letter 607. Letters 600–608 were a refutation of certain Origenist doctrines in Seridos's monastery. Barsanuphius and John respond to questions from monks who admitted to reading Origen and Evagrius among others. Daniël Hombergen has discussed this issue in Daniël Hombergen, "The Question of Dorotheus of Gaza's Position in the Second Origenist Controversy," in *Church, Society and Monasticism: Acts of the International Symposium, Rome, May 31–June 3, 2006: The Monastic Institute of the Faculty of Theology in the Pontifical Athenaeum S. Anselmo*, ed. E. López-Tello García and B. S. Zorzi (Rome: Pontificio Ateneo S. Anselmo, 2009); Hombergen, "Barsanuphius and John of Gaza and the Origenist Controversy."; Daniël Hombergen, *The Second Origenist Controversy: A New Perspective on Cyril of Scythopolis' Monastic Biographies as Historical Sources for Sixth-Century Origenism* (Roma: Centro studi S. Anselmo, 2001).

113. Barsanuphius and John, *Letters*, 191, Letter 607; Barsanuphius and John, *Correspondance*, 830, Letter 607.

114. Barsanuphius and John, *Letters*, 191, Letter 607; Barsanuphius and John, *Correspondance*, 832–834, Letter 607.

115. Barsanuphius and John, *Letters*, 191, Letter 607; Barsanuphius and John, *Correspondance*, 834, Letter 607.

116. Barsanuphius and John, *Correspondance*, 834, Letter 607.

117. Barsanuphius and John, *Letters*, 191–192, Letter 607; ibid., 834, Letter 607.

118. Ibid., 192, Letter 607.

119. Ibid.; Barsanuphius and John, *Correspondance*, 836, Letter 607.

120. Irénée Hausherr, *Spiritual Direction in the Early Christian East*, trans. Anthony P. Gythiel (Kalamazoo: Cistercian Publications Inc., 1989), 77.

121. Dorotheos of Gaza, *Abba Dorotheos*, 58, Life of Dositheos.

122. Ibid., 57–58, Life of Dositheos; Dorotheos of Gaza, Œuvres spirituelles, 130, Life of Dositheos.

123. Dorotheos of Gaza, Œuvres spirituelles, 144, Life of Dositheos.

124. Dorotheos of Gaza, *Abba Dorotheos*, 63, Life of Dositheos; Dorotheos of Gaza, Œuvres spirituelles, 144, Life of Dositheos.

125. Dorotheos of Gaza, *Abba Dorotheos*, 61, Life of Dositheos.

126. Ibid., 295, Letter 10; Dorotheos of Gaza, Œuvres spirituelles, 518, Letter 10.

127. Dorotheos of Gaza, *Abba Dorotheos*, 171, Discourse 10; Dorotheos of Gaza, Œuvres spirituelles, 342, Discourse 10. "

128. Dale B. Martin, *The Corinthian Body* (New Haven: Yale University Press, 1995), 161.

129. Ibid. In the invasion etiology, disease is caused by alien forces—either personal (demons, gods) or impersonal (pollutants, tiny animals)—that invade the body. Martin asserts that "For both these etiologies, the body is continually pervaded by cosmic forces and is even constituted by those forces; it is a vacillating moment in an energy field. For those convinced by the logic of balance, this is not necessarily bad: the body is simply a microcosm of

the balanced universe and is naturally constituted of the same substances. Others perceive the penetrability of the body as threatening, however necessitating protection against invasion, manipulation, and disintegration." Ibid.

130. Dorotheos mentioned demonic or diabolic influences, but these influences were extensions of evil thoughts already entertained by the monks. A devil (διάβολος) or demon (δαίμονος) amplified a disharmony already present in the soul. The enemy was defeated by humility, "This is why [the devil 'ὁ διάβολος'] is not only called enemy but adversary, too. However, every action of the adversary is destroyed by humility." Dorotheos of Gaza, *Abba Dorotheos*, 90, Discourse 2; Dorotheos of Gaza, Œuvres spirituelles, 188, Discourse 2.

131. Dorotheos of Gaza, *Abba Dorotheos*, 256, Letter 1; Dorotheos of Gaza, Œuvres spirituelles, 494, Letter 1.

132. Dorotheos of Gaza, *Abba Dorotheos*, 256, Letter 1; Dorotheos of Gaza, Œuvres spirituelles, 494, Letter 1.

133. Dorotheos of Gaza, *Abba Dorotheos*, 179, Discourse 11; Dorotheos of Gaza, Œuvres spirituelles, 356, Discourse 11.

134. Dorotheos of Gaza, *Abba Dorotheos*, 179, Discourse 11; Dorotheos of Gaza, Œuvres spirituelles, 356, Discourse 11.

135. Dorotheos of Gaza, *Abba Dorotheos*, 193, Discourse 12.

136. Ibid., 323, Saying 3; Dorotheos of Gaza, Œuvres spirituelles, 526, Saying 3.

137. Dorotheos of Gaza, *Abba Dorotheos*, 139, Discourse 6; Dorotheos of Gaza, Œuvres spirituelles, 282–284, Discourse 6.

138. Dorotheos of Gaza, *Abba Dorotheos*, 139, Discourse 6; Dorotheos of Gaza, Œuvres spirituelles, 282–284, Discourse 6.

139. Dorotheos of Gaza, *Abba Dorotheos*, 261, Letter 2; Dorotheos of Gaza, Œuvres spirituelles, 498, Letter 2.

140. Dorotheos of Gaza, *Abba Dorotheos*, 271, Letter 4.

141. Brown, *The Body and Society*, 236. "Ascetic struggles of exhortation continued to stress the sharp opposition between the pure spirit and the sensual body. The Great Old Man did not mince his words to young Dorotheos: 'Torture your senses, for without torture there is no martyrdom…Trample on the passions by meditating on this letter.' (Letter 256)"

142. Ibid.

143. Dorotheos of Gaza, *Abba Dorotheos*, 98, Discourse 2; Dorotheos of Gaza, Œuvres spirituelles, 206, Discourse 2.

144. Brown, *The Body and Society*, 235.

145. Dorotheos of Gaza, *Abba Dorotheos*, 192, Discourse 12; Dorotheos of Gaza, Œuvres spirituelles, 384, Discourse 12.

146. Dorotheos of Gaza, *Abba Dorotheos*, 191, Discourse 12; Dorotheos of Gaza, Œuvres spirituelles, 382, Discourse 12. See, Evagrius of Pontus, *Les six centuries des "Kephalaia gnostica"*, trans. Antoine Guillaumont, Patrologia orientalis (Paris: Firmin-Didot, 1958), 168–169, 4.76.

147. Dorotheos of Gaza, *Abba Dorotheos*, 192, Discourse 12; Dorotheos of Gaza, Œuvres spirituelles, 384, Discourse 12.

148. Dorotheos of Gaza, *Abba Dorotheos*, 192, Discourse 12; Dorotheos of Gaza, Œuvres spirituelles, 384, Discourse 12.

149. Dorotheos of Gaza, *Abba Dorotheos*, 191, Discourse 12; Dorotheos of Gaza, Œuvres spirituelles, 382, Discourse 12.

150. Dorotheos of Gaza, *Abba Dorotheos*, 193, Discourse 12; Dorotheos of Gaza, Œuvres spirituelles, 384, Discourse 12.

151. Dorotheos of Gaza, *Abba Dorotheos*, 194, Discourse 12; Dorotheos of Gaza, Œuvres spirituelles, 388, Discourse 12. Translation slightly altered.

152. Dorotheos of Gaza, *Abba Dorotheos*, 71, Discourse 1; Dorotheos of Gaza, Œuvres spirituelles, 152, Discourse 1.

153. Dorotheos of Gaza, *Abba Dorotheos*, 69, Discourse 1.

154. Ibid.

155. Ibid., 101, Discourse 3.

156. Dorotheos of Gaza, Œuvres spirituelles, 430, Discourse 14.

157. Ibid.

Chapter 7: Conclusion

1. Pauli, *Menschsein und Menschwerden*, 89.

2. Dorotheos of Gaza, *Abba Dorotheos*, 179, Discourse 11.

3. Pauli, *Menschsein und Menschwerden*, 89. "For every ailment of the soul Christ holds an appropriate "medicine" ready."

4. Ibid., 65. "Through Christ, the new Adam, the nature of man is being renewed, and his senses regain their original health."

5. Dorotheos of Gaza, *Abba Dorotheos*, 74, Discourse 1.

6. Ibid., 186, Discourse 11.

7. Ibid., 217–218, Discourse 14.

8. Ibid., 217, Discourse 14; Dorotheos of Gaza, Œuvres spirituelles, 430, Discourse 14.

9. Dorotheos of Gaza, *Abba Dorotheos*, 229, Discourse 15.

10. Ibid., 98, Discourse 2.

11. Pauli, *Menschsein und Menschwerden*, 78. "Used positively the body is now the instrument through which the soul can be purified from the passions. Dorotheos illustrates this in the relationship of physical effort and humility."

12. Dorotheos of Gaza, *Abba Dorotheos*, 192, Discourse 12.

13. Bitton-Ashkelony and Kofsky, *The Monastic School of Gaza*, 223.

Bibliography

Primary Sources

Barsanuphius, and John. *Letters*. Translated by John Chryssavgis. Vol. 1. Fathers of the Church. Washington, D.C.: Catholic University of America Press, 2006.

———. *Letters*. Translated by John Chryssavgis. Vol. 2. Fathers of the Church. Washington, D.C.: Catholic University of America Press, 2007.

———. *Correspondance*. Edited by François Neyt and Paula de Angelis-Noah. Sources Chrétiennes vol. 426, Paris: Éditions du Cerf, 1997.

———. *Correspondance*. Edited by François Neyt and Paula de Angelis-Noah. Sources Chrétiennes vol. 427, Paris: Éditions du Cerf, 1998.

———. *Correspondance*. Edited by François Neyt and Paula de Angelis-Noah. Sources Chrétiennes vol. 450, Paris: Éditions du Cerf, 2000.

———. *Correspondance*. Edited by François Neyt and Paula de Angelis-Noah. Sources Chrétiennes vol. 451, Paris: Éditions du Cerf, 2001.

———. *Correspondance*. Edited by François Neyt and Paula de Angelis-Noah. Sources Chrétiennes vol. 468, Paris: Éditions du Cerf, 2002.

Basil of Caesarea. *The Asketikon of St. Basil the Great*. Translated by Anna M. Silvas. New York: Oxford University Press, 2005.

———. "Homily 9: On the Hexaemeron." Translated by Agnes Clare Way. In *Saint Basil: Exegetical Homilies*. The Fathers of the Church. Washington, D.C.: The Catholic University of America Press, 1963.

————. "Homily 10: A Psalm on the Lot of the Just Man (Psalm 1)." Translated by Agnes Clare Way. In *Saint Basil: Exegetical Homilies*. The Fathers of the Church. Washington, D.C.: The Catholic University of America Press, 1963.

————. "Homily 10: Against Those Who Are Prone to Anger." Translated by M. Monica Wagner. In *Ascetical Works*. The Fathers of the Church. New York: Fathers of the Church, 1950.

————. "Homily 11: A Psalm of David Which He Sang to the Lord, for the Words of Chusi, the Song of Jemini (on Psalm 7)." Translated by Agnes Clare Way. In *Saint Basil: Exegetical Homilies*. The Fathers of the Church. Washington, D.C.: The Catholic University of America Press, 1963.

————. "Homily Explaining That God Is Not the Cause of Evil." Translated by Nonna Vernon Harrison. In *On the Human Condition*. Popular Patristics Series, 65–80. Crestwood, N.Y.: St. Vladimir's Seminary Press, 2005.

————. *Saint Basil: Letters (186–368)*. Translated by Agnes Clare Way. The Fathers of the Church. Vol. 2, New York: Fathers of the Church, Inc., 1955.

Dorotheos of Gaza. *Abba Dorotheos: Practical Teaching on the Christian Life*. Translation, introduction, and glossary by Prof. Constantine Scouteris. Athens: Constantine Scouteris, 2000.

————. *Dorotheos of Gaza: Discourses and Sayings*. Translated by Eric P. Wheeler. Kalamazoo: Cistercian Publications, 1977.

————. *Doctrinae Diversae: Die geistliche Lehre*, 2 vols. Translated by Judith Pauli. Freiburg: Herder, 2000.

————. Œuvres Spirituelles. Translated by Lucien Regnault and J. de Préville. Sources Chrétiennes. Vol. 92, Paris: Éditions du Cerf, 1963.

————. *S. Dorotheus, Archimandrita* Patrologiae Cursus Completus, Series Graeca. edited by J. -P Migne. Vol. 88, Paris: J.-P. Migne, 1860.

Eusebius of Caesarea. *The History of the Church from Christ to Constantine*. Translated by G. A. Williamson. New York: New York University Press, 1966.

Evagrius of Pontus. *Euagrius Ponticus*. Translated by Wilhelm Frankenberg. Abhandlungen Der Königlichen Gesellschaft Der Wissenschaften Zu Göttingen, Philologische-Historische Klasse. Vol. 13.2, Berlin: Weidmannsche Buchhandlung, 1912.

————. *Evagrius of Pontus: Talking Back: A Monastic Handbook for Combating Demons*. Translated by David Brakke. Trappist, KY: Cistercian Publications, 2009.

————. *Evagrius of Pontus: The Greek Ascetic Corpus*. Translated by Robert E. Sinkewicz. Oxford: Oxford University Press, 2003.

————. *Les Six Centuries Des "Kephalaia Gnostica"*. Translated by Antoine Guillaumont. Patrologia Orientalis. Paris: Firmin-Didot, 1958.

Evagrius Scholasticus. *The Ecclesiastical History of Evagrius Scholasticus*. Translated by Michael Whitby. Liverpool: Liverpool University Press, 2000.

Galen. *Galen: Method of Medicine*. Translated by Ian Johnston and G. H. R. Horsley. Loeb Classical Library. Vol. 1, Cambridge, M.A.: Harvard University Press, 2011.

————. *Selected Works*. Translated by P. N. Singer. New York: Oxford University Press, 1997.

Gregory Nazianzen. *Funeral Orations*. Translated by Leo P. McCauley. The Fathers of the Church. New York: Fathers of the Church, Inc., 1953.

Gregory of Nyssa. *Saint Gregory of Nyssa: Ascetical Works*. Translated by Virginia Woods Callahan. The Fathers of the Church. Washington D.C.: The Catholic Universtiy Press, 1967.

Hippocrates. *Hippocrates*. Translated by W. H. S. Jones. The Loeb Classical Library. Vol. 2, Cambridge, MA: Harvard University Press, 1959.

Isaiah of Scetis. *Abba Isaiah of Scetis: Ascetic Discourses*. Translated by John Chryssavgis and Pachomios Penkett. Kalamazoo: Cistercian Publications, 2002.

———. *Abbé Isaïe: Recueil Ascétique*. Translated by Les moines de Solesmes. Spiritualité Orientale. Vol. 7, 1970.

———. *Les Cinq Recensions De L'ascéticon Syriaque D'abba Isaïe*. Corpus Scriptorium Christianorum Orientalium. Vol. 289–290, 293–294, Louvain: Secrétariat du Corpus scriptorum Christianorum Orientalium, 1968.

———. *Tou Hosiou Patros Hēmōn Abba Esaiou Logoi Xxix*. 2nd ed. Volos: Typographeion tēs Hagioreitikēs Bibliothēkēs, 1962.

———. *Του Οσιου Πατρος Ημων Αββα Ησαιου Λογοι ΚΘ*. Jerusalem: Augoustinos Hilarion Monachoi, 1911.

John Moschos. *The Spiritual Meadow*. Translated by John Wortley. Kalamazoo, Mich: Cistercian Publications, 1992.

John Rufus. *John Rufus: The Lives of Peter the Iberian, Theodosius of Jerusalem, and the Monk Romanus*. Translated by Cornelia B. Horn and Robert R. Phenix. Atlanta: Society of Biblical Literature, 2008.

John the Dwarf. *Appendix Ad Palladium*. Patrologiae Cursus Completus, Series Graeca. edited by J. -P Migne. Vol. 65, Paris: J.-P. Migne, 1864.

Origen of Alexandria. *Contra Celsum*. Translated by Henry Chadwick. New York: Cambridge University Press, 1980.

———. "Genesis Homily Xiii." Translated by Ronald E. Heine. In *Origen: Homilies on Genesis and Exodus*. The Fathers of the Church, 185–195. Washington D.C.: The Catholic University of America Press, Inc., 1982.

Palladius. *The Lausiac History*. Translated by Robert T. Meyer. Westminster: Newman Press, 1965.

Plato. *The Republic of Plato*. Translated by Allan Bloom. United States of America: Basic Books, 1991.

Zosimas. "Alloquia." In *Νέα Σιών*, edited by Augoustinos Iordanites, 697–701, 1912.

———. "Alloquia." In *Νέα Σιών*, edited by Augoustinos Iordanites, 854–865, 1913.

———. "Reflections." Translated by John Chryssavgis. In *In the Heart of the Desert: The Spirituality of the Desert Fathers and Mothers: With a Translation of Abba Zosimas' Reflections*. Bloomington: World Wisdom, Inc., 2008.

———. *ΤΟΥ ΟΣΙΟΥ ΠΑΤΡΟΣ ΗΜΩΝ ΑΒΒΑ ΖΩΣΙΜΑ ΚΕΦΑΛΑΙΑ ΠΑΝΥ ΩΦΕΛΙΜΑ*. Jerusalem: Augustinos Monachos Iordanitos, 1913.

Secondary Sources

Amundsen, Darrel W. "Medicine and Faith in Early Christianity." In *Medicine, Society, and Faith in the Ancient and Medieval Worlds*, 127–157. Baltimore: The Johns Hopkins University Press, 1996.

Amundsen, Darrel W., and Gary B. Ferngren. "Virtue and Medicine from Early Christianity through the Sixteenth Century." In *Virtue and Medicine: Explorations in the Character of Medicine*, edited by Earl E. Shelp, 23–62. Boston: D. Reidel Publishing Company, 1985.

Asceticism. edited by Vincent L. Wimbush and Richard Valantasis New York: Oxford University Press, 1995.

Avi-Yonah, Michael. *The Madaba Mosaic Map: With Introduction and Commentary* Jerusalem: Israel Exploration Society, 1954.

Baldauf, Christa. "Sprachliche Evidenz Metaphorischer Konzeptualisierung: Probleme Und Perspektive Der Kognitivistischen Metapherntheorie." In *Bildersprache Verstehen: Zur Hermeneutik Der Metapher Und Anderer Bildlicher Sprachformen*, 117–132. München: W. Fink, 2000.

Bazzana, Giovanni Battista. "Early Christian Missionaries as Physicians: Healing and Its Cultural Value in the Greco-Roman Context." *Novum Testamentum* 51 (2009): 232–251.

Binns, John. *Ascetics and Ambassadors of Christ: The Monasteries of Palestine, 314–631.* Oxford: Clarendon Press, 1994.

Bitton-Ashkelony, Brouria, and Aryeh Kofsky. *The Monastic School of Gaza.* Leiden: Brill, 2006.

Brown, Peter. *The Body and Society: Men, Women, and Sexual Renunciation in Early Christianity.* 2nd ed. New York: Columbia University Press, 2008.

———. "The Rise and Function of the Holy Man in Late Antiquity." *Journal of Roman Studies* 61 (1971): 80–101.

Burton-Christie, Douglas. *The Word in the Desert: Scripture and the Quest for Holiness in Early Christian Monasticism.* New York: Oxford University Press, 1993.

Cameron, Averil. *Christianity and the Rhetoric of Empire: The Development of Christian Discourse.* Berkeley: University of California Press, 1991.

Canivet, Pierre. "Dorothée De Gaza: Est-Il Un Disciple D'évagre?". *Revue des Études Greques* 78 (1965): 336–346.

Chitty, Derwas J. "Abba Isaiah." *Journal of Theological Studies* 22, no. 1 (April 1971): 47–72.

———. *Barsanuphius and John: Questions and Answers.* Translated by Derwas J. Chitty. Patrologia Orientalis. Vol. 31/3, Paris: Firmin-Didot et C Éditeurs, 1966.

———. *The Desert a City: An Introduction to the Study of Egyptian and Palestinian Monasticism under the Christian Empire.* Oxford: Blackwell, 1999.

Chryssavgis, John. "Abba Isaiah of Scetis: Aspects of Spiritual Direction." *Studia Patristica* 35 (2001): 30–40.

———. "Barsanuphius and John: The Identity and Integrity of the Old Men of Gaza." *Studia Patristica* 39 (2006): 307–313.

———. "From Egypt to Palestine: Discerning a Thread of Spiritual Direction." In *Abba: The Tradition of Orthodoxy in the West. Festschrift for Bishop Kallistos (Ware) of Diokleia*, edited by John Behr, Andrew Louth and Dimitri Conomos, 299–315. Crestwood, NY: St. Vladimir's Seminary Press, 2003.

———. *In the Heart of the Desert: The Spirituality of the Desert Fathers and Mothers: With a Translation of Abba Zosimas' Reflections.* Bloomington: World Wisdom, Inc., 2008.

———. *Soul Mending: The Art of Spiritual Direction.* Brookline, Mass.: Holy Cross Orthodox Press, 2000.

Chryssavgis, John, and Pachomios Penkett. *Abba Isaiah of Scetis: Ascetic Discourses.* Translated by John Chryssavgis and Pachomios Penkett. Kalamazoo: Cistercian Publications, 2002.

Clark, Elizabeth A. *Reading Renunciation: Asceticism and Scripture in Early Christianity.* Princeton: Princeton University Press, 1999.

Clark, Gillian. "The Health of the Spiritual Athlete." In *Health in Antiquity*, edited by Helen King, 216–229. New York: Routledge, 2005.

Constans, David. *The Emotions of the Greeks: Studies in Aristotle and Greek Literature.* Toronto: University of Toronto Press, 2006.

Crislip, Andrew T. *From Monastery to Hospital: Christian Monasticism & the Transformation of Health Care in Late Antiquity.* Ann Arbor: University of Michigan Press, 2005.

———. *Thorns in the Flesh: Illness and Sanctity in Late Ancient Christianity.* Philadelphia: University of Pennsylvania Press, 2013.

D'Irsay, Stephen. "Patristic Medicine." *Annals of Medical History* 9 (1928): 364–378.

Di Segni, Leah. "Monk and Society: The Case of Palestine." In *The Sabaite Heritage in the Orthodox Church from the Fifth Century to the Present*, edited by Joseph Patrich. Orientalia Lovaniensia Analecta, 31–36. Leuven: Uitgeverij Peeters in Departement Oosterse Studies, 2001.

Dörnemann, Michael. *Krankheit Und Heilung in Der Theologie Der Frühen Kirchenväter.* Studien Und Texte Zu Antike Und Christentum. Tübingen: Mohr Siebeck, 2003.

Edelstein, Ludwig. "The Relation of Ancient Philosophy to Medicine." Translated by Lilian C. Temkin. In *Ancient Medicine: Selected Papers of Ludwig Edelstein*, edited by Owsei Temkin and Lilian C. Temkin. Baltimore: The Johns Hopkins Press, 1967.

Egender, Nikolas. "Dorotheus of Gaza and Benedict of Nursia." *Cistercian Studies Quarterly* 44, no. 2 (2009): 145–160.

———. "Dorotheus Von Gaza Und Benedikt Von Nursia." *Regulae Benedicti Studia Annuarium Internatioale* 17 (1992): 39–52.

Elm, Susanna. *Virgins of God: The Making of Asceticism in Late Antiquity.* New York: Oxford University Press, 1994.

Ferngren, Gary B. *Medicine and Health Care in Early Christianity.* Baltimore: Johns Hopkins University Press, 2009.

Ferngren, Gary B., and Darrel W. Amundsen. "Virtue and Health/Medicine in Pre-Christian Antiquity." In *Virtue and Medicine: Explorations in the Character of Medicine*, edited by Earl E. Shelp, 3–22. Boston: D. Reidel Publishing Company, 1985.

Finn, Richard Damian. *Asceticism in the Graeco-Roman World.* New York: Cambridge University Press, 2009.

Flood, Gavin. *The Ascetic Self: Subjectivity, Memory and Tradition.* Cambridge University Press, 2005.

Flusin, Bernard. *Miracle Et Histoire Dans L'œuvre De Cyrille De Scythopolis.* Paris: Études Augustiniennes, 1983.

Foucault, Michel. *The Hermeneutics of the Subject: Lectures at the Collège De France, 1981–1982.* Translated by Graham Burchell. New York: Picador, 2004.

Goehring, James E. *Ascetics, Society, and the Desert: Studies in Early Egyptian Monasticism.* Harrisburg, PA: Trinity Press International, 1999.

Gould, Graham. "A Note on the Apophthegmata Patrum." *Journal of Theological Studies* 37, no. 1 (1986): 133–138.

Guy, Jean-Claude. "Educational Innovation in the Desert Fathers." *Eastern Churches Review* 6 (1974): 44–51.

Hadot, Pierre. *Philosophy as a Way of Life: Spiritual Exercises from Socrates to Foucault.* Translated by Michael Chase. Malden, MA: Wiley-Blackwell, 1995.

———. *What Is Ancient Philosophy?* Translated by Michael Chase. Cambridge, MA: Belknap Press of Harvard University Press, 2004.

Hagman, Patrik. *The Asceticism of Isaac of Nineveh.* New York: Oxford University Press, 2010.

Harmless, William. "Monasticism." In *The Oxford Handbook of Early Christian Studies*, edited by Susan Ashbrook Harvey and David G. Hunter, 493–517. New York: Oxford University Press, 2008.

Harnack, Adolf. *Medicinisches Aus Der Ältesten Kirchengeschichte.* Leipzig: J. C. Hinrichs'sche Buchhandlung, 1892.

———. *The Mission and Expansion of Christianity in the First Three Centuries.* Translated by James Moffatt. Vol. 1, New York: G. P. Putnam's Sons, 1908.

Harpham, Geoffrey Galt. *The Ascetic Imperative in Culture and Criticism.* Chicago: University of Chicago Press, 1987.

Harris, William V. *Restraining Rage: The Ideology of Anger Control in Classical Antiquity.* Harvard: Harvard University Press, 2004.

Harvey, Susan Ashbrook. "Physicians and Ascetics in John of Ephesus: An Expedient Alliance." In *Symposium on Byzantine Medicine*, edited by John Scarborough. Dumbarton Oaks Papers, 87–93. Washington, D.C.: Dumbarton Oaks Research Library and Collection, 1984.

Hausherr, Irénée. "La "Doctrine Xxiv" De Saint Dorothée." *Orientalia christiana periodica* 6 (1940): 220–221.

———. *Spiritual Direction in the Early Christian East.* Translated by Anthony P. Gythiel. Kalamazoo: Cistercian Publications Inc., 1989.

Hay, Kathleen. "Impact of St. Sabas: The Legacy of Palestinian Monasticism." In *The Sixth Century, End or Beginning?*, edited by Pauline Allen and Elizabeth Jeffreys, 118–125. Brisbane: Australian Association for Byzantine Studies, 1996.

Henschennio, Godefrido, and Daniele Papebrochio, ed. *Acta Sanctorum.* Vol. April, Tome 2, Paris: Victorem Palmé, 1866.

Hevelone-Harper, Jennifer. "Anchorite and Abbot: Cooperative Spiritual Authority in Late Antique Gaza." *Studia Patristica* 39 (2006): 379–384.

———. "Ecclesiastics and Ascetics: Finding Spiritual Authority in Fifth- and Sixth-Century Palestine." *Hugoye: Journal of Syriac Studies* 9, no. 1 (January 2006): 1–28.

———. "Letters to the Great Old Man: Monks, Laity, and Spiritual Authority in Sixth Century Gaza." phD diss., Princeton University, 2000.

Hevelone-Harper, Jennifer Lee. *Disciples of the Desert: Monks, Laity, and Spiritual Authority in Sixth-Century Gaza*. Baltimore: Johns Hopkins University Press, 2005.

Hirschfeld, Yizhar. *The Judean Desert Monasteries in the Byzantine Period*. New Haven: Yale University Press, 1992.

———. "The Monasteries of Gaza: An Archaeological Review." In *Christian Gaza in Late Antiquity*, edited by Bruria Bitton-Ashkelony and Aryeh Kofsky, 61–88. Boston: Brill, 2004.

———. "The Monasteries of Palestine in the Byzantine Period." In *Christians and Christianity in the Holy Land: From the Origins to the Latin Kingdoms*, edited by Ora Limor and Guy G. Stroumsa, 402–419. Turnhout: Brepols, 2006.

Hombergen, Daniël. "Barsanuphius and John of Gaza and the Origenist Controversy." In *Christian Gaza in Late Antiquity*, edited by Bruria Bitton-Ashkelony and Aryeh Kofsky, 173–182. Boston: Brill, 2004.

———. "The Question of Dorotheus of Gaza's Position in the Second Origenist Controversy." In *Church, Society and Monasticism: Acts of the International Symposium, Rome, May 31–June 3, 2006: The Monastic Institute of the Faculty of Theology in the Pontifical Athenaeum S. Anselmo*, edited by E. López-Tello García and B. S. Zorzi, 475–485. Rome: Pontificio Ateneo S. Anselmo, 2009.

———. *The Second Origenist Controversy: A New Perspective on Cyril of Scythopolis' Monastic Biographies as Historical Sources for Sixth-Century Origenism*. Roma: Centro studi S. Anselmo, 2001.

Horden, Peregrine. "The Death of Ascetics: Sickness and Monasticism in the Early Byzantine Middle East." In *Monks, Hermits and the Ascetic Tradition: Papers Read at the 1984 Summer Meeting and the 1985 Winter Meeting of the Ecclesiastical History Society*, edited by W. J. Sheils, 25–40. Oxford: Blackwell, 1985.

Horn, Cornelia B. *Asceticism and Christological Controversy in Fifth-Century Palestine: The Career of Peter the Iberian*. Oxford: Oxford University Press, 2006.

"Incipit Vita Sancti Barsanorii Abbatis." In *Catalogus Codicum Hagiographicorum Latinorum Antiquiorum Saeculo Xvi Qui Asservantur in Bibiotheca Nationali Parisiensi, Ediderunt Hagiographi Bollandiani*, 525–535. Bruxellis: Apud Editores, 1889.

King, Helen, ed. *Health in Antiquity*. New York: Routledge, 2005.

Kleinman, Arthur. *The Illness Narratives: Suffering, Healing, and the Human Condition*. New York: Basic Books, 1988.

Kofsky, Aryeh. "The Byzantine Holy Person: The Case of Barsanuphius and John of Gaza." In *Saints and Role Models in Judaism and Christianity*, edited by Marcel Poorthuis and Joshua Schwartz, 261–285. Boston: Brill, 2004.

Lakoff, George, and Mark Johnson. *Metaphors We Live By*. Chicago: University of Chicago Press, 1980.

Larchet, Jean-Claude. *Thérapeutique Des Maladies Spirituelles: Une Introduction À La Tradition Ascétique De L'église Orthodoxe*. 2 ed. Suresnes: Éditions de l'Ancre, 1993.

Lavere, George J. "Virtue." In *Augustine through the Ages: An Encyclopedia*, edited by Allan D. Fitzgerald, 871–874. Grand Rapids: Wm. B. Eerdmans Publishing Company, 2009.

Martin, Dale B. *The Corinthian Body*. New Haven: Yale University Press, 1995.

Meredith, Anne Elizabeth. "Illness and Healing in the Early Christian East." PhD diss., Princeton University, 1999.

Miller, Timothy S. *The Birth of the Hospital in the Byzantine Empire*. Baltimore: Johns Hopkins University Press, 1997.

Neyt, François. "A Form of Charismatic Authority." *Eastern Churches Review* 6 (1974): 52–65.

———. "La Formation Au Monastère De L'abbé Séridos À Gaza." In *Christian Gaza in Late Antiquity*, edited by Bruria Bitton-Ashkelony and Aryeh Kofsky, 151–164. Boston: Brill, 2004.

Neyt, François, and Paula de Angelis-Noah. "Introduction." Translated by Lucien Regnault. In *Correspondance*. Paris: Éditions du Cerf, 1997.

Nutton, Vivian. *Ancient Medicine*. New York: Routledge, 2004.

———. "From Galen to Alexander: Aspects of Medicine and Medical Practice in Late Antiquity." In *Symposium on Byzantine Medicine*, edited by John Scarborough. Dumbarton Oaks Papers, 1–14. Washington, District of Columbia: Dumbarton Oaks Research Library and Collection, 1984.

Parrinello, Rosa Marie. *Comunità Monastiche a Gaza: Da Isaia a Doroteo (Secoli Iv–Vi)*. Temi E Testi. Roma: Edizioni di Storia e Letteratura, 2010.

Patrich, Joseph. *Sabas, Leader of Palestinian Monasticism: A Comparative Study in Eastern Monasticism, Fourth to Seventh Centuries*. Washington: Dumbarton Oaks Research Library and Collection, 1995.

Patrich, Joseph, ed. *The Sabaite Heritage in the Orthodox Church from the Fifth Century to the Present*. Leuven: Peeters, 2001.

Pauli, Judith. *Doctrinae Diversae: Die Geistliche Lehre*. 2 vols. Vol. 37, Freiburg: Herder, 2000.

———. *Menschsein Und Menschwerden Nach Der Geistlichen Lehre Des Dorotheus Von Gaza*. St. Ottilien: EOS Verlag, 1998.

Perkins, Judith. *The Suffering Self: Pain and Narrative Representation Inearly Christianity*. London; New York: Routledge, 1995.

Perrone, Lorenzo. "Byzantine Monasticism in Gaza and in the Judaean Desert: A Comparion of Their Spiritual Traditions." *Proche-Orient Chrétien* 62 (2012): 6–22.

———. "Monasticism in Gaza: A Chapter in the History of Byzantine Palestine." In *Zwischen Polis, Provinz Und Peripherie: Beiträge Zu Byzantinischen Geschichte Und Kultur*, edited by Lars M. Hoffmann and Anuscha Monchizadeh, 59–74. Wiesbaden: Harrassowitz Verlag, 2005.

———. "The Necessity of Advice: Spiritual Direction as a School of Christianity in the Correspondence of Barsanuphius and John of Gaza." In *Christian Gaza in Late Antiquity*, edited by Bruria Bitton-Ashkelony and Aryeh Kofsky, 131–150. Boston: Brill, 2004.

————. "Scripture for a Life of Perfection. The Bible in Late Antique Monasticism: The Case of Palestine." In *The Reception and Interpretation of the Bible in Late Antiquity: Proceedings of the Montréeal Colloquium in Honour of Charles Kannengiesser, 11–13 October 2006*, edited by Lorenzo DiTommaso and Lucian Turcescu, 393–417. Boston: Brill, 2008.

Porterfield, Amanda. *Healing in the History of Christianity*. New York: Oxford University Press, 2005.

Regnault, Lucien. *Barsanuphe Et Jean De Gaza, Correspondance*. Sable-sur-Sarthe: Abbaye Saint-Pierre de Solesmes, 1972.

————. "Les Apophtegemes Des Pères En Palestine Aux Ve-Vie Siécles." *Irénikon* 54 (1981).

————. "Théologie De La Vie Monastique Selon Barsanuphe Et Dorothée." In *Théologie De La Vie Monastique; Études Sur La Tradition Patristique*, 315–322. Paris: Aubier, 1961.

Regnault, Lucien, and Jacques de Préville. *Œuvres Spirituelles*. Sources Chrétiennes. Paris: Éditions du Cerf, 1963.

Risse, Guenter B. *Mending Bodies, Saving Souls: A History of Hospitals*. New York: Oxford University Press, 1999.

Rousseau, Philip. "Ascetics as Mediators and as Teachers." In *The Cult of Saints in Late Antiquity and the Middle Ages: Essays on the Contribution of Peter Brown*, edited by Paul Antony Hayward and J. D Howard-Johnston, 45–59. New York: Oxford University Press, 1999.

————. *Ascetics, Authority, and the Church in the Age of Jerome and Cassian*. 2nd ed. Notre Dame: University of Notre Dame Press, 2010.

————. *Basil of Caesarea*. Berkeley: University of California Press, 1994.

Rubenson, Samuel. "'As Already Translated to the Kingdom While Still in the Body' the Transformation of the Ascetic in Early Egyptian Monasticism." In *Metamorphoses: Resurrection, Body, and Transformative Practices in Early Christianity*, edited by Turid Karlsen Seim and Jorunn Økland, 271–289. New York: W. de Gruyter, 2009.

————. "Christian Asceticism and the Emergence of the Monastic Tradition." In *Asceticism*, edited by Vincent L. Wimbush and Richard Valantasis, 49–57. New York: Oxford University Press, 1995.

————. "The Egyptian Relations of Early Palestinian Monasticism." In *The Christian Heritage in the Holy Land*, edited by Anthony O'Mahony, Göran Gunner and Kevork Hintlian. London: Scorpion Cavendish Ltd., 1995.

Shaw, Teresa M. *The Burden of the Flesh: Fasting and Sexuality in Early Christianity*. Minneapolis, MN: Fortress Press, 1998.

Sorabji, Richard. *Emotion and Peace of Mind: From Stoic Agitation to Christian Temptation: The Gifford Lectures*. New York: Oxford University Press, 2000.

Stewart, Columba. "Evagrius Ponticus on Monastic Pedagogy." In *Abba: The Tradition of Orthodoxy in the West. Festschrift for Bishop Kallistos (Ware) of Diokleia*, edited by John Behr, Andrew Louth and Dimitri Conomos, 241–271. Crestwood, NY: St. Vladimir's Seminary Press, 2003.

Temkin, Owsei. *Hippocrates in a World of Pagans and Christians*. Baltimore: The Johns Hopkins University Press, 1991.

Vailhé, Siméon. "Saint Dorothée Et Saint Zosime." Échos d'*Orient* 4 (1905): 359–363.

Valantasis, Richard. "Construction of Power in Asceticism." In *The Making of the Self: Ancient and Modern Asceticism*, 14–59. Eugene, OR: Cascade Books, 2008.

———. "A Theory of the Social Function of Asceticism." In *The Making of the Self: Ancient and Modern Asceticism*, 3–13. Eugene, OR: Cascade Books, 2008.

———. "A Theory of the Social Function of Asceticism." In *Asceticism*, edited by Vincent L. Wimbush and Richard Valantasis, 544–552. New York: Oxford University Press, 1995.

Vlahogiannis, Nicholas. "'Curing' Disability." In *Health in Antiquity*, edited by Helen King, 180–191. New York: Routledge, 2005.

Ward, Benedicta. *The Sayings of the Desert Fathers: The Alphabetical Collection*. London: Mowbrays, 1975.

Wheeler, Eric P. *Discourses and Sayings*. Translated by Eric P. Wheeler. Kalamazoo: Cistercian Publications, 1977.

Williams, Rowan. *The Wound of Knowledge: Christian Spirituality from the New Testament to St. John of the Cross*. 2nd. ed. Cambridge, MA: Cowley Pubications, 1990.

Wimbush, Vincent L. *Ascetic Behavior in Greco-Roman Antiquity: A Sourcebook*. Minneapolis: Fortress Press, 1990.

Wimbush, Vincent L., and Richard Valantasis. "Introduction." In *Asceticism*, edited by Vincent L. Wimbush and Richard Valantasis, xix–xxxiii. New York: Oxford University Press, 1995.

Zachariah the Rhetor. "Vita Isaiae Monachi." Translated by E. W. Brooks. In *Vitae Virorum Apud Monphysitas Celeberrimorum*. Corpus Scriptorum Christianorum Orientalium. Louvain: L. Durbecq, 1955.

Zecher, Jonathan L. "The Symbolics of Death and the Construction of Christian Asceticism: Greek Patristic Voices from the Fourth through the Seventh Centuries." PhD diss., Durham University, 2011.